Microsoft®

First Look 2007 Microsoft® Office System

Katherine Murray

PUBLISHED BY
Microsoft Press
A Division of Microsoft Corporation
One Microsoft Way
Redmond, Washington 98052-6399

Library of Congress Control Number 2005939242
ISBN-13: 978-0-7356-2265-4
ISBN-10: 0-7356-2265-5

Printed and bound in the United States of America.

2 3 4 5 6 7 8 9 QWE 1 0 9 8 7 6

Distributed in Canada by H.B. Fenn and Company Ltd.

A CIP catalogue record for this book is available from the British Library.

Microsoft Press books are available through booksellers and distributors worldwide. For further information about international editions, contact your local Microsoft Corporation office or contact Microsoft Press International directly at fax (425) 936-7329. Visit our Web site at www.microsoft.com/mspress. Send comments to mspinput@microsoft.com.

Acquisitions Editor: Juliana Aldous Atkinson
Developmental Editor: Sandra Haynes
Project Editor: Valerie Woolley
Technical Editor: Steve Sagman
Editorial and Production: Studioserv

Body Part No. X12-33283

Contents at a Glance

Table of Contents

Acknowledgments

Putting together a book like this is an exciting, challenging, and hopeful mix of possibility, probability, and practicality. In that respect, it's not unlike software development—we start with a vision, put research and planning and effort and talent behind it, and continue to check, revise, and enhance as long as we've got the time to make changes.

This project has been fascinating, fast, and fruitful—thanks to the talent and effort of the following great people:

Valerie Woolley, our fun and fearless project leader at Microsoft Press, keeper of schedules and deadlines, and great opener of doors;

Steve Sagman, of Studioserv, who regularly does the impossible by pulling together pieces of manuscript in varying stages of readiness and turns them into the great-looking, technically accurate, and on-time book you now hold in your hands (or see on your screen);

Thanks also to Nancy Sixsmith at Studioserv for her careful, conscientious, and friendly edit.

And special thanks to my agent, Claudette Moore, for all the amazing things she does on my behalf, and to Juliana Aldous, my acquisitions editor at Microsoft Press, for giving me the opportunity to write in detail about this awesome new release.

Thanks also to the group of talented and busy application program managers at Microsoft who took the time to answer questions (sometimes many questions) and share their experiences in our Q&A interviews. Specifically, thanks go to

- Jared Anderson
- Jessica Arnold
- Leslie Cole
- Daniel Escapa
- Mor Hezi
- Ryan Hoppe
- Gary Knowlton
- Alex Robinson
- Eric Rockey
- Mary Sobcyzk

Introduction

"I wish my programs worked together better."

"I wish there were an easier way to keep track of all the information—documents, messages, schedules, and more—related to my projects."

"I wish it was easier to learn how to use these applications."

"I wish I could do something about my e-mail!"

"I wish it wasn't so hard to find what I need when I'm doing something new."

"I wish I felt like I was getting more out of these programs. As it is, I just do the same things over and over, producing the same results."

Your wishes are granted! The new release that is the focus of this book—2007 Microsoft Office system—has been designed to answer just these kinds of needs for people working with information the world over. The 2007 release not only offers better integration, enhanced communication, professional presentation, and expanded collaboration but it also offers these improvements in a greatly simplified and smart user interface that fits naturally into the way you work.

Research has shown that people who use the Microsoft Office system today perform specific tasks with their favorite applications. One person produces a quarterly income statement in Microsoft Office Excel; another writes the company newsletter in Microsoft Office Word; another creates presentations for the monthly sales meeting. They all use Microsoft Office Outlook for e-mail: some use it to create tasks; others use Office Outlook with Business Contact Manager to track sales leads, contacts, and accounts for their small businesses. But research has also shown that most of us use only certain features. We don't often venture out into the unknown, try new things, or explore the full capabilities of the programs. We run the risk of getting stuck in a technological rut—the same old tasks, using the same old program, in the same old way.

The 2007 Microsoft Office system is changing all that. This newest version is a radical departure from the menu option approach of its predecessors. For the new user interface, the Office team went back to the drawing board and brought to bear everything they knew and all the research they'd done about the best way to create an intuitive interface that works just the way the user wants it. Combine the new look and feel with context-based tools, new formats, an amazing level of integration between applications, server supports, and a focus on what we need to do today, and you have a powerful system that saves you time, expands your reach, and helps you work both faster and smarter by leveraging your work among your favorite applications.

We're living at the edge of a major shift in the way technology is used throughout our lives. Today's computers are much more than number-crunching or data-organizing tools; they are an integral part of the way we live, work, and play. Twenty years ago, desktop PCs were just beginning to appear on desks; ten years ago everybody had a computer at work, and increasing numbers of us had them at home; today we have not only computers at work and at home but also in our briefcases, backpacks, pockets, and watches. We rely on technology not only to ensure the efficiency and accuracy of our business decisions and processes but also to help organize our time, improve our relationships, maximize our potential, and express our creativity. And when all those goals are met, we use technology to have fun!

This is an exciting time for those of us riding the wave of changing technology. Our lives are becoming increasingly integrated—the lines between home and work, online and offline, in touch or unreachable are dissolving, enabling us to create a seamless, connected experience supported by the best technology has to offer. At the front of that wave is the 2007 Microsoft Office system, the exciting new version of the world's most popular suite of applications. This version of the Microsoft Office system is radical in that it takes major steps toward working the way you do—intuitively sensing the tools you need and offering you context-related options, whether you are creating a report, printing marketing materials, or working on a financial statement.

Introducing the 2007 Microsoft Office System

The 2007 Microsoft Office system goes far beyond previous releases in helping you run your business and expand your reach. More than a set of tools for the everyday essentials (word processing, spreadsheets, communication, and more), the 2007 release offers a whole set of integrated new capabilities that support you in marketing and sales functions; offer professional templates for high-quality presentations and documents; and assist you in more efficient, effective, and—in some cases, instant—communications.

Here are just a few of the features you'll want to make sure to try in the 2007 Microsoft Office system (and you'll find many more features to try described throughout this book):

- Throughout the 2007 release, you'll find a new, simplified, and results-oriented user interface that gives you just the tools you need when you need them; enhanced integration among all the applications; great new templates; support for PDF and XPS file formats; and features to make sharing your work easier—and safer—than ever.
- In Office Outlook 2007, the new To-Do Bar enables you to see at a glance all your upcoming tasks and appointments. You can flag messages to turn them into tasks and also color-categorize contacts, tasks, and messages. The integration of tasks on your daily calendar helps you schedule time to complete important tasks.

- In Microsoft® Office Word 2007, find the style you like by letting Quick Styles show you a fast rendering of the choices you're thinking about making; use building blocks of content for boilerplate text in your documents; add references now with a single click; improve the graphics in your document by using SmartArt; publish to your blog directly from within Office Word 2007; explore the major enhancements in document review and comparison; and create large mailings more easily using the Mail Merge tab.
- In Microsoft® Office Excel® 2007, try out dramatically increased processing speed and power, larger worksheets, the powerful charting enhancements, conditional formatting, Web dashboard, and enhanced PivotTable support.
- In Microsoft® Office PowerPoint® 2007, experiment with the great new themes, custom layouts, SmartArt and text effects, and style galleries.
- In Microsoft® Office Publisher 2007, use Publisher Tasks to walk you step-by-step through creating your publication, use dynamic previews to see how your publication will look before you finalize options, reuse content you create in other applications in your Publisher materials, and finish your publication with full four-color commercial printing support. Additionally, Office Publisher 2007 is seamlessly integrated with Office Outlook 2007 with Business Contact Manager so that you can create, track, and evaluate marketing campaigns.
- In Microsoft Office Access 2007, work with the dramatically improved user interface to switch among data views, and create tables, reports, lists, queries, macros, and forms easier than ever. New full-featured templates enable you to begin building your own solution based on trackable applications that are ready right out of the box. Gather information by using e-mail forms and add the information directly to the related tables in your Office Access 2007 database.
- In Microsoft Office OneNote 2007, use the new OneNote Guide to learn all about the ins and outs of the program; work with multiple notebooks and sync your notebooks on your desktop, laptop, and mobile devices; add tables, files, and documents easily; share notes in real time using the Shared Live worksessions.
- In Microsoft Office Groove 2007, learn to create a collaborative workspace that brings together the resources and communication support your team needs whether they are all online together or not. Office Groove 2007 works with Windows SharePoint Services and Microsoft Office SharePoint Server 2007 so that you can easily check out documents from SharePoint document libraries, work on them in your Office Groove 2007 workspace, and return them to the SharePoint site when you're through.

2007 Microsoft Office System Requirements

- A PC with an Intel Pentium 500 MHz (or higher) processor. 1 gigahertz (GHz) and 512 MB of RAM or higher for Microsoft Office Outlook 2007 with Business Contact Manager.
- Microsoft Windows Server 2003 or later, or Microsoft Windows XP Service Pack 2.
- 256 MB RAM or higher.
- 2 GB required for installation
- DVD drive
- Super VGA (800x600) or higher-resolution monitor (1024x768 recommended).
- Mouse, touchpad, trackball, or other pointing device (optional).
- Peripheral devices as needed: printer, scanner, digital camera, microphone, and so on (optional).
- Broadband Internet connection

What Is *First Look 2007 Microsoft Office System*?

First Look 2007 Microsoft Office System is designed to help you get a quick sense of the huge range of changes and enhancements in the Microsoft Office system and inspire you to try out some of the new features as you're working with the early versions of the software on your own systems. Some of the biggest work challenges we face today–information overload, knowledge management, collaboration limitations, localization issues, and more–are directly addressed by new and revamped features in 2007 Microsoft Office system. This book seeks to introduce you to those features. In short, we want to help the 2007 release make your life easier!

The design of the 2007 Microsoft Office system really puts you at the center of things by providing technology that fits intuitively into your work style instead of forcing you to continue to learn, remember, and master complicated, disjointed tasks for carrying out what could be a more natural, integrated workflow. In Chapter 2, "A New Look," you find out how the dramatic changes in the user interface all gear toward the end result–giving you just what you need to complete the task at hand, *First Look 2007 Microsoft Office System* shines a light on the great benefits of this new program and helps you make the connection to your own daily work so you can begin to see how your own work efforts could be more productive, effective, and far-reaching with the 2007 Microsoft Office system.

This Book Is for You

We wrote this book early in the process of the 2007 Microsoft Office system beta cycle because we wanted to share ideas and inspiration—and show you how to find features that will knock your socks off—right from the start. If you are weighing the decision of whether to upgrade to the 2007 release, you will find examples and ideas to help you evaluate the benefit of the new features and make an educated choice. Hopefully you'll find lots of good ideas you'll want to try along the way.

What You'll Find in This Book

The style and approach of *First Look 2007 Microsoft Office System* is business casual—focused and clear about getting the job done, but full of stories, insight, and suggestions meant to inspire, and in some cases, entertain. One of the goals of the 2007release is to fit naturally into *your* projects and processes rather than insist you adapt to the dictates of the software. The focus is on your vision and need, not the capabilities or limits of the tools. In keeping with that goal, *First Look 2007 Microsoft Office System* includes a special feature with the intention of making the features real and relevant to the work you're trying to do: "Three Things To Try" are short sidebars provided by leading Office experts, cluing you in to their favorite new or improved capabilities.

Additionally, because the changes in the 2007 Microsoft Office system are so dramatic, and because the Microsoft Office system is a bit of an institution in itself, we thought it would be fun to provide some "Office 2007 Backstory" sidebars offering Q&A interviews with some of the folks behind the major changes in this release. These fun and interesting interviews give you a sense of what life is like "inside" a major release like this one and lets you get to know some of the people who are directly responsible for the changes in the software you'll be using today.

Now that you have the map for the special features in this book, here's a quick overview of what you'll find in the chapters:

Part I, "Introducing the 2007 Microsoft Office System," focuses on familiarizing you with the approach and interface of the new Office. Chapter 1, "Time for Something New," introduces you to the research and new opportunities driving the changes in the 2007 release. You'll find out what research has shown about the way people work with information today and discover the approach behind the major changes in the 2007 Microsoft Office system user interface. This chapter also introduces you to the primary applications in the different 2007 Microsoft Office system versions and gives you an overview of what has changed in each one.

Chapter 2, "A New Look," is all about the new user interface. Find out about the new command tab design, contextual tool sets, live previews, galleries, and much more. Chapter 3, "Important Systems: Help and Security," talks about changes in the seamless way you'll be able to get help while working with your data and documents. You'll also get a bird's-eye view of the enhanced security features in 2007 Microsoft Office system.

Part II, "Preparing and Producing Professional Results," is all about the core applications and the documents, databases, and communications you'll create using them. Chapter 4, "Create Professional Documents with Office Word 2007," spotlights the features you'll use during the concept-to-completion process of creating a high-quality, professional document. Create a professional and consistent look with new themes, let the Document Inspector help you check your work, and learn to work collaboratively to create a team project in Office Word. Chapter 5, "Extend Your Insight with Office Excel 2007," shows you how to make the most of a wide range of new and improved features, including improved formatting, styles, and charting tools; the new SmartArt diagramming tool; faster calculations and a larger worksheet; enhanced sorting and filtering features; and seamless integration with Excel Services. Chapter 6, "Design Attention-Getting Presentations with Office PowerPoint 2007," introduces you to the eye-popping new custom layouts, slide libraries, improved styles, and more. Chapter 7, "Produce Quality Business Materials with Office Publisher 2007," shows you how you can produce high-quality professional marketing materials, which rival those created by top marketing firms, for a fraction of the cost (and time!). Chapter 8, "Gather, Find, and Share Information with Microsoft Office OneNote 2007," shows you how to create and work with multiple notebooks, capture text, audio, and ink notes–and include file attachments, tables, and more--whether you're working solo or as part of a team. Chapter 9, "Track Information Quickly and Effectively with Office Access 2007," shows you the amazing new changes in Office Access and demonstrates the assortment of new built-in templates and easy-to-find tools, ready to help you manage all kinds of business data management needs.

Part III, "Communicating and Collaborating: People and Processes," is all about staying in touch with others–at work and at home–and making sure your collaborative projects succeed. Chapter 10, "Manage Your Time, Tasks, and E-Mail with Office Outlook 2007," shows you the new changes in Office Outlook 2007, enabling you to better control your calendar and organize tasks, coordinate your efforts using the To-Do Bar, locate messages, tasks, and contacts with lightning speed (and more). Chapter 11, "Enhance Team Effectiveness with Office Groove 2007," introduces you to the exciting new tool that enables you to create a collaborative space in which you can discuss, trade files, chat, and prioritize tasks with your teammates.

An appendix rounds out the book, by introducing you to additional components of the 2007 Microsoft Office system, and lists ways in which the new 2007 Microsoft Office system makes the most of features in Microsoft Windows Vista.

As you can see, we have a lot of ground to cover! The next chapter gets things started with a bit about the history of the changes in the 2007 Microsoft Office system and an overview of all things new.

Part I
Introducing the 2007 Microsoft Office System

In this part:

Chapter 1

Time for Something New

What you'll find in this chapter:

- The changing way we work
- The evolution of the Microsoft Office system
- Meeting today's work challenges
- The 2007 Microsoft Office system–tools for today
- The new 2007 Microsoft Office system versions
- Benefits of upgrading to the new release

In this world, there always seems to be a tension between the old and the new. Businesses, schools, religious institutions, and even governments feel the future pulling them forward and the roots of tradition pulling them back. We as individuals feel it too. We lean forward into our futures, eager to see what's coming, to make things better, to further our careers, and to accomplish our goals. But we remain grounded in our history–what we've learned, where we came from, what we value, who we are.

That also is the story of the new 2007 Microsoft Office system. What makes the 2007 release so exciting is that it represents the best of that forward-leaning future while staying connected to the roots of functionality and core values that have made the program the dependable, powerful mainstay it is today. Throughout this book, you'll see how the 2007 Microsoft Office system has been designed to help you respond to the very real challenges we face in getting our work done in an effective, efficient way that actually enables us to feel that we accomplished something at the end of the day. Straighten out the clutter, establish your priorities, and step out into the future. The Microsoft Office system will keep pace right alongside.

The Changing Way We Work

Over the last two decades, technology has changed everything about the way we work. Twenty-five years ago, connecting with customers meant calling them on the phone, mailing them a letter, or going to their place of business. Today, connecting with customers might mean firing off a quick e-mail message, distributing an electronic newsletter, posting information on the Web, giving a custom presentation via an Internet connection, or–the good old-fashioned way–calling on the phone or showing up on the doorstep with a laptop and a folder tucked under your arm.

Today we have a whole new set of expectations around what we consider "productive and effective" uses of our time:

- Thanks to e-mail, voice mail, and instant messaging, we expect to be able to communicate directly and quickly–if not instantly.
- Thanks to desktop applications with publishing and data merge capabilities, we expect to be able to control and complete in-house projects we used to outsource.
- Thanks to shared document technologies, the Internet, and e-mail, we expect to work collaboratively with others outside our immediate circle of coworkers and peers, or with our peers back in the office when we're traveling.
- Thanks to application-independent file formats, we expect to be able to share information–regardless of computer type and application used.
- Thanks to integration among applications, we expect to be able to leverage data and documents we have previously created.

In this chapter–and throughout this book–you'll see how this latest version of the Microsoft Office system is designed to help you meet your goals in a reliable, trackable, and efficient way. What's more, you'll see how the Microsoft Office system helps you get the clutter off your desktop (and out of your mind) and focus your energies on what's most important: making sound decisions, producing high-quality materials, and working effectively with others to meet and surpass the expectations of a fast-moving marketplace.

The Changing Nature of the Microsoft Office System

The earliest versions of Microsoft Office were revolutionary in that they gave us the digital means to do tedious tasks more efficiently and–best of all–to save our work and continue to benefit from the results of our efforts. Typing a report no longer required a spool of correction tape on the old Smith-Corona typewriter; now you could make changes in the file–instantly!–before it ever went to the printer.

The first version of Microsoft® Office Word for Windows, released in 1989, had only two toolbars. We were impressed with the most basic functionality (making words bold so they would stand out; centering a heading; adding a page number). When the next version of Office Word arrived three years later, it still had only two toolbars, but the new additions were (drum roll, please!) nested dialog boxes–that is, dialog boxes *within* dialog boxes.

Between 1989 and 2003, Microsoft Office experienced a growth spurt in the features department. In fact, the suite grew into a set of software tools that became mammoth in size. Power and flexibility are two great qualities in software; and knowing that you had a suite of programs that could "do it all" created a sense of security. But with 31 toolbars, 19 task panes, context menus, dockable menus, hierarchical menus, and expanding menus, how would you ever find the commands you needed to accomplish what you set out to do today? What about those projects you did infrequently–such as producing a quarterly manager's report? Remembering how to find the options you needed for tasks you did infrequently became a bit like looking for a needle in a haystack. See Table 1-1 for an interesting look at the evolution of Microsoft Office over the last 17 years.

Table 1-1 Microsoft Office—Kong-Sized Growth

Release	Date	Screen Resolution	Toolbars	Added Features
Office Word for Windows 1.0	1989	640x480	2	
Office Word for Windows 2.0	1992	640x480	2	Nested dialog boxes
Office Word 6.0	1994	800x600	8	Right-click contextual menus; ToolTips; tabbed dialog boxes; toolbars on bottom of screen; Wizards
Office Word 95	1995	800x600	9	Auto spelling checker; Auto features (AutoCorrect)
Office Word 97	1996	1024x768	18	Toolbars all around screen and floating; menu bar redockable; multilevel context menus; icons on menus; grammar checking; hierarchical pull-down menus
Office Word 2000	1999	1024x768	23	Expanding menus, default toolbars on a single row, help pane
Office Word 2002	2001	1024x768	30	Task panes, Type a question for help box; Smart Tags; Paste options
Office Word 2003	2003	1024x768	31	11 new task panes; Research features

Survival of the Smartest

In a study conducted by scientists at the University of Oregon,[1] researchers found that what affects a person's memory capacity most is the ability to disregard irrelevant or unnecessary details. In other words, it's not what you know–it's what you *ignore*–that might be a major factor in your success.

If you work with information, you know how true that is. Daily, you are barraged with facts and files, and buried in a mountain of e-mail messages. Some items are urgent and require immediate action, but most are simply notes you need to respond to reasonably soon, reports you need to comment on, leads you need to follow up with, or junk mail you need to delete. Your first task in getting a handle on all this information is to weed out the items that have nothing to do with the task at hand. The 2007 Microsoft Office system can help you with that.

1. Ward Leslie, Melody. *Discovery Disproves Simple Concept of Memory as "Storage Space."* Available on the Internet: *www.eurekalert.org/pub_releases/2005-11/uoo-dds111805.php.*

Meeting Today's Work Challenges

Whether you feel successful in your work probably depends on many factors. If you are a business owner or manager, success likely has a lot to do with your ability to lead—to make good decisions, to focus on the important things, to gather and act on accurate data, and to delegate and follow up in a way that continues to move your company or your department toward the overall goal. If you are an information worker who focuses mainly on projects and timeframes, you might feel successful when you can complete the tasks and projects you're working on, collaborate with those who have information or input you need, and produce the output you (and your supervisors) are hoping for.

No matter what our roles at work, to be successful today we need to somehow balance the following critical needs:

- To gather and process information accurately and efficiently to make sound business decisions (and weed out the irrelevant data we receive)
- To connect with others (customers, vendors, employees, peers, managers, and stakeholders) in a timely and effective way
- To learn and use tools that help us schedule and complete tasks, manage relationships, track business processes, and demonstrate professional results
- To produce quality materials that help move our company or department toward established goals (increased market awareness, improved customer satisfaction, enhanced business partnerships, and so on)

The following sections go into a little more detail about each of these items and introduce a few possibilities for the way the Microsoft Office system can help you address them.

Finding What You Need to Make Educated Business Decisions

Because of the fast-moving nature of business today, it is crucial that owners and managers be able to track the results of their business decisions. Having the capacity to evaluate actions—did that last marketing campaign result in new leads for your company?—in a timely way helps ensure that you are doing more of what works and less of what doesn't. Microsoft® Office Outlook® with Business Contact Manager 2007 includes a Marketing Campaign feature that enables you to create a campaign, distribute it by using Office Word 2007 or the Microsoft® Office Publisher Mail Merge functionality, and then track the results of the campaign by gathering customer account data. Microsoft® Office Excel® 2007 also includes tools designed to help you gather Business Intelligence (BI) that will give you the information you need to make decisions that will affect your business or department.

> **Note** Office Outlook with Business Contact Manager 2007 is available in Microsoft® Office Professional 2007, Microsoft® Office Small Business 2007, and Microsoft® Office Small Business Management 2007.

Prioritizing Your Work Efforts—Weeding Out the Irrelevant

The fact that we have the option of being connected 24/7 brings with it additional challenges. We want access to information–but we need it simple. We have to be able to prioritize what we need to work on–and then find quickly what we need to do the work, and then move on to other things. Otherwise, we are buried in a mountain of extraneous data that never gets us where we need to go.

As Microsoft Office evolved over the years, it grew dramatically in the number of features and tools it made available for users. But until now, one thing the software could not do was to help us prioritize–what's most important to do first? Which tools do I need in order to do that? With the new look and feeling of the Microsoft Office system, you will be able to find and use the tools you need for the task at hand, which helps you focus on accomplishing the next step–while still keeping the big picture in mind.

The command tabs in the core applications follow the life-cycle stages of a document or project, so the programs are organized to provide the support you need in each step of document creation. For example, in Office Word 2007, the command tabs are (from left to right) Home, Insert, Page Layout, References, Mailings, Review, and View (see Figure 1-1). (If you have installed Office Outlook with Business Contact Manager 2007, you also see a Business Tools tab.)

Chances are that as you create a document, you will want to write first (Home tab); add charts, clip art, or diagrams (Insert tab); then finalize the page layout (Page Layout tab). For some projects, you might need to add more specialized items, such as footnotes or citations (Reference tab), add mail merge components for a mass mailing (Mailings tab), or work collaboratively with others as you go through a review cycle with the document (Review tab). Of course, along the way you'll want to be able to see your evolving document from different perspectives (View). This life-cycle progression is similar in Office Excel 2007, Microsoft Office® PowerPoint® 2007, and Microsoft® Office Access 2007 as well. With this approach, you always know where to find things–and you always remember which step comes next!

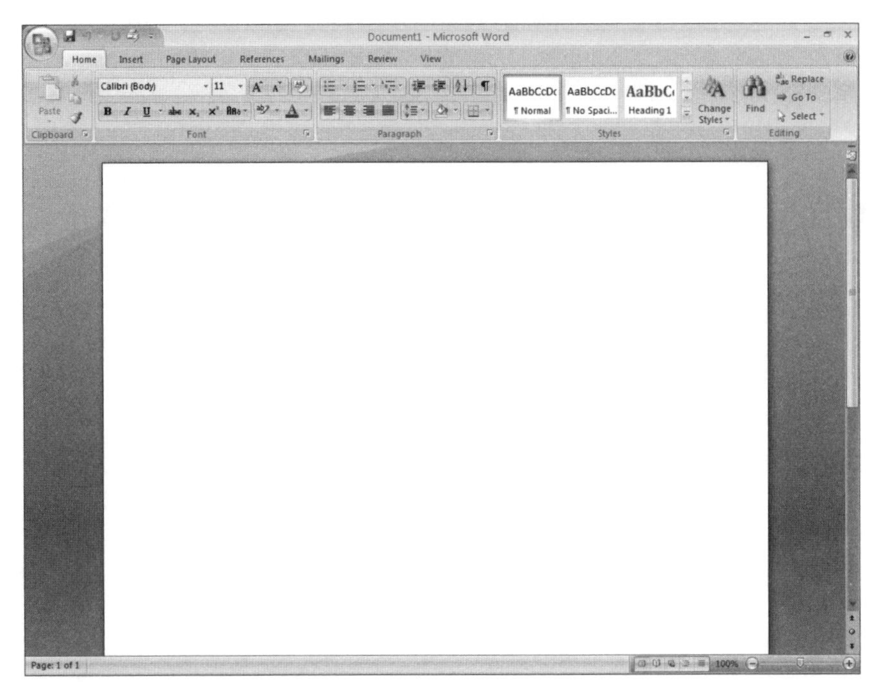

Figure 1-1 Each command tab is designed to represent a different stage in the life cycle of a document or project.

Connecting to the Right People and Getting the Job Done

Today's business is connected. When is the last time you felt completely out of touch with the outside world? That means no cell phone, no television, no Internet. We have grown accustomed to staying in touch with the flow of information throughout our workdays and into our evenings at home. Everywhere we go, it seems, we have the option of connecting to the information we need–via our cell phones, our PDAs, and laptops. You can schedule meetings on your Pocket PC while your daughter finishes at soccer practice; you can download the files you need for a presentation while you sit in a drive-through waiting for your mocha latte. The coffee shop isn't just a quiet place to "get away from it all" anymore–now it's a place to surf the Web, answer e-mail, or finish your review of the team's report for this Friday's stakeholder's meeting. Office Outlook 2007 includes a great new To-Do Bar that helps you see at a glance all the appointments you have and tasks that are due for the next few days. Office Outlook 2007 functions more than ever before as your command center, enabling you to identify and prioritize tasks so you can get more done in less time.

Learning and Using Flexible Tools for Varying Experience Levels

The workplace today represents a dramatic range of ages and experience levels. Companies include people who began working before the IBM PC arrived on the scene and they may still work to get comfortable with new technology; while at the other end of the spectrum, workers coming out of college today have grown up with access to computers, video games, and more. The difference in their comfort level can be dramatic–and it means that there might be a great mix of attitudes in your own workplace. How can you meet the needs of both groups of users–and all those in-between–so each person can be more productive while working, no matter the experience or comfort level? Design a simple, elegantly powerful suite of programs that works the way they do.

> **Tip** The Microsoft Office system offers training, templates, clip art, and more online at *office.microsoft.com*.

The 2007 Microsoft Office System—Tools for Today

As you will learn throughout this book, the exciting changes in the 2007 release were designed to meet the very real challenges in the lives of real people. From school to home to office, we need fast, efficient, and simple ways to work with hectic schedules, manage information, run businesses, and manage global operations. That's no small task!

The Microsoft Office system development team has been listening and learning from users for years, conducting detailed studies, hosting focus groups, and compiling data from the Office 2003 Customer Experience Improvement Program. The extensive amount of study and feedback is paying off in the 2007 Microsoft Office system–a radical change in a powerful suite of applications that not only provides the tools you need to accomplish important business tasks but also grows with you as a business analysis and development tool.

> **Tip** For a fascinating look at the early stages of 2007 Microsoft Office system design and implementation (as told to Channel 9 by Office Program Manager Julie Larson-Green), go to *channel9.msdn.com/Showpost.aspx?postid=114720*.

The 2007 Microsoft Office system was designed specifically with the following goals in mind:

Make the product easier to use. The dramatic and smart redesign of the look and feel of the Microsoft Office system does away with the overabundance of toolbars and the layers of nested dialog boxes. As you learn in Chapter 2, the design of the majority of the applications (Office Word 2007, Office Excel 2007, Office PowerPoint 2007, and Office Access 2007) now brings to you the tools you need to complete the task you're working on. It's easy to discover new features you didn't see before because of the contextual display, but you don't have to go searching through multiple levels of menus to uncover that one command you vaguely remember but can't find.

Help you become more efficient. The redesign of the look and feel saves you time by making the options you need easier to find; the flexibility in the way you can work with the Microsoft Office system (choosing primary mouse-based or keyboard-based techniques) enables you to choose the work style you like best. Faster search capabilities help you locate what you need more quickly than ever; increased integration among the applications makes it faster and easier to share data and objects between programs.

Make it easier to find what you need. Super ToolTips help you understand how to use a feature and provide a link for more detailed help; Live Preview enables you to try an option (such as a style, font, or color) before selecting it. Galleries display a range of choices you can select quickly without digging through multilayered menus.

Make it easier to create great professional quality documents. A large collection of professionally designed templates is now part of all the core Microsoft Office system applications. Additionally, process-related help (such as Publisher Tasks, the Design Checker, the Document Inspector, and more) help you ensure that your documents and projects are as accurate and professional as possible before you share them with others.

BI and ECM in the 2007 Microsoft Office System

It's easy to get caught up in the dramatic new look and feel of the new Microsoft Office system and overlook some of the more powerful behind-the-scenes features that don't get the same level of press. But the 2007 release of the Microsoft Office system moves the suite out of the realm of "power software tools" you can use to accomplish specific tasks and into the category of a powerful suite of applications that strategically help you grow your business. Two dynamics that are key to the business development capabilities of the Microsoft Office system are features that support Business Intelligence (BI) and Enterprise Content Management (ECM).

BI is the process of evaluating, reflecting on, and assessing the business environment in which a company operates. To collect the BI that a travel agency needs, for example, the owner or manager might do considerable marketing and industry research and then analyze all the competition to see how those companies are distinguishing themselves. The information gathered through BI helps business leaders plot out the appropriate course to achieve the company goals. BI helps companies answer these questions, among others: How well are we doing? Did that marketing campaign hit the mark? Are we in sync with the demands of our marketplace? How do we stand out from the crowd?

ECM is really about managing the content of an enterprise. What does your company do with the content you produce? These content pieces might include digital content such as text, video, audio, or photos; transactions; catalogs; data; code. Planning the way you create, manage, publish, share, present, and store content is the function of an ECM system.

> New features built into the core applications–Office Word 2007, Office Publisher 2007, Office Excel 2007, and more–help you get better results from your efforts and plan long-term for the protection and dissemination of the content you produce with the 2007 Microsoft Office system.

New 2007 Microsoft Office System Versions

The Microsoft Office system is available in a variety of versions, each designed with a specific user group in mind. Here's a quick overview of the different versions, along with the applications included in each one:

- Office Professional 2007 includes Office Word 2007, Office Excel 2007, Office PowerPoint 2007, Office Outlook 2007 with Business Contact Manager, Office Access 2007, and Office Publisher 2007.
- Office Professional Plus 2007 includes Office Word 2007, Office Excel 2007, Office PowerPoint 2007, Office Outlook 2007, Office Access 2007, Office Publisher 2007, Microsoft® Office InfoPath® 2007, Microsoft® Office Communicator 2007, Integrated Enterprise Content Management, Electronic Forms, and Advanced Information Rights Management and Policy Capabilities.
- Microsoft® Office Basic 2007 includes Office Word 2007, Office Excel 2007, and Office Outlook 2007.
- Microsoft® Office Home and Student 2007 includes Office Word 2007, Office Excel 2007, Office PowerPoint 2007, and Office OneNote® 2007.
- Microsoft® Office Standard 2007 includes Office Word 2007, Office Excel 2007, Office PowerPoint 2007, and Office Outlook 2007.
- Office Small Business 2007 includes Office Word 2007, Office Excel 2007, Office PowerPoint 2007, Office Publisher 2007, and Office Outlook 2007 with Business Contact Manager.
- Office Small Business Management 2007 includes Office Word 2007, Office Excel 2007, Office PowerPoint 2007, Office Publisher 2007, Office Outlook 2007with Small Business Contact Manager, Office Access 2007, and Microsoft® Office Small Business Accounting 2007.
- Microsoft® Office Enterprise 2007 includes Office Word 2007, Office Excel 2007, Office PowerPoint 2007, Office Outlook 2007, Office Access 2007, Office Publisher 2007, Office InfoPath 2007, Microsoft® Office Communicator, Integrated Enterprise Content Management, Electronic Forms, Advanced Information Rights Management and Policy Capabilities, and Microsoft® Office Groove® 2007.

For more information about the various 2007 Microsoft Office system versions, go to *office.microsoft.com*.

Upgrading to the 2007 Microsoft Office System

The question of when to upgrade to a new software system is something each individual group considers when weighing the benefit of the new version compared with the comfort level of the old. As dramatic a change as the new user interface (UI) is in the 2007 Microsoft Office system, users will likely find that the switch to the 2007 release is a much easier transition than the move to previous versions.

One of the main reasons for this ease of transition is that the 2007 release is built on a cornerstone of simplicity. When developers went back to the drawing board on the UI, it was with the intention of designing software that works the way we do. Rather than adding more features and commands to an already overburdened and complicated menu system, designers created the system around a core of ease-of-use and easy access. This means that learning to use the program is more intuitive for users than previous versions because the programs are designed to work the way we do.

Value Benefits of the 2007 Microsoft Office System

Much more than just a set of new-and-improved features (which you'll discover in more detail throughout the rest of this book), the 2007 Microsoft Office system is a combination of powerful core applications that enable you to respond more effectively to the following challenges in your work:

- Finding what you need–instantly
- Uncovering the tools you need when you return to a task you do infrequently
- Standing out from the crowd
- Dealing with information overload
- Collaborating in a "wall-less" workplace
- Creating professional materials in-house and at less cost
- Pulling together flexible workgroups to accomplish a specific goal
- Discovering and using the full capabilities of your software investment
- Tracking and analyzing your business efforts
- Managing, using, and archiving the content you create

A Lower Learning Curve

Because of the nature of the new look and feel of the 2007 Microsoft Office system, new users can accomplish tasks right away. No long arduous searches for one rarely used command hidden four levels down in a menu system. When users begin working on a new worksheet, for example, options for all the tasks they might need when creating a new worksheet become available in the user interface (see Figure 1-2). Options related to other worksheet tasks (for example, sorting or filtering data) are completely out of the way (not simply grayed-out). This simplifies the work area and shows users only what they need related to the task at hand.

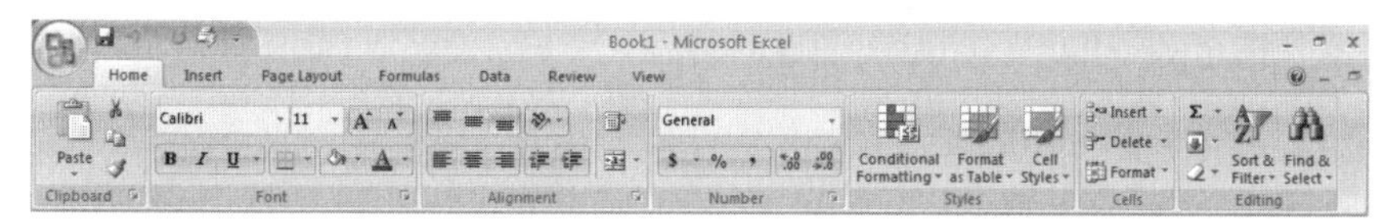

Figure 1-2 The user interface displays only what you need to accomplish a specific task.

> **Tip** For a detailed look at each of the features in the new Microsoft Office system user interface, see Chapter 2.

Legacy Mode and Keyboard Support

If you are the type of user who prefers using the keyboard over the mouse (and there are many of us out here!), you will be pleased to know that the 2007 Microsoft Office system includes a number of features for keyboard lovers.

- First, every keyboard shortcut you use in previous versions of Microsoft Office works exactly the same way in the 2007 release.
- Second, new KeyTips show you quick keys you can use to navigate through the user interface without using the mouse.
- And finally, the Microsoft Office system includes a *Legacy mode* that users can turn on to bring keyboard accelerators to life. All the keyboard accelerators you're familiar with will work with the 2007 Microsoft Office system.

Create It Once; Use It Many Times

Because the 2007 Microsoft Office system is built completely on the new Office Open XML file format, you can use the documents and data files you create in the Microsoft Office system in a variety of other applications. Consider this: you spend a lot of time perfecting the annual report for your small business. You've got the phrasing just right; you love the images you selected; the template includes all the formats you want to use in your other business documents.

As you create marketing brochures throughout the year, you can use the text you created in your annual report without cutting and pasting. Why? Because it's saved as XML data, and you can pull that data directly into your brochure template in Office Publisher 2007. When you want to create an Office PowerPoint 2007 presentation to show potential investors how efficient your operation is, you can pull from that annual report (and the Office Excel 2007 worksheets that provided the financial data) because everything is saved as XML data.

Not only does the new Office Open XML format save you time and trouble but it also decreases the margin for error that is introduced when you have to rekey information or copy and paste portions of files from one document to another. You can work smarter, easier, and faster–and produce more accurate results because of the Office Open XML format in the 2007 Microsoft Office system.

Coming Next

In the next chapter, you'll learn more about that various aspects of the new 2007 Microsoft Office system user interface. Read on to find out about the changes in the UI, as well as the new contextual commands, Galleries, Live Preview, and much more.

Chapter 2

A New Look

What you'll find in this chapter:

- Learning the landscape: The new user interface
- The new File menu
- Using the Quick Access toolbar
- New view controls
- Keyboard support

The most talked-about change in the 2007 Microsoft® Office system—the one the public was so excited to see for the first time—is the revolutionary change in the Microsoft Office system user interface. As you learned in Chapter 1, a great amount of research, testing, thought, and effort went into designing an end user experience that puts the needs of the information worker (or business owner or manager) at the center. In other words, the software is supposed to work the way you do. To accomplish that goal, the way the programs interact with you must be smooth and seamless. Commands need to be easy to find; the right tools must show up when you need them; and the work area must be open and uncluttered so you can focus on the most important task at hand—completing your project, not wrangling with multilevel menus and bottomless nests of dialog boxes.

Learning the Landscape: The 2007 Microsoft Office System User Interface

The design of the 2007 Microsoft Office system user interface includes fully a dozen new features that will ultimately make working with your favorite applications less work. If that seems counterintuitive (12 new features will make things easier?), keep reading. This section shows you how each component fits into the overall goal of simplifying and streamlining your options so you always have what you need for your current task.

Tip Why do we need an easier interface? When you consider that the original version of Microsoft® Office Word (1.0) had only about 100 commands, and the most recent version, Office Word 2003, includes more than 1500, it's easy to understand how the sheer number of features has outgrown the original menu system. To find some commands, you have to hunt through menus, multiple submenus, and dialog boxes. The new 2007 release user interface brings the commands to you—with more power, more flexibility, and software that anticipates what you need and when you need it.

Using the New User Interface

If you've been working with Beta 1 of the 2007 Microsoft Office system or if you read any of the press coverage or blog posts about the new release, you've heard about the new user interface, which is the dramatic new replacement for the customary menu system in previous versions of Microsoft Office. The user interface stretches across the top of the work area in most of the core applications, giving you tabs, contextual commands, and more that are related to the current operation you are performing (see Figure 2-1).

The user interface is actually a collection of a number of components:

- Command tabs (such as Home, Insert, Page Layout, Formulas, Data, Review, and View in Microsoft® Office Excel® 2007) stretch across the screen just below the window title bar.
- Command sets are the commands available for the selected tab that relate to what you're trying to do. The name of the command set appears below the commands (for example, Clipboard, Font, and Alignment are shown in Figure 2-1).
- Contextual commands appear only when an object (table, chart, and so on) is selected.

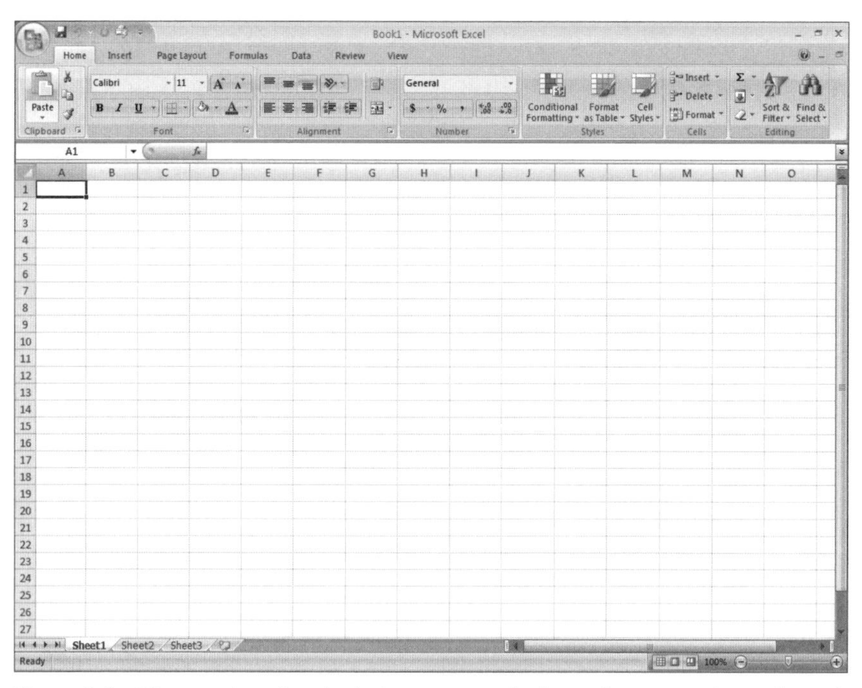

Figure 2-1 The user interface includes command tabs and command sets that relate to a specific aspect of your project.

Command Tabs

The menu system you are used to seeing in Microsoft Office has now been replaced with a series of *command tabs* that relate directly to the tasks you need to accomplish. For example, the new command tabs in Microsoft® Office Word 2007 are File (marked by the 2007 release logo), Home, Insert, Page Layout, References, Mailings, Review, and View (see Figure 2-2). In Office Excel 2007, the command tabs are File, Home, Insert, Page Layout, Formulas, Data, Review, and View.

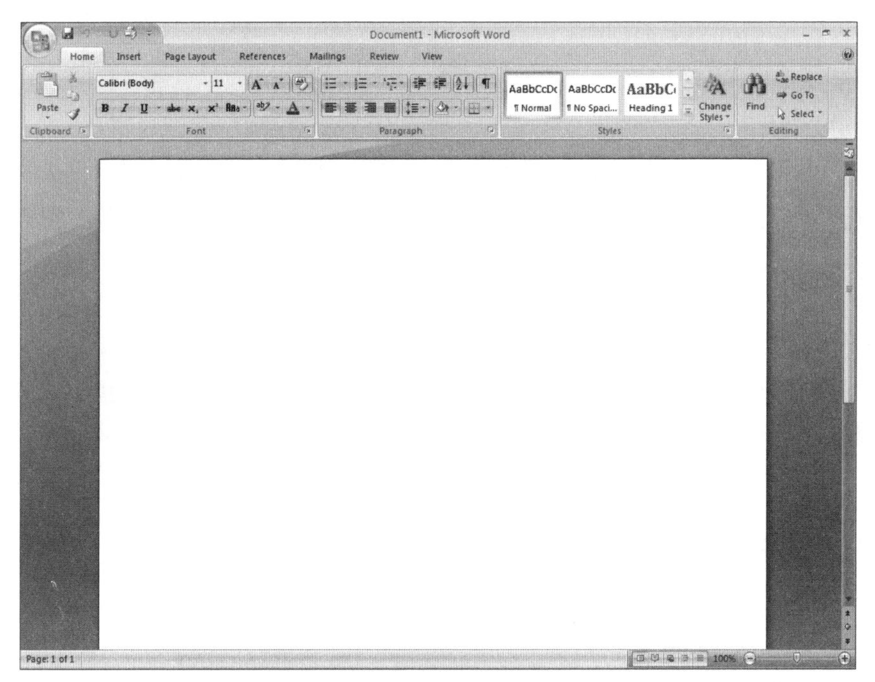

Figure 2-2 The command tabs in Office Word 2007 correspond to the different tasks of preparing a document.

The tabs correspond directly to the stages of the process you're likely to follow as you create a project in an application. For example, when you're creating a worksheet, you need commands related to data entry, editing, and formatting. Further on in the process, you might want to work with the information on the worksheet by sorting, filtering, consolidating, or validating it. These commands are available in the Data tab, further down the row in the Office Excel 2007 command tab display.

Command Sets

Different commands appear in the user interface, depending on the tab you selected. If you click the Home tab in Office Word 2007, one set of commands appears in the user interface; if you click the Review tab, a different set is displayed. This type of filtered tool display cuts down on the number of menus, commands, and dialog boxes you have to sort through to find the items you want. Each *command set* is grouped according to its function. In Figure 2-3, the Page Setup, Themes, Background, and Arrange groups are all command sets for the Design tab in Microsoft® Office PowerPoint® 2007.

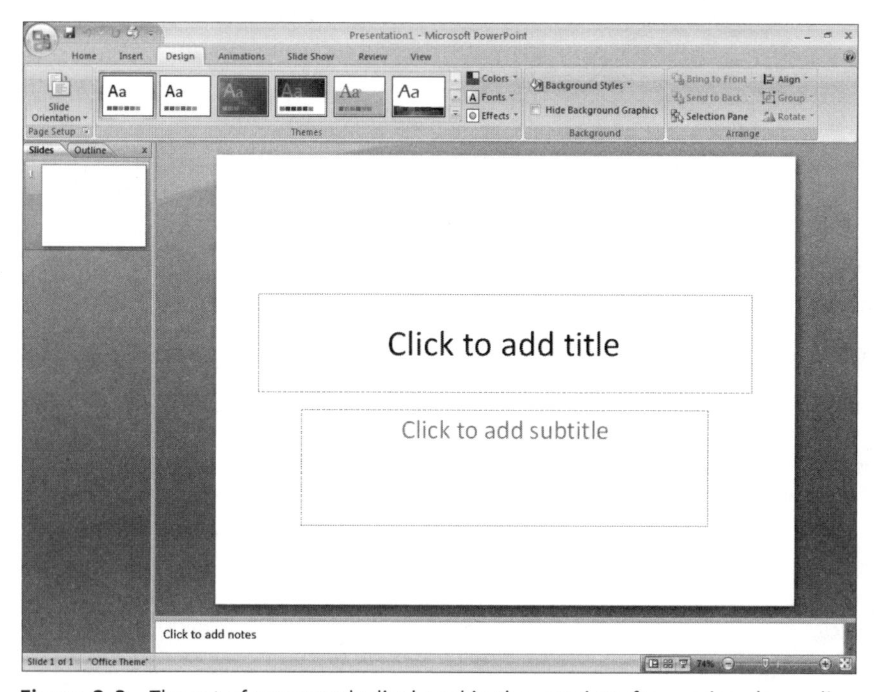

Figure 2-3 The set of commands displayed in the user interface varies, depending on the command tab you select.

Contextual Tools

To keep the design uncluttered and relevant to what you're doing, contextual command sets appear only when a specific object is selected. Figure 2-4 shows a set of *contextual tools* that become available after you add a diagram with the SmartArt tool (available in the Insert tab). The name of the displayed contextual tool set appears above the user interface and is highlighted so that you can recognize it easily.

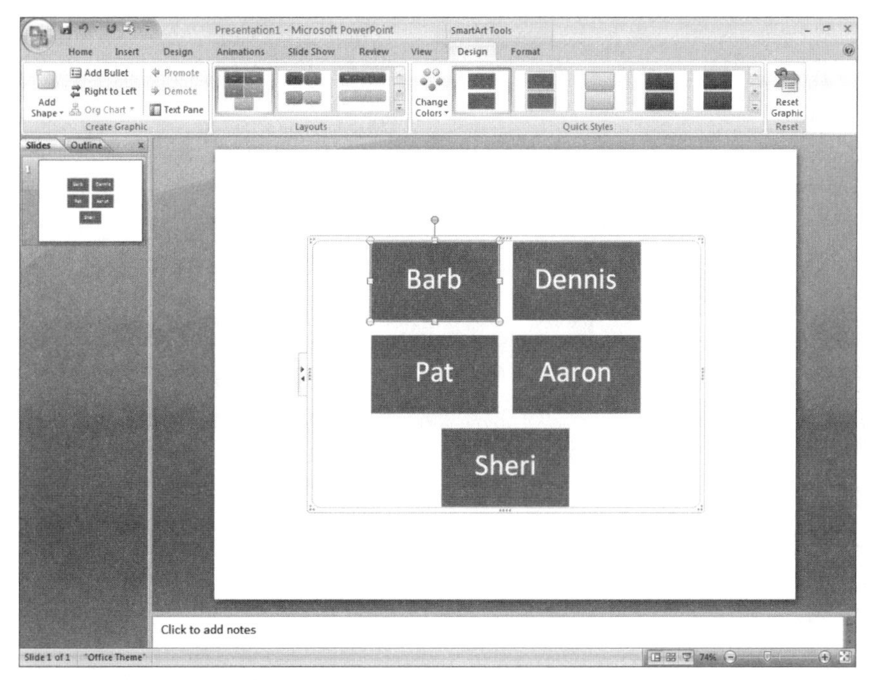

Figure 2-4 Contextual commands display only the commands you need that are related to the currently selected object.

Dialog Launchers

Some command sets on the user interface are also available in traditional style dialog boxes. You can display the dialog box by clicking the *dialog launcher* in the lower-right corner of the command set. Here's how it works. Click the command tab you want (for example, Home in Office Word 2007). Now click the small arrow symbol in the lower-right corner of the command set you want to display, which launches the dialog box for that set of commands, as Figure 2-5 shows.

Dialog launchers are also available at the bottom of any gallery that shows advanced options. For example, when you choose the Page Layout command tab and click the Columns down arrow, a gallery of column-wrapping settings appears. Click the More Columns option at the bottom of the gallery to launch the Columns dialog box (see Figure 2-6).

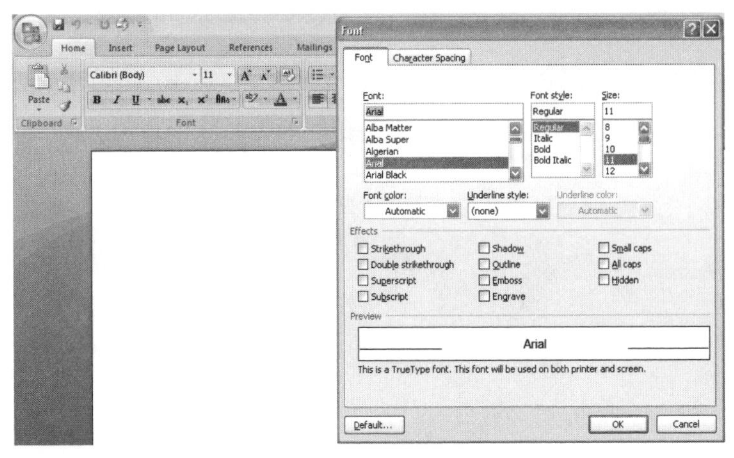

Figure 2-5 Dialog launchers display some command sets in traditional dialog boxes.

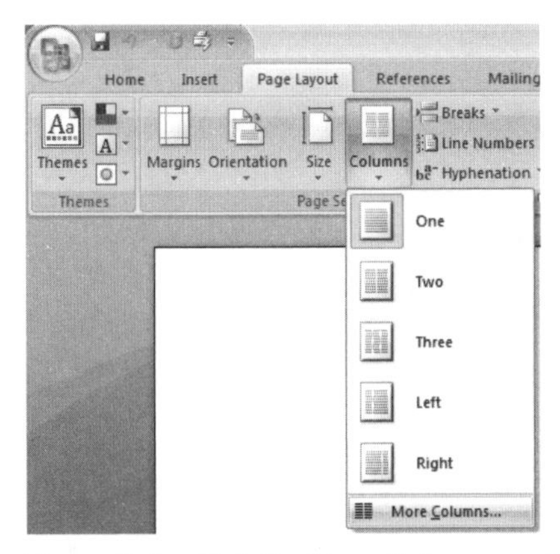

Figure 2-6 Click the More Columns option at the bottom of a gallery to display a dialog box of additional options.

Galleries

Galleries are a great visual addition to the design of the new program windows–they make finding the look you want as simple as point and click. The 2007 Microsoft Office system includes two types of galleries. Galleries with only a few selections are typically shown as part of a command set in the user interface; but galleries with multiple selections (such as Themes, Margins, and Position in Office Word 2007) display as drop-down galleries in which you can make your selection.

When you select a command that has a down arrow next to it (which means that additional choices are available), the palette of options appears (see Figure 2-7). You can see at a glance which color combination, format, color scheme, transition, or chart type you want. Just click your choice (or point to it if you want to use the Live Preview feature, described next), and the setting is applied to the current document or a selected object.

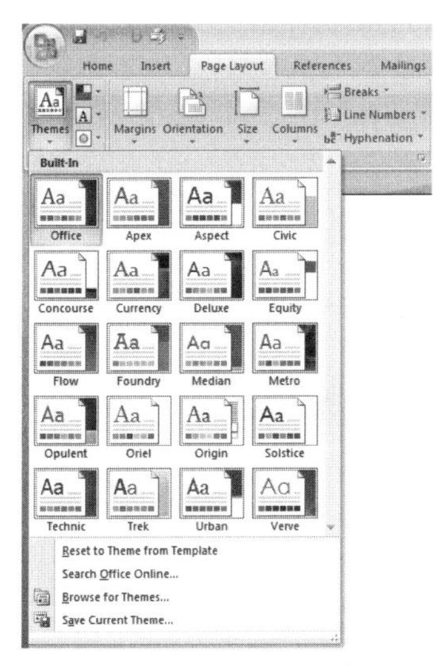

Figure 2-7 Galleries enable you to easily find and select the choice that's right for your project.

Live Preview

Live Preview enables you to try a choice on for size before you select it. Now when you consider an option (such as the Page Color gallery shown in Figure 2-8), you can point to it. The effect is then applied to your document, worksheet, or presentation so you can see how it will look. If you want to keep the change, click the option. If you want to keep looking, point to a different option.

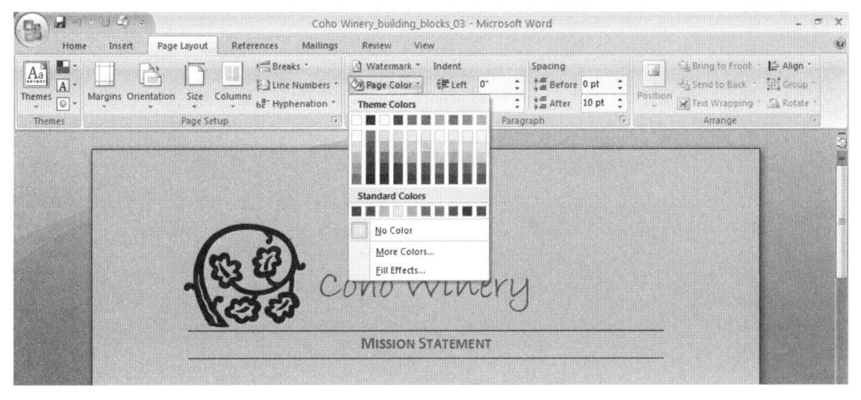

Figure 2-8 Live Preview shows you what the result of your choice will look like before you actually select it.

The new Office 2007 system user interface changes are currently available in Office Word 2007, Office Excel 2007, Office PowerPoint 2007, and Microsoft® Office Access 2007. Some aspects of Microsoft® Office Outlook® 2007 also incorporate the new features.

The New File Menu

The File menu has had a major bit of cosmetic surgery–instead of the word "File," the 2007 Microsoft Office system logo now marks the spot where the File menu resides. And the changes in the File menu aren't only cosmetic–functional changes help you focus on the file-related tasks you need. The new File menu includes two panels. On the left, you see the major file tasks; on the right, the choices related to those tasks appear when you point to one of the commands on the left. For example, when you position the mouse over Save As, the options shown in Figure 2-9 appear.

Figure 2-9 The File menu displays additional choices when you point to its major commands.

In each of the applications, the tasks in the File menu follow the basic progression of the life cycle of your document. One great new addition is the Finish command, which provides you with options for completing the document–whether the file is an Office Word document, an Office Excel worksheet, or an Office PowerPoint presentation (see Figure 2-10). The Publish command, also in the File menu, gives you the means to publish your files to a shared document workspace, Excel Services, or your blog (perhaps the best-kept secret in Office Word 2007!)

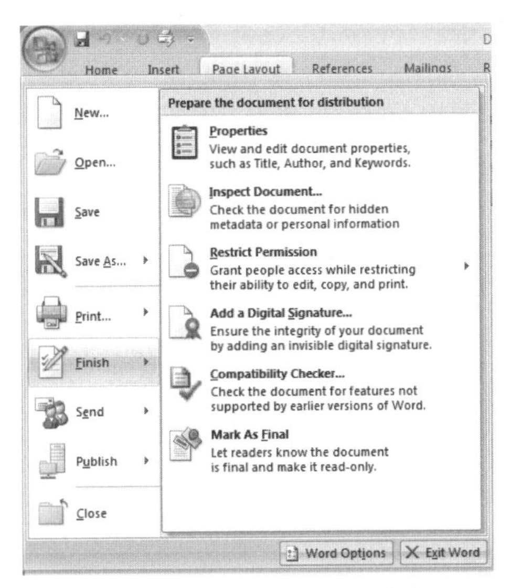

Figure 2-10 The Finish command gives you options for checking and protecting your file.

Quick Access Toolbar

To the right of the File menu on the user interface you see three familiar tools: Save, Undo, and Redo. The Print tool is a smart addition to this group, placed along with the other tools for easy access. These tools are part of the *Quick Access Toolbar*, which travels with you from application to application. These four tools are available in the same spot in all the Office 2007 core applications that have the new user interface. You can customize the Quick Access Toolbar to add other tools you use regularly. For example, you might want to add the Hyperlink tool to the Quick Access Toolbar so it is available in all your applications.

To add a tool to the Quick Access Toolbar, right-click the tool and select Add To Quick Access Toolbar (see Figure 2-11).

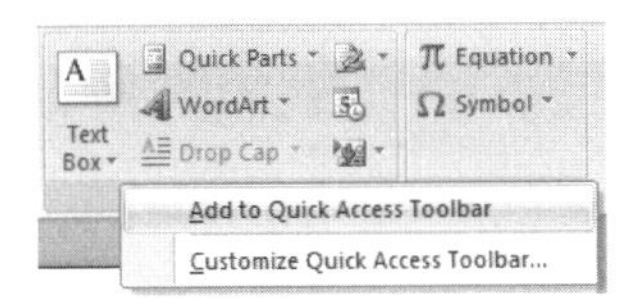

Figure 2-11 Add your favorite tools to the Quick Access Toolbar.

> **Tip** If you put a number of tools on the Quick Access Toolbar, you might want to display it in its own row in the user interface. Right-click anywhere on the Quick Access Toolbar and choose Place Quick Access Toolbar Below The User Interface. To return the display of the toolbar to its original state, right-click the Quick Access Toolbar a second time and choose Place Quick Access Toolbar Above The User Interface.

New View Controls

With all the changes in the 2007 Microsoft Office system interface, you might wonder where some of your favorite tools have gone. How do you work with other open files, which used to be the function of the Window menu? How do you move among views so that you can work with your document outline, display Slide Sorter view in Office PowerPoint, or zoom in for a closer look at a document?

The 2007 release uses the View tab to organize the controls you need for viewing your documents. Everything you formerly found in the Window or View menus, you'll now find by clicking the View tab (see Figure 2-12). The familiar View tools appear in the lower-right corner of the document window, to the left of a handy Zoom tool that enables you to enlarge or reduce the display of your document incrementally while you work.

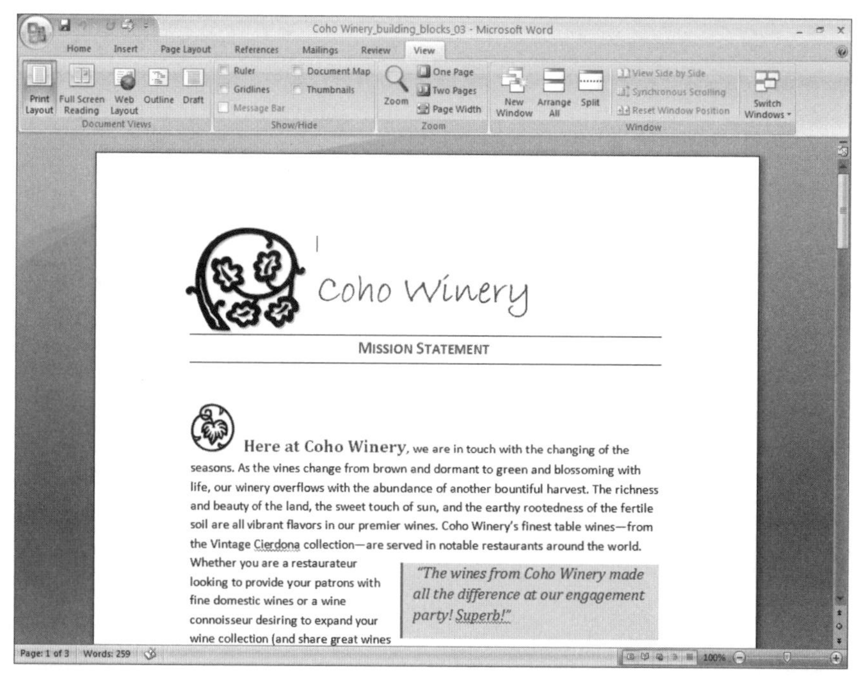

Figure 2-12 Switch between windows and change the view by using the commands in the View tab.

Tip To magnify or reduce the size of the document displayed on the screen, drag the slider in the Zoom tool until the document is the size you want.

Keyboard Support

People who become proficient with software often look for (or create!) shortcuts to help them cut down on wasted keystrokes and mouse clicks when they do routine tasks. The 2007 Microsoft Office system includes a number of keyboard features that will make even the most ardent shortcut key lover happy. Three different levels of keyboard support are available:

- KeyTips enable you to toggle on the display of keystrokes you can press to navigate the user interface using the keyboard.
- Keyboard shortcuts in the 2007 release work exactly the same way they worked in Office 2003 (see Table 2-1).

KeyTips

KeyTips in the 2007 release display all the available shortcut keys so you can choose the one you want. To toggle the display of the shortcut keys, simply press Alt and wait a moment. The KeyTips appear on top of the commands wherever they're found; simply press the letter of the command you want to select (see Figure 2-13).

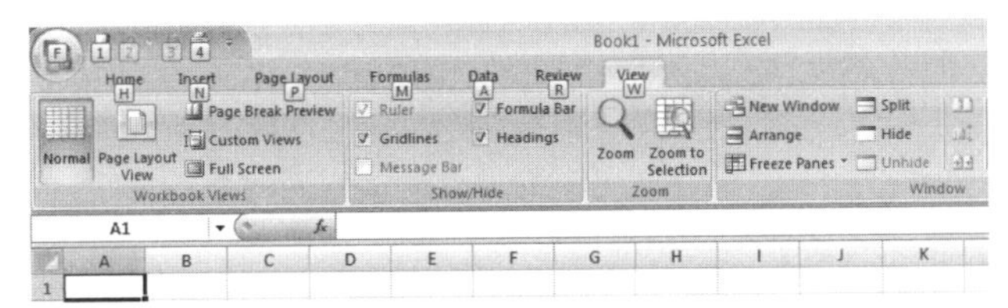

Figure 2-13 Press Alt to toggle on the display of KeyTips.

Keyboard Shortcuts

There are so many keyboard shortcuts in the 2007 Microsoft Office system that it's possible to use your favorite applications without ever touching a pointing device. These keyboard shortcuts are carryovers from Microsoft Office 2003—but the important thing is that if you're a shortcut fan, you'll be pleased to know that every keyboard shortcut works the way it did in the previous release (no unlearning required). Table 2-1 provides a list of the shortcuts that are common to all the core applications, but each application has its own huge range of keyboard shortcuts for you to put into service.

Table 2-1 Common Keyboard Shortcuts in the 2007 Microsoft Office system

Shortcut	Command	Shortcut	Command
Ctrl+O	Open	Ctrl+E	Align Center
Ctrl+Z	Undo	Ctrl+C	Copy
Ctrl+Y	Redo	Ctrl+X	Cut
Ctrl+S	Save	Ctrl+V	Paste
Ctrl+P	Print	Ctrl+F	Find
Alt+F4	Close the Active Window	Ctrl+H	Replace
Ctrl+B	Bold	Ctrl+A	Select the Entire Document
Ctrl+I	Italic	F7	Start the Spell Checker
Ctrl+U	Underline	Shift+F7	Display the Thesaurus
Ctrl+R	Align Right	Ctrl+Shift+S	Style dialog box
Ctrl+Shift+F	Font dialog box		

Coming Next

Now that you know the basic lay of the land in the 2007 Microsoft Office system, it's time to get into some of the systems. The next chapter shows you what's changed in the Help system and walks you through the ways to safeguard your files in your favorite applications.

Chapter 3

Important Systems: Help and Security

What you'll find in this chapter:

- Finding help in all the right places
- Using Super Tooltips
- Changes in Microsoft Office Online
- Safeguarding your files

Productivity is all about movement–moving forward, creating documents, crossing tasks off your To Do list, getting things done. Whether you are the manager of a large business or a sole proprietor working alone in an office, the way you meet and resolve obstacles in your day has a lot to do with how productive you–or your department or your company–can be.

This chapter is all about two important systems that help keep you moving on the road to productivity using the 2007 Microsoft® Office system. The help system in the 2007 release has been moved out of the task pane and now links users instantly to expanded and improved resources. And improvements in the way you finish and protect your completed documents give you a variety of ways to control who has access to your documents and how far that access will let them go in modifying, sharing, or printing the files they receive.

Finding Help in All the Right Places

Software help systems usually get a pretty bad rap. The users who rely on them (oddly enough, statistics show they are often more experienced users) are quick to point out what's missing, what doesn't work, what isn't helpful. And because help systems are where people go when they are up against an obstacle and want an answer fast, there's a level of frustration built into pressing F1 and looking through a help system for the answers.

If you are the type of user who prefers to find your own way through a new program, you will most likely click through all the menus and explore the available options, trying to figure things out yourself instead of consulting a resource like help. If you are the type of user who reads the manual (Hello! This book is for you!), you are likely to turn to the printed page (or keep the book handy while you explore the software on your own). So where does the help system fit in? Help is where you go when none of these other resources is producing what you need to get unstuck; and when help is one of your last stops, you really want it to produce the answer you need. Fast.

For administrators, help that's done well can be a first line of support for their users who are new or unfamiliar with a Microsoft Office system application. A brief introduction to the help system can plug users in to a steady stream of troubleshooting ideas (and creative resources such as templates, online training, and more) that in the long run can save your company valuable time and money that might have been spent chasing down an answer that was just a few clicks away. And a help resource that meets users where they are and offers a range of detail in the help that is provided–from a simple tool name (tooltips) to how-to articles, templates, community newsgroups, videos, and training–provides a level of continuing support beyond the reach of most stand-alone applications.

Changes in the 2007 Release Help System

The changes in the 2007 release help system are designed to get you the best answer for your questions as quickly as possible. The new Microsoft Office system help viewer has been designed to provide a variety of ways to find, display, and preserve the help information relevant to what you're trying to accomplish.

Figure 3-1 shows the Microsoft Office system Help window. The toolbar includes the familiar navigation tools—Back, Forward, and Stop–as well as a new Refresh tool you can click to update the content of the window as needed. The Application Home tool gives you the option of accessing additional information related to the program you are currently using.

Four additional tools help you find and view help information, and then preserve the information you find. The TOC button enables you to display a listing of help topics related to the current application (as shown in Figure 3-2), the Text Size tool increases (or decreases) the size of the text in the Help window, the Print tool prints the current window, and the Pin tool lets you "pin" the current Help page open so that you can refer to it while you work.

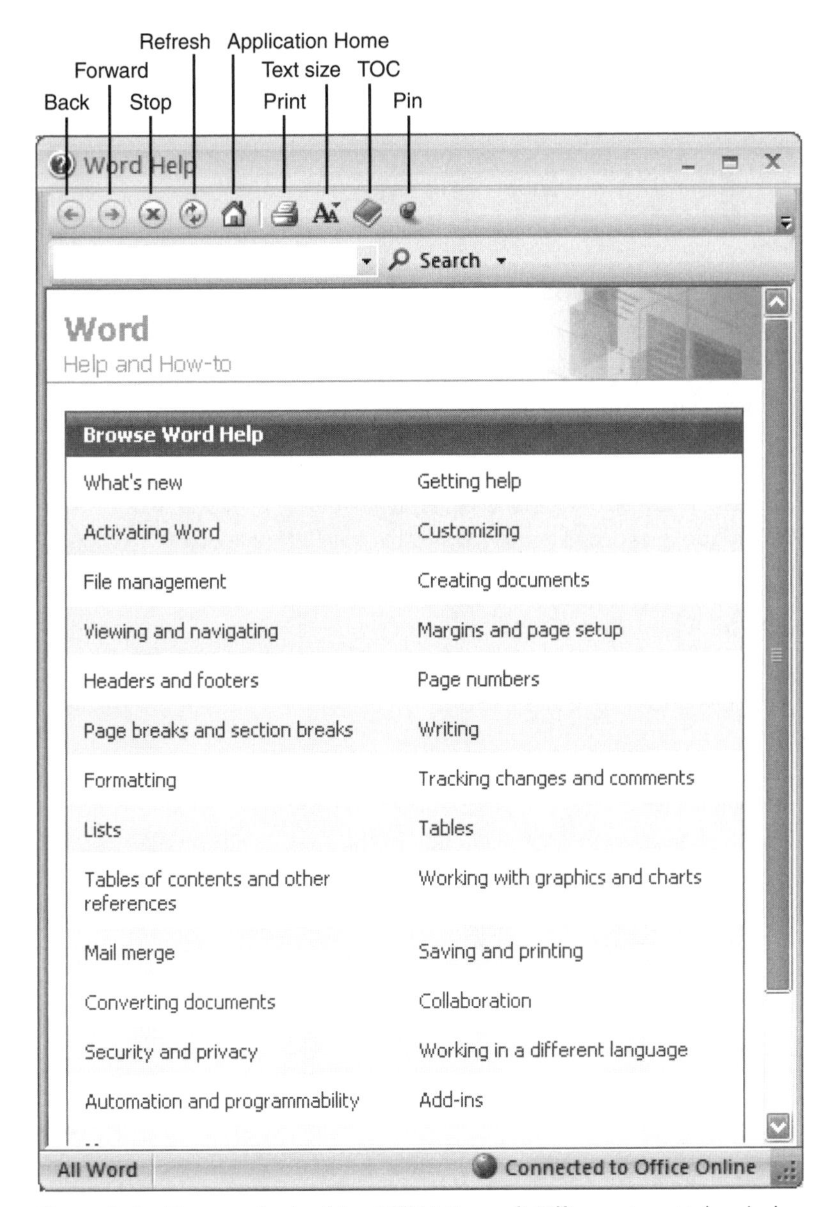

Figure 3-1 The new look of the 2007 Microsoft Office system Help window

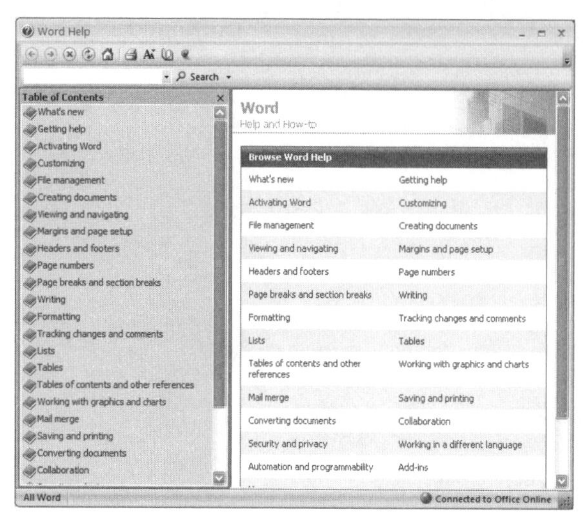

Figure 3-2 The TOC tool gives you links to task-related help information.

The Return of F1

If you're a fan of pressing F1 to get context-sensitive help while you're working with your favorite application, you'll be pleased to know that F1 is back in the Microsoft Office system. According to Mike Kelly from Microsoft Office Online, "There was a technical reason why it was difficult to do in 2003 that we fixed in 12. So while you won't always see context-sensitive links when you press F1, you will always get to help where you can search...and we will do context-sensitive links for the most common dialogs (one of the other advantages of online help–we know what are the most popular searches and context-sensitive requests and can focus on improving those first)." [1]

1. Mike Kelly, from Office Online, commenting on Jensen Harris's blog: *http://blogs.msdn.com/jensenh/archive/2005/11/29/497861.aspx*.

More than a Name: Super Tooltips

One of the important design goals of the new look and feel of the Microsoft Office system was to unclutter the work area and give you only the tools and options you need to accomplish your current task. Super Tooltips offer a new way to get contextual help that comes and goes without taking up a lot of room on the screen.

Super Tooltips give you more information than traditional tooltips (which display only the name of the tool at the mouse pointer position). Although tooltips display for all tools in the the 2007 release interface, Super Tooltips are used only for those items that need a little more explanation. For example, consider the Super Tooltip displayed when the pointer is positioned on the Format Painter tool (see Figure 3-3).

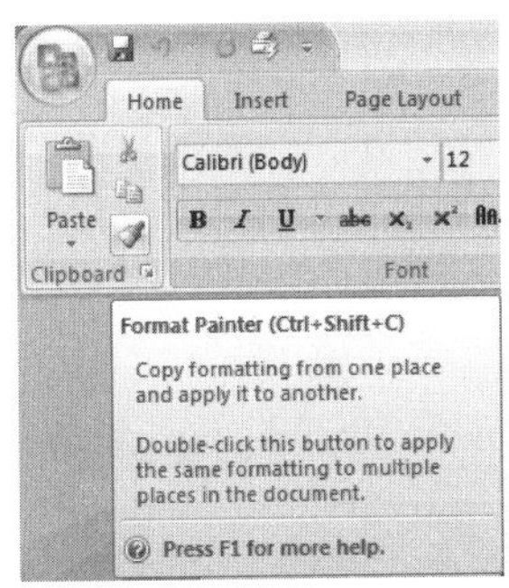

Figure 3-3 Super Tooltips provide more information than the simple tool name.

The developers of the help system in the 2007 release have envisioned Super Tooltips as the missing link between the user interface and the help system. Not only do Super Tooltips provide the expanded descriptions, contextual suggestions, and sometimes even images but they also link back to the help system so you can press F1 for more detailed information about that particular command. When you finish with the Super Tooltip, click outside the box to close it.

A Tip for a Launcher

Just so you'll never have to wonder whether clicking a dialog launcher in the bottom-right corner of a command set will produce the dialog box you want, you can position the pointer over the launcher, and a Super Tooltip will show you which dialog box will open when you click the launcher.

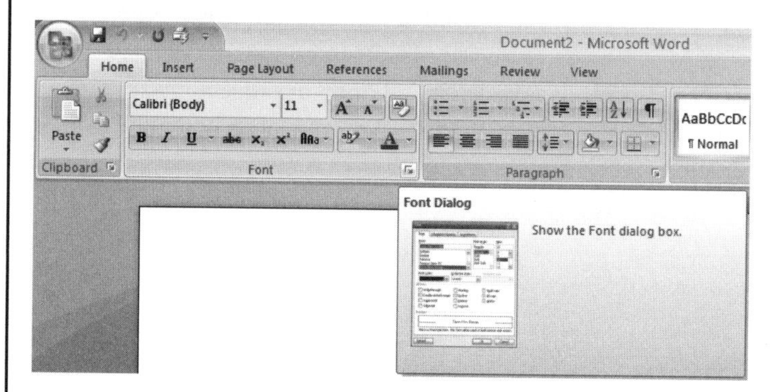

Previewing the dialog box in this way saves you at least one mouse click (and possible frustration when you open two or three dialog boxes looking for the one you want).

New Offerings from Microsoft Office Online

Microsoft Office Online has new and improved visibility in the core applications–Microsoft® Office Word® 2007, Microsoft® Office Excel® 2007, Microsoft® Office PowerPoint® 2007, and Microsoft® Office Access® 2007. When you create a new document by choosing New from the File menu, the opening window gives you several choices: You can choose a template; select an existing file; start with a blank document; or scroll down to the Microsoft Office Online area and click links there to find tips, tutorials, downloads, and additional templates for your application.

Microsoft Office Online has been totally redesigned to streamline and expand the support experience. In addition to detailed help information, you'll find how-to articles, training links, demonstrations, quizzes, IT and developer pages, Microsoft Security, Ask The Community, and more. Additionally, you can find resources to help you with specific needs, such as Work Essentials, Enterprise Solutions, Microsoft Learning, and Microsoft® Office Small Business 2007. Be sure to check out Microsoft Office Online and take advantage of the resources available to help you get the most out of the 2007 release.

Safeguarding Your Files

Not long ago, the phrase *global workplace* seemed like just a concept–something far-off and fuzzy about the way we could one day work together to get things done. Today the global workplace is a reality. We work with teams all over the world; we connect with call centers on different continents; we send files back and forth (or work together in a shared workspace on the Web) to finish group projects and presentations.

This global sharing of data is a great benefit for businesses large and small, but it also brings a heightened need for protecting sensitive documents. Businesses need to be able to secure proprietary documents and sensitive data; users need to know that the documents they create are making it into the right hands (and *only* the right hands). Information workers need a way of ensuring that only those with the necessary permissions can modify, print, or send a document they receive. No matter what the size of your organization, the enhancements in the file security and protection features of the Microsoft Office system give you additional ways to ensure that the work you create and share is secure.

Finishing and Protecting Your Files

In Office Word 2007, Office Excel 2007, and Office PowerPoint 2007, the File menu includes a new Finish command that provides a number of ways to safeguard finished documents, worksheets, and presentations (see Figure 3-4). Here's a quick introduction to the tools:

- The Properties option enables you to add identifying information about the open file, including the author name, keywords, subject, and more (See Figure 3-5).
- Use the Inspect Document option to find and remove any personal or sensitive information in your document before you share it.
- Choose Restrict Permission to set and control access you give others to your files.
- Select Add A Digital Signature to attach a hidden signature to the document so that only authorized recipients can view it.
- Use Mark As Final to save a read-only version of your file so that the document you share with others cannot be modified by the recipients.

Tip The Compatibility Checker available in the Finish submenu reviews the current document to make sure that your version of the file is compatible with other versions of the software.

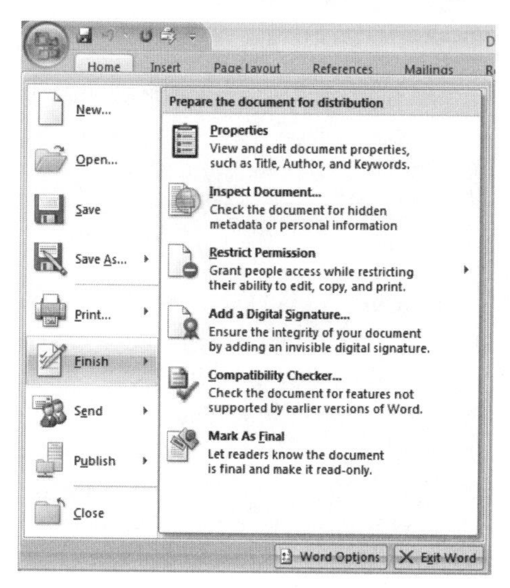

Figure 3-4 The Finish command provides a number of options you can use to finalize and secure your files.

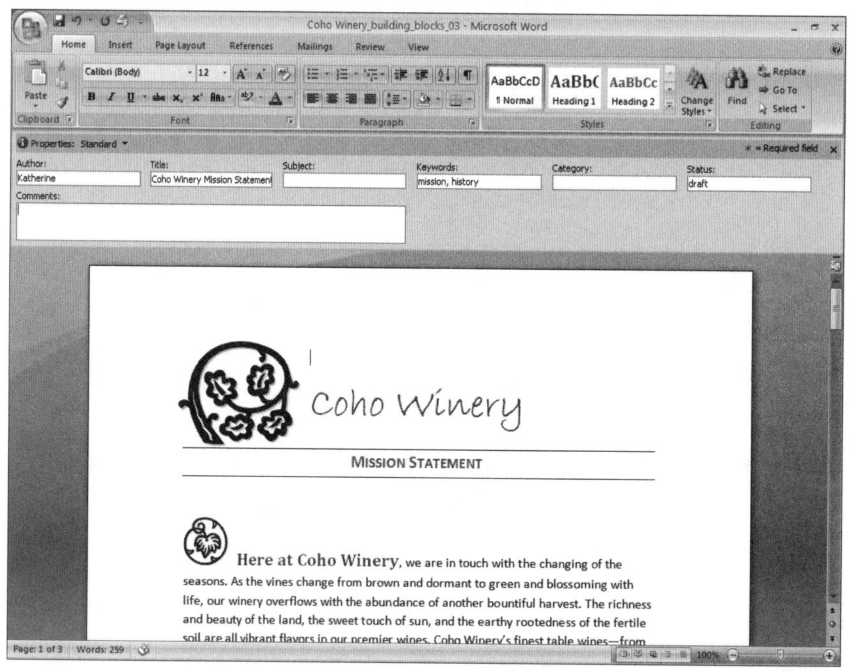

Figure 3-5 Add identifying information to the file using the Properties command.

Removing Personal or Private File Information

The Document Inspector (available in Office Word 2007, Office Excel 2007, and Office PowerPoint 2007) searches your file for information that could be inadvertently included in the finished file. When you click Finish and then Document Inspector in the File menu, the Document Inspector provides you with the inspection choices shown in Figure 3-6

After you click Inspect, the tool evaluates the document and displays a results window (see Figure 3-7). If you want to remove the information, click the Remove All button for any items you want to remove; then click Reinspect to review the document again. Repeat this as many times as necessary until the file is in the finished form you want.

Tip The procedure for setting file permissions in the Microsoft Office system is identical to the process in Microsoft Office 2003; but now you can set and control file permissions from the File menu. To work with permissions for your file, open the File menu, choose Finish, and click Restrict Permissions. Choose the option from the submenu that applies to the settings you want to use.

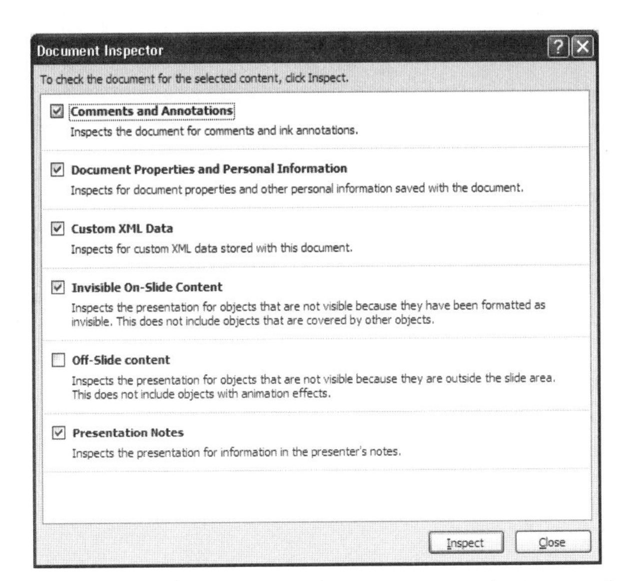

Figure 3-6 The Document Inspector can evaluate your document, worksheet, or presentation for a number of potential problems.

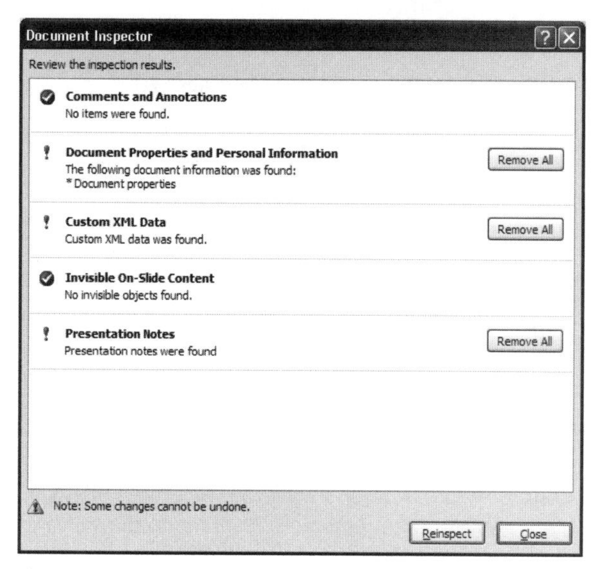

Figure 3-7 The Document Inspector displays the results of its review.

Adding a Digital Signature

A digital signature, also called a *digital ID*, is an electronic identification that authenticates a document and lets others know it is from a reputable source. To add a digital signature to the files you create in the Microsoft Office system, you need either to sign up for a digital ID from a Microsoft partner or create one yourself.

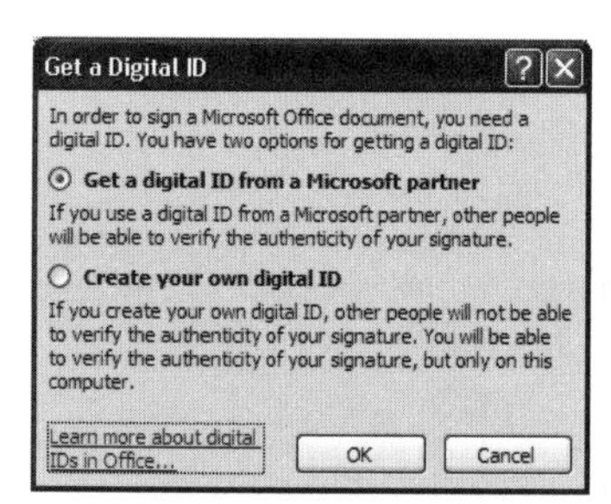

Marking a Document as Final

When you complete a document and want to save it as a read-only file (so others can view but not modify it), use Mark As Final from the Finish submenu. The application prompts you to save the file first; when you click Yes, the file is saved as a final file. Now any commands that would make it possible for users to modify and resave the file have been disabled, preserving your file in the state you intended.

Note You can reach the Trust Center from within Office Word 2007, Office Excel 2007, Office PowerPoint 2007, and Office Access 2007 by opening the File menu and choosing the Options tool in the lower-right corner of the menu. Click Trust Center in the Options window to get to the security and privacy options within the individual applications.

Old-Fashioned Document Protection

In addition to these new security options in the Microsoft Office system, you can still use the tried-and-true Protect Document tool, now available by clicking the Review command tab in Office Word 2007, and the Protect Sheet and Protect Workbook tools in the Review command tab of Office Excel 2007. Both of these commands enable you to set varying degrees of protection and to assign passwords to your files to further ensure that your files are accessible only to those with the necessary permissions.

Coming Next

This chapter gave you a bird's-eye-view of two important systems that work behind the scenes as you create documents, prepare worksheets, and design presentations. With improvements such as Super Tooltips and far-reaching security options, the new applications are geared to giving you just what you need for your daily work.

The next chapter begins Part II of the book by exploring the new features and improvements designed to help you create professional documents in Office Word 2007.

Part II
Preparing and Producing Professional Results

In this part:

Chapter 4

Create Professional Documents with Office Word 2007

What you'll find in this chapter:

- New views, new tools
- The design of the Office Word 2007 window
- Create better documents, faster
- Fast, professional diagrams with SmartArt
- Counting your words
- A professional look, instantly
- Simplified collaboration
- Mail merge improvements

Microsoft® Office Word 2007 has always been a powerful program. In fact, from its earliest version, Microsoft Office Word has included more features than most people need (or know how to find) to create the documents they work with every day. Creating a full-featured, flexible, powerful program that doesn't overwhelm, restrict, or frustrate users has been a key goal for the developers of Office Word 2007. The idea is to simplify the way users of varying experience levels find, learn, and use the tools they need while continuing to increase the capability of the program to connect to the real demands of our professional, always-on business world. The result is that we will spend less time hunting for features we rarely use and more time producing high-quality documents that can be leveraged in a variety of ways.

New Views, New Tools

Perhaps the biggest news in Office Word 2007 is the story most of the applications share–the new look and feel of the program window. The user interface makes it easy to find just what you need (and *only* what you need) in the command tabs; the contextual tabs appear when you select an object; the command sets relate to the command tab that is currently selected. In addition to the new look, a new live Word Count toolbar enables you to know how long your document is getting and gives you a new full-screen viewing experience.

The Design of the New Office Word 2007 Window

The command tabs on the Office Word 2007 user interface are arranged according to the sequence of tasks you are likely to accomplish as you move through the different stages of document creation (see Figure 4-1). Here's a quick rundown of the command tabs and what you'll find in each one:

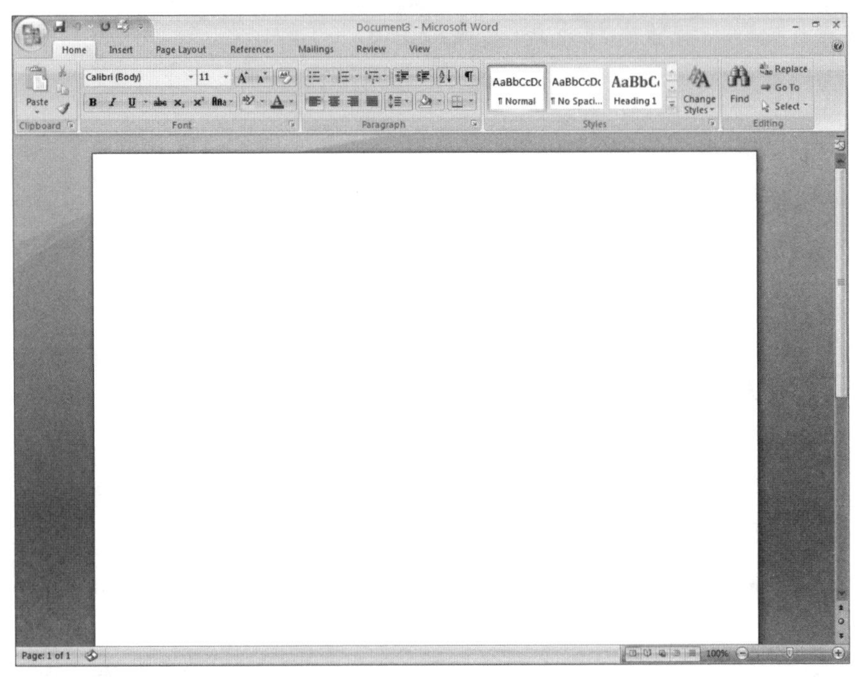

Figure 4-1 The new look of the Office Word 2007 window

- The **Home** tab includes commands related to the Clipboard, font selections, paragraph settings, styles, and editing.
- The **Insert** tab includes what you need to add pages, tables, illustrations, links, headers and footers, text objects, and symbols in your document.
- The **Page Layout** tab contains the commands for working with themes, page backgrounds, and paragraph spacing in your document. Additionally, you choose page setup options and arrange the order of elements on your page using this tab.
- The **References** tab includes special elements you will use when you create longer or more complete documents. On this tab, you'll find what you need to create a table of contents, footnotes, citations and bibliographies, captions, an index, and a table of authorities.
- The **Mailings** tab is a new addition in the Office Word 2007 interface. Here you can find everything you need related to creating, previewing, and producing a mail merge project.

- The **Review** tab houses all the commands you need for checking (spelling, thesaurus, and more) your document and sharing it with others for review. Here's where you find commands for adding comments, tracking and working with changes, comparing versions, and protecting the document.
- The **View** tab is where you'll find all the options for displaying your document in different ways: from basic document views, to a set of display tools for adding rulers and gridlines, to options for working with multiple documents in multiple windows.

View controls are placed in the bottom-right corner of the Office Word 2007 window so you can move among views easily. The new Zoom slider is a great addition, enabling you to magnify or reduce the display incrementally while you work.

Tip For more about working with the different features in the new 2007 Microsoft Office system user interface—including command sets, contextual tools, live preview (which really shines in Office Word 2007), dialog launchers, and more—see Chapter 2, "A New Look."

Better Documents, Faster

Not everyone is comfortable sitting down at the keyboard and pounding out a 10-page document in a single afternoon. Some people suffer from the memory of the seventh grade English teacher (the one with the red pen that never ran dry) and agonize over their choice of words, punctuation, and sentence style. Office Word 2007 includes tools that help users of all comfort levels create documents quickly by using ready-made templates and document parts, lessening the guesswork (and the fear of failure) involved in the creative process. This section introduces some of the features that help us get more done, more quickly with Office Word 2007.

Quick Cover Pages

Presenting a core message in the best possible light is an important part of communicating what any business, organization, or department is all about. A professional look and feel says a lot about a group's standards, commitment, and even hints at the possible quality of its services. Adding a sophisticated cover page to a report, sales prospectus, or business plan can convey a solid sense of professionalism–or at least attention to detail.

In Office Word 2007 you can now create a professionally designed cover page in two clicks of the mouse. Click Cover Page in the Insert tab to display a gallery of cover page styles; then simply click the page you like best (see Figure 4-2). Office Word 2007 adds the page to your current document, and you can click in the text boxes and add your own text to the page.

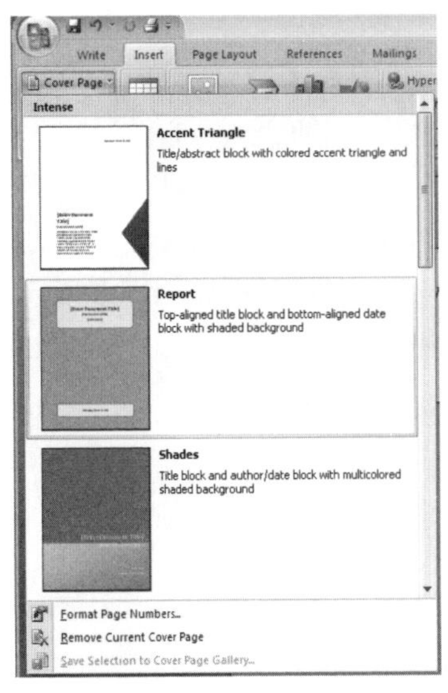

Figure 4-2 Creating a cover page is as simple as point, click, and edit.

> **Tip** You can customize the cover page you select by adding your logo, adding a photo of your facility, or choosing the color scheme and font style that matches your business brand. Then save the cover as an item you will reuse with other reports to give your documents a consistent look and feel.

Working with Building Blocks

Building Blocks are great new tools in Office Word 2007 that are based on the idea of reusable content. If you have a logo, letterhead, mission statement, or disclaimer that you use again and again on your professional documents, why not save those items as document parts you can insert quickly into new documents you create? This saves you the time and trouble of recreating the content and reduces the margin for error (because any time you draft something new you open up the possibility of typos and grammatical errors).

The Building Blocks feature is available in the Text command set of the Insert tab. When you click the Quick Parts arrow, a gallery displays any parts you created and saved and offers options for adding fields, page numbers, or inserting other parts from the Building Blocks Organizer (see Figure 4-3).

> **Note** During the beta program for Office Word 2007, Building Blocks were originally referred to as Quick Parts.

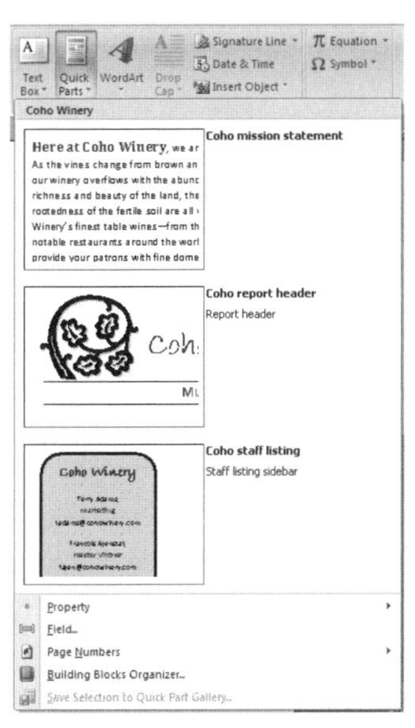

Figure 4-3 The Building Blocks gallery contains pieces of reusable content you can add to your own documents.

Built-in Building Blocks

Office Word 2007 comes with dozens of ready-made building blocks you can use to add pull quotes, equations, tables, and more to your own documents. These building blocks appear as selections in the various galleries you'll find throughout Office Word 2007. For example, when you click the Text Box arrow in the Insert tab, the gallery that appears is populated with the building blocks included with Office Word 2007. You can use these building blocks as they are or modify them to fit your own content and design and then resave them as a Building Block.

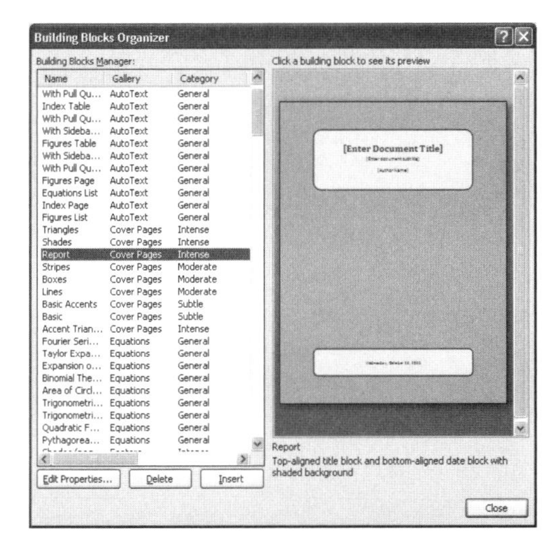

Choose Building Blocks Organizer from the Building Blocks Gallery to view the whole collection. You can click Edit Properties to change the settings associated with that item, click Delete to remove it from the list, or click Insert to add it to your document at the cursor position.

New Format, New Flexibility

Office Word 2007 includes support for the new Open XML format, the new default file format for Office Word 2007, Microsoft® Office Excel® 2007, and Microsoft® Office PowerPoint® 2007. Open XML format enables you to save a huge amount of file space (up to 50 percent) and makes the content you create reusable in a potentially unlimited number of ways. Here's a little bit about XML in Office Word 2007:[1]

- Open XML in Office Word 2007, Office Excel 2007, and Office PowerPoint 2007 is backward compatible, which means you can use files saved in XML format from Microsoft Office 2000, Microsoft Office XP, and Microsoft Office 2003.
- The file created by default in Office Word 2007 uses a new extension to reflect the change (.docx).
- Files saved in previous versions of Office Word (non-XML formats) are fully supported in Office Word 2007.

Tip The new Publish command in the File menu enables you to create a document workspace for the current document, share the document on a document management server (such as Microsoft Office SharePoint Server 2007), or post the document as an entry on your blog.

Fast Professional Diagrams with SmartArt™ Graphics

SmartArt graphics provide a great way for users who are outside their comfort zone creating drawings or diagrams to illustrate data concepts in their documents. With SmartArt graphics, you can create sophisticated diagrams that show data processes, hierarchies, cycles, and relationships.

Choose SmartArt from the Insert tab to start the process; then select one of the four basic layout styles (Process, Hierarchy, Cycle, and Relationship) to find the diagram type that is right for your document. Each diagram style offers dozens of style possibilities (see Figure 4-4).

---

1. For more information on XML in the Microsoft Ofice system applications, see Microsoft Office system Product Manager Brian Jones' blog at *http://blogs.msdn.com/brian_jones/*.

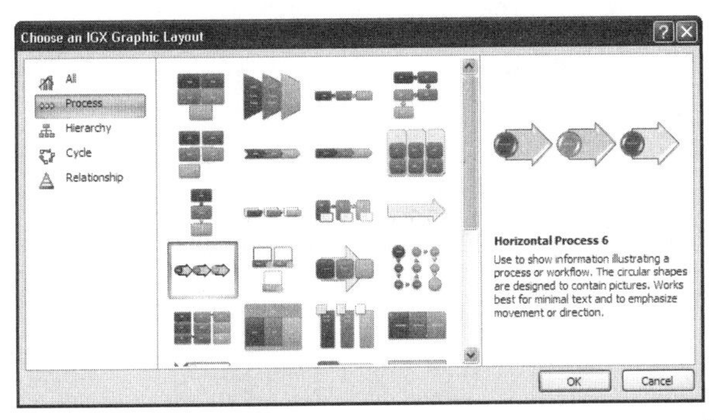

Figure 4-4 SmartArt graphics enable you to create sophisticated diagrams quickly by customizing them with pictures, descriptive text, and more.

> **Tip** Flexibility is one of the best features of SmartArt graphics. Whether you are creating a diagram to illustrate a sales process or designing the new organizational chart for your department, a wide range of styles and options are available to help you convey your ideas in just the right way.

Counting Your Words

If you are responsible for writing to a particular specification, the live Word Count tool makes it easy to keep an eye on how long your document is getting while you're writing it. What's even better is that you don't have to do anything to make the count appear; it appears naturally, by default, in the lower-left corner of the Office Word 2007 window (see Figure 4-5).

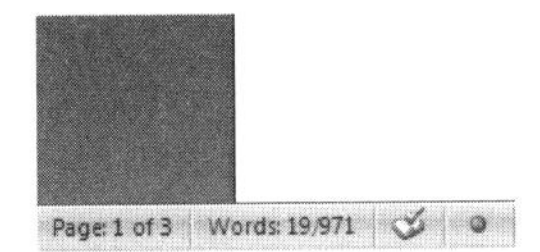

Figure 4-5 The new live Word Count tool enables you to keep an eye on the length of your document while you're writing it.

As you compose your document, Office Word 2007 displays the number of words in your document and also does a spelling and grammar check while you work. (This feature is similar to the wavy underline features in Office Word 2003 that alerted you to spelling and grammar errors in a document.)

> **Tip** You can find the number of words in an article or a text box by selecting only the text you want to count. The status bar displays two numbers (for example, 35/1250), showing the number of words in the selected text first and the count for the entire document second.

Quick Document Stats

If you want to get a quick sense of the different elements in your document, right-click the status bar of the Office Word 2007 window. A pop-up menu appears and shows various items, including the number of lines, columns, and sections; the status of features such as signatures, permissions, and track changes; and input and display options.

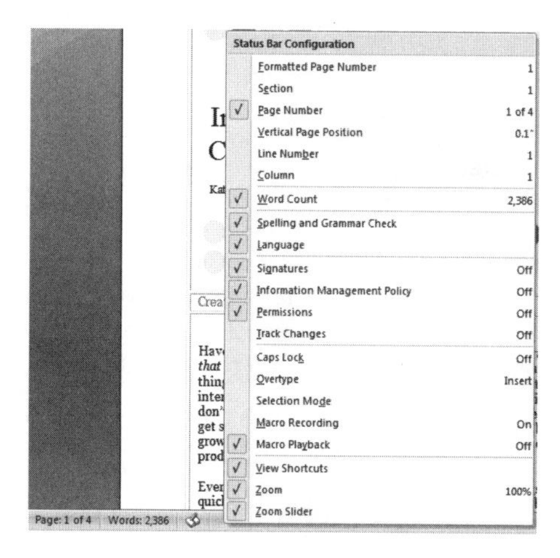

You can add any of the display controls to the status bar by clicking them. For example, clicking Line Number adds it to the status bar to the left of the live word count. To remove items from display, right-click the bar a second time and deselect the item you want to hide.

A Professional Look, Instantly

Have you ever spent hours laboring over a report and then took a look at it in Print Preview and decided you didn't like what you saw? Great new features in Office Word 2007 make it easy for you to try on several different styles before you commit to one you want to use. You can see how a publication will look before you go through changing font styles, colors, tables, and more. This section introduces the new features in Office Word 2007 that help you hit that professional look right off the bat.

Applying Quick Styles

Office Word 2007 includes a new Quick Styles feature that enables you to preview a number of styles before you select the one you want to apply to your document. Click to position the mouse cursor in your document at the point you want to apply the new style; then point to the selection in the Style command set that you want to preview. To see additional styles, click More in the lower-right corner of the style examples; a gallery of style choices appears (see Figure 4-6).

Tip You can create your own Quick Styles by formatting text in the font, style, and color you want; then highlight the text and right-click it. In the context menu that appears, choose Save Selection as a New Quick Style. In the Create New Style From Formatting dialog box, type a name for the new style and click OK. The style is now available for selection in the Style gallery.

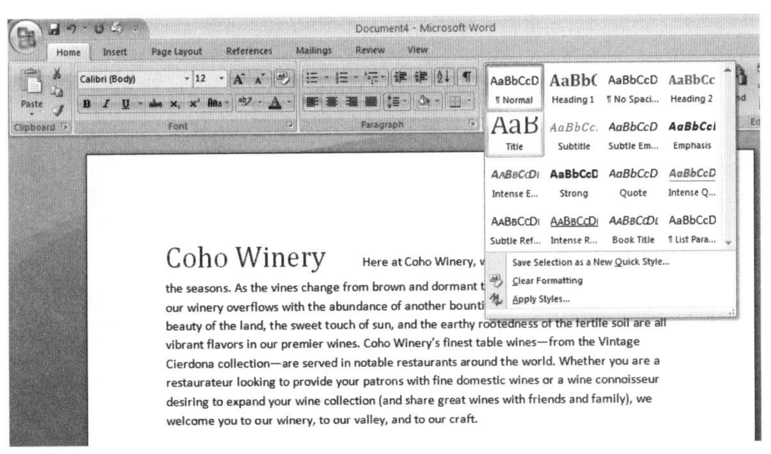

Figure 4-6 Preview a style by pointing to it in the Styles command set; apply a style by clicking it.

Three Things to Try

Mary Millhollon and Katherine Murray, authors of *Microsoft Office Word 2007 Inside Out*, recommend these as their favorite new "must try" features in Office Word 2007:

1. Building Blocks enable you to create, save, and use building blocks of content in your documents.
2. Document themes give your documents a professional look quickly.
3. Full Screen Reading view lets you review the document in a clean workspace.

Choosing a Document Theme

Document Themes enable you to change the way text, tables, and special elements are displayed throughout your document. A theme includes the typeface of headings and body text (including color, style, and spacing) as well as graphics such as rules, boxes, brackets, and borders. To preview different styles in your document, select the Page Layout tab and click Themes. The Themes gallery opens, displaying a number of different theme choices. Point to a theme style you want to preview, and the changes appear in the document window (see Figure 4-7). When you find a theme you want to use, click the theme to apply it to your document.

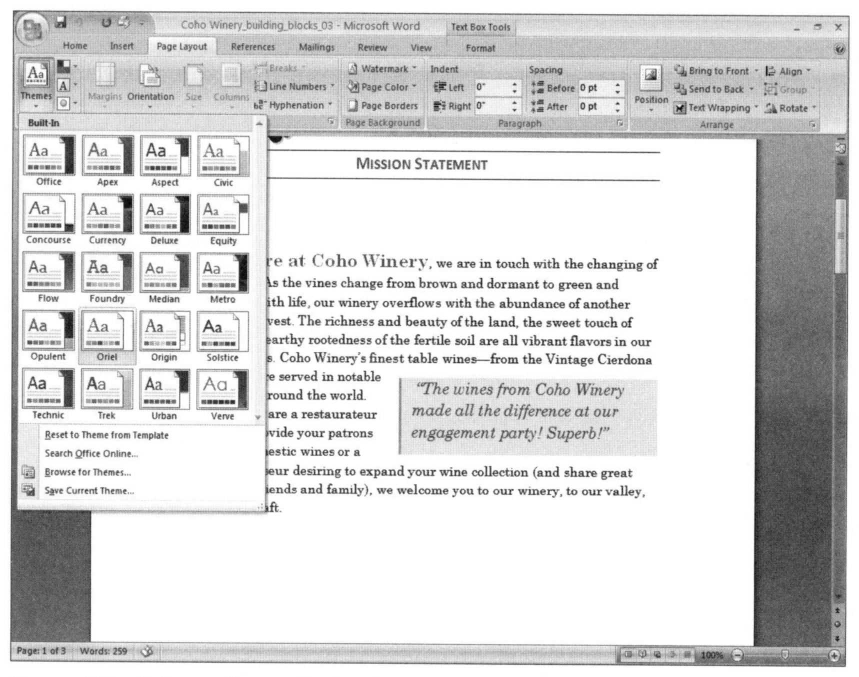

Figure 4-7 Point to themes in the Theme gallery to preview them in your document.

Late-Breaking Feature: Blogging in Office Word 2007

The hottest new feature in beta 2 of Office Word 2007 is the new blogging feature. Now you can blog directly from Office Word 2007 by opening the File menu, pointing to Publish, and clicking Blog. The Blog Post tab provides you with the commands you need to publish posts, set up blog accounts, format, and proof your blog entries.

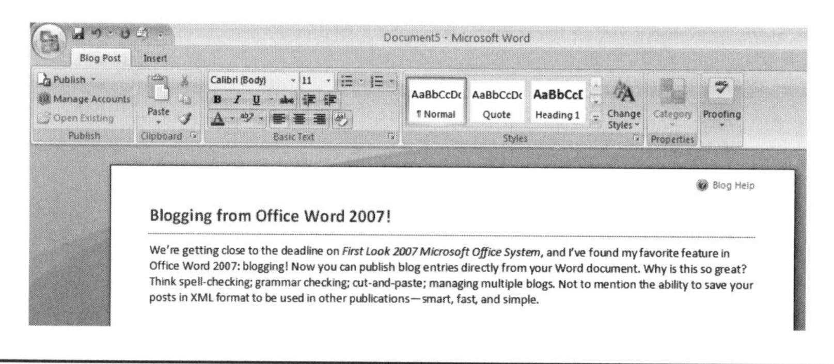

List Improvements

Bullets and numbering styles are now easier to apply because of the new Bullet Library and Numbering Library. There's no more navigating through menus and submenus to get what you need; now you can easily choose a new bullet or numbered list or create a new style by choosing the options in the Library windows.

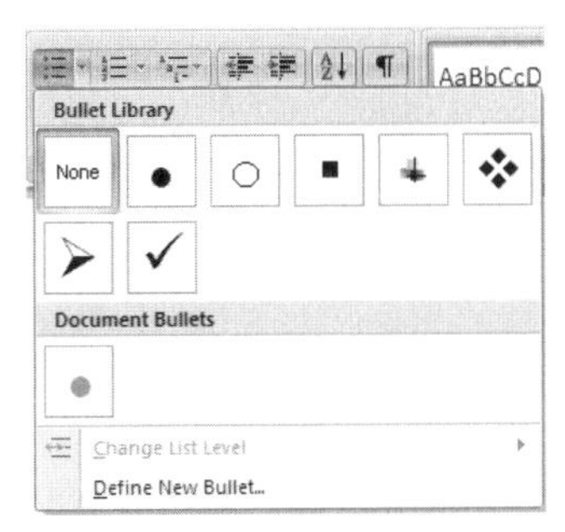

The new Bullet Library displays a gallery of graphical or simple document bullets. You can also create your own or make changes to the bullet level from this gallery.

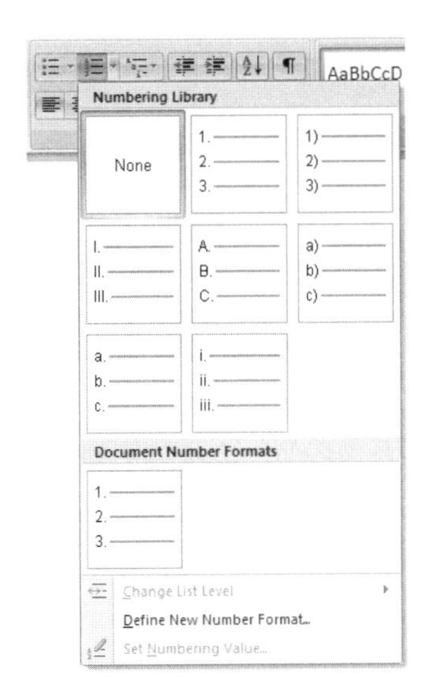

The Numbering Library gives you a choice of various numbering styles and also provides the means for creating a new number format, changing list levels, and setting numbering values.

Simplified Collaboration

If it takes a village to raise a child, it takes a team to create an effective document. The writing task might fall to you, but there will no doubt be others–associates, managers, marketing professionals, and perhaps financial personnel–who will take a look at what you've done and make comments, suggestions, and edits. Although this collaboration process at first glance might seem to make things more complicated, in reality it enhances the quality of our documents. Different people with different areas of emphasis view the document through different lenses–and ultimately that means a more fully developed document for your reader.

The document-sharing features in Office Word 2007 have been given additional power, so the experience of working collaboratively in Office Word 2007 is more natural than it seemed in previous versions. This section shines a light on the new or improved features you and your team can use in Office Word 2007.

Improved Document Comparison

When you are working on a document that is making the rounds among team members, it is sometimes hard to see how the versions have changed. Improvements in Document Comparison enable you to compare two versions of the same document, checking for changes in a number of features (see Figure 4-8).

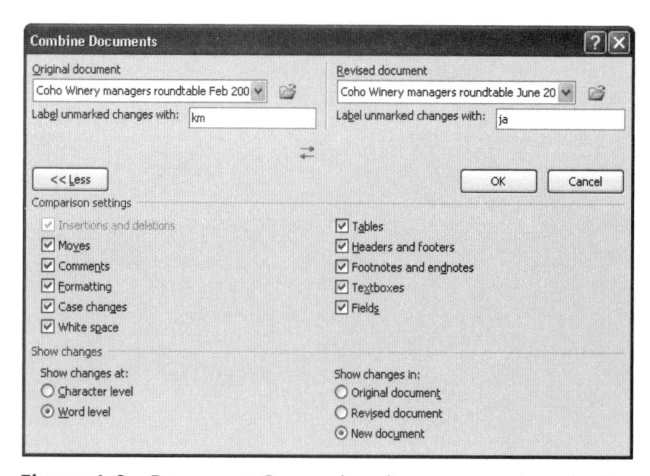

Figure 4-8 Document Comparison improvements make it easier to see which changes have been made—and by whom.

After you select the documents and the comparison features, the results window displays both documents, the merged document, and a Summary panel to highlight the changes made in the document (see Figure 4-9).

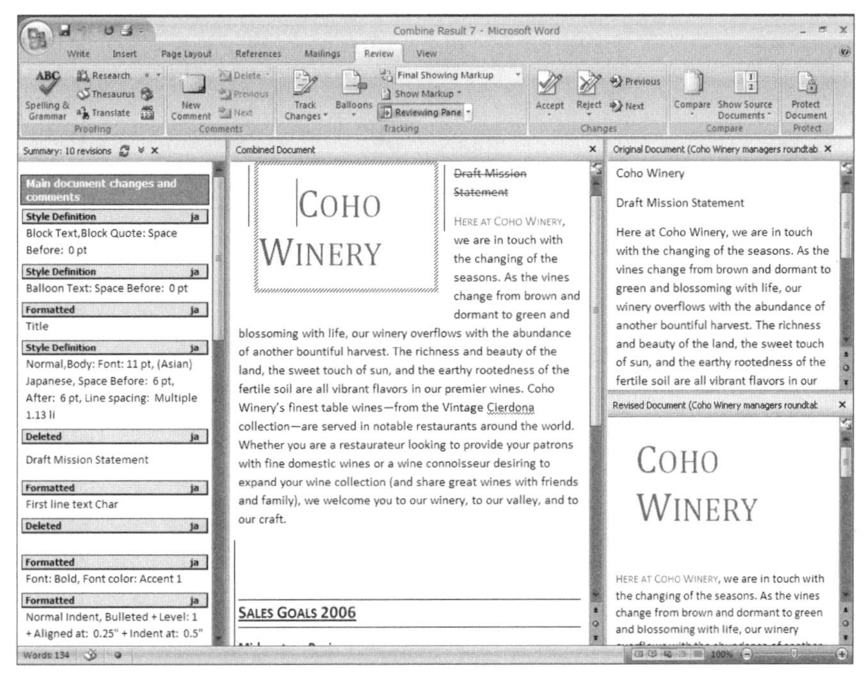

Figure 4-9 A tripanel display enables you to review the merged document and both versions of the file at the same time.

Reviewing Documents in Full-Screen Reading View

Depending on the types of documents you create in Office Word 2007, you might be relieved to know that you can hide the menus and scrollbars to get the maximum amount of room on screen. To view your document in full-screen view, click the View tab and choose Full Screen Reading. The document is displayed in two-page format, and a toolbar across the top of the display gives you options for printing, saving, reviewing, and changing the view of the displayed document (see Figure 4-10).

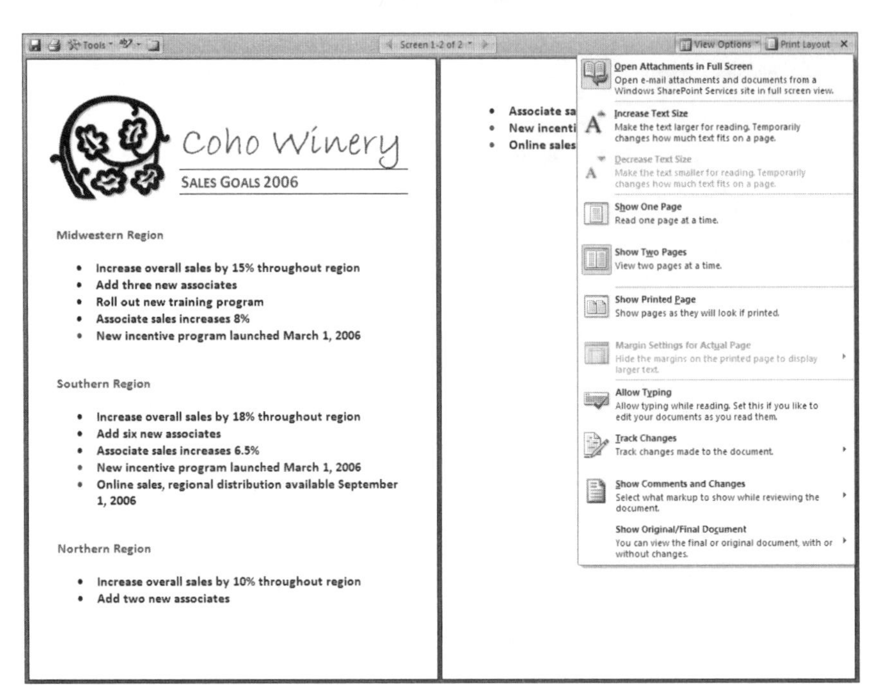

Figure 4-10 The Full Screen Reading view is perfect for reviewing and commenting on documents in progress.

> ### Reviewing Tools in Full Screen Reading View
> Full Screen Reading view in Office Word 2007 is different from Full Screen view in Office Word 2003 in that it offers a full array of document review and viewing tools, but editing individual words is not possible in this view. Instead, when you highlight a word or phrase on the document displayed in Full Screen Reading view, a context menu offering the Highlight, New Comment, and Research tools appears.

Inspecting Your Document

When you're working on a document collaboratively, it's not unusual to have several different people inserting comments, changing phrases, modifying formats, and deleting text and images. With all the inserting and deleting, it's possible that some things that need to be removed can be inadvertently left in the document. To make sure that your finished document includes only the information you really want to share with your readers, you can use the Inspect Document option that's available when you choose Finish from the File menu.

The Document Inspector provides a set of five different checks you can run on your document (see Figure 4-11). When you click Inspect, the Document Inspector does the selected reviews and displays a results window alerting you to any problems that are found in the document. Simply click Remove All to correct the problem and click Reinspect to make sure there are no lingering problems in the document before you finalize it.

Finalizing Your Document

After you finish the document (and have run the Document Inspector), you can mark the file as read-only so readers can't modify it in any way. Open the File menu and point to the Finish command. In the submenu that appears, click Mark As Final. Now readers can open and read, print, and e-mail the document, but they can't modify the content or formatting in any way.

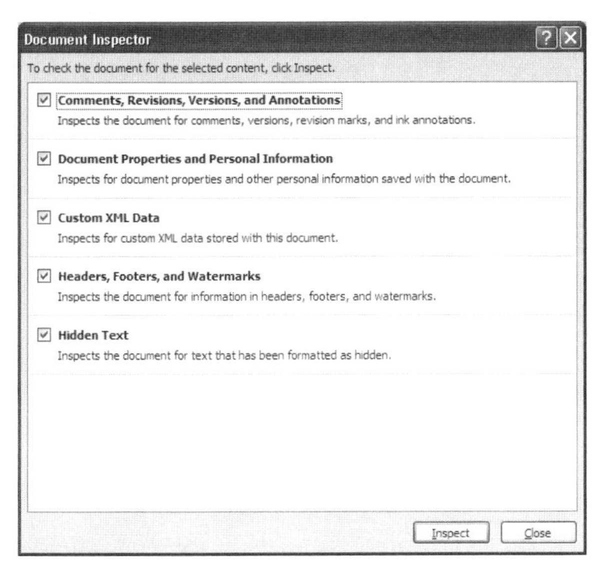

Figure 4-11 The Document Inspector runs five different sets of checks to ensure that your document includes only the information you want to share.

Better Integration with Office SharePoint Server 2007

If your company uses Microsoft® Office SharePoint® Server 2007, you will enjoy the improved integration that Office Word 2007 shares with Microsoft® Windows® SharePoint® Services and Office SharePoint Server 2007. With Office SharePoint Server 2007 you can create, track, and manage document workflow and task assignments, create libraries of resource materials, communicate with other members of your team, streamline review cycles, and much more.

Mail Merge Improvements

Whether you used mail merge rarely or frequently in the previous versions of Office Word, you no doubt realized that mail merge was hard to find and work with, buried as it was inside the Tools menu. Today's mail merge process is given greater visibility and easier access–now a Mailings command tab on the user interface enables you to create, preview, organize, and send a mailing quickly and efficiently. Click the Mailings tab to start the process; then click Start Mail Merge (see Figure 4-12) to find the familiar document choices. Each of the commands on the user interface enables you to follow the sequence of preparing your mailing for distribution.

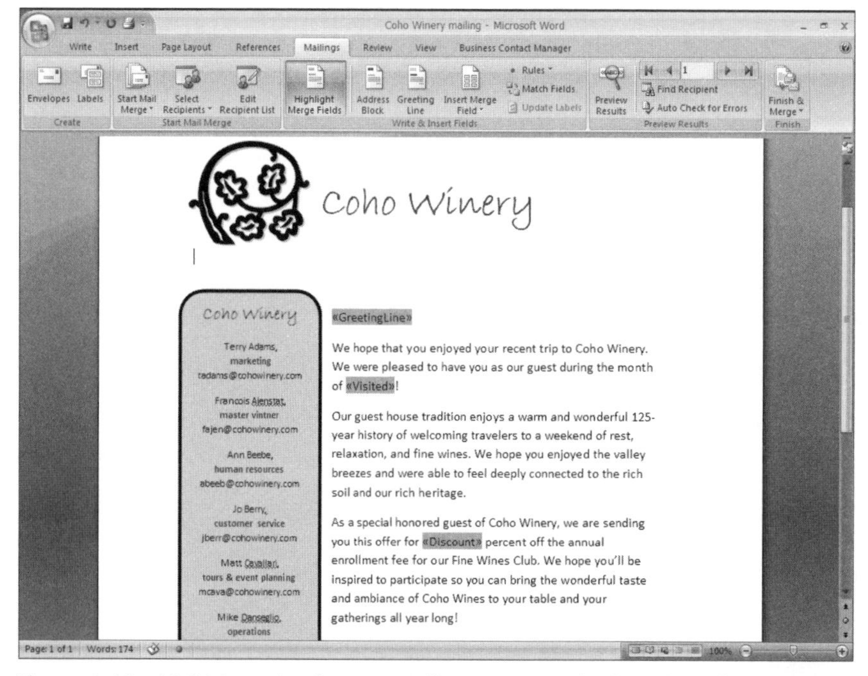

Figure 4-12 Mail Merge has its own Mailings command tab in the Office Word 2007 user interface.

Tip If you prefer having the Mail Merge Wizard lead you through the steps involved in creating a mass mailing, you can start the wizard by clicking Start Mail Merge and selecting Step By Step Mail Merge Wizard.

Simplifying Special Elements

One challenge of using a full-featured application such as Office Word 2007 is that it can be difficult to remember how to do things you use only once in a while. For example, when you need to add a sophisticated equation in the annual report you're producing, how do you find and use the Equation Builder? And what exactly is the difference between an endnote and a footnote, and how do you know when to use which one?

The new Equation Builder makes it easy for you to add sophisticated equations to your document. You can choose ready-made equations from the Equation Gallery or create a new equation using the contextual tab of equation tools:

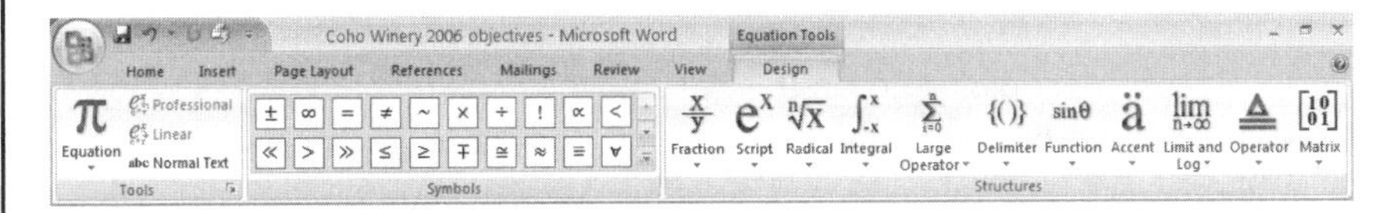

Additionally, citations and other references are easier to add and use. You can choose a specific citation style, use the Resource Manager to organize your references, and create a bibliography automatically from the resources used in your document.

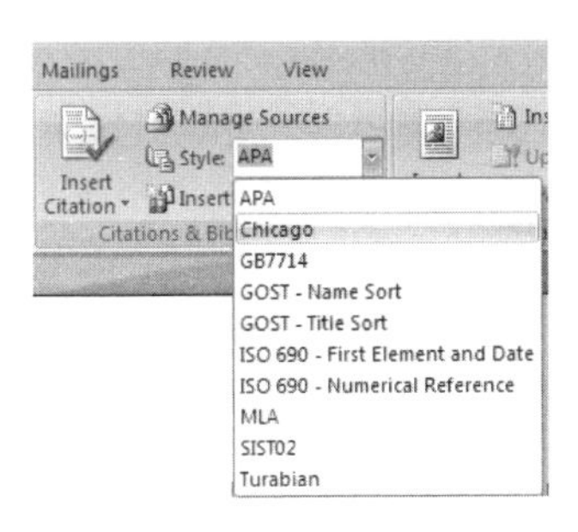

2007 Microsoft Office System Behind-the-Scenes Interview

Leslie Cole, Content Publisher for Office Word 2007

What are your favorite new features in Office Word 2007? I am very excited about the new content controls for making templates and forms. But I'm also excited about the new cover page and predesigned page layout options; the new equation, and citation and bibliography features; changes to lists, styles, and tables; and of course, the fabulous new user interface that gets you to all of those great Office Word 2007 features.

How long have you been working with the new release? Do you have a special area of emphasis? Developing documentation for a new product comes later in the release cycle, after most of the product development has been finished. I've been working on some aspect of the Office Word documentation for this release since April 2005. I'm one of three individuals who develop documentation for the new Office Word 2007.

Did the new page layout changes come about as a result of user feedback? How so? While a lot of the features aren't new to Office Word 2007, what the features look like and how much easier they'll make your job most certainly is new. The entire development of Office Word 2007 was based on customer feedback. Some of that feedback came from customers who were looking at online articles, demos, training, and help topics and gave us feedback that many features were buried or too hard to use.

Do you have a sense of who a "typical" Office Word 2007 user is? What is this person producing? I'm in the business of creating assistance content for users who tell us every single day in their online feedback who they are and what they need. The typical user has a task they're trying to accomplish and wants answers right now. We try to produce content that meets those needs as much as we can.

Coming Next

Now that you know how to find and experiment with the new and expanded capabilities of Office Word 2007, prepare to take a closer took at Office Excel 2007. The next chapter shows you the ways in which the new philosophy of streamlined use for increased productivity can have a significant impact on the quality of your financial documents.

Chapter 5

Extend Your Insight with Office Excel 2007

What you'll find in this chapter

- The design of the Office Excel 2007 window
- Page layout: A better view for printing
- More room, more speed, more choices
- Create better worksheets, faster
- Share workbooks and manage information with Excel Services
- PivotTables views—more support, better insight

For many people, Microsoft® Office Excel® 2007 is one of those programs you grow into. Unless their job responsibilities demand a detailed working knowledge of spreadsheets right from the start, their earliest experiences with Office Excel 2007 might have been creating simple financial documents–maybe in response to a request from a manager, a need in their own business, or a question from a financial advisor.

Over the years, Office Excel has evolved from a basic spreadsheet tool to a major business application that enables information workers to create, analyze, consolidate, report on, and share critical information that affects the entire business life cycle. This is not your grandmother's calculator! Office Excel 2007 faces the same challenge that Microsoft® Office Word 2007 takes on: offering powerful, sophisticated tools in an accessible way that enables both experts and novices to find what they need easily and produce professional-quality, accurate, and insightful results.

The major changes in Office Excel 2007 offer exciting possibilities that can simplify and extend the way users create, work with, and share financial documents–spreadsheets, workbooks, reports, and more. Specifically, the additions and enhancements in Office Excel 2007 help users create better spreadsheets faster; understand, visualize, and share important information more easily with others; and make data analysis easier and more effective, resulting in better insight for those decisions that affect the bottom line. This chapter introduces some of these significant changes.

The Design of Office Excel 2007

The new results-oriented look of Office Excel 2007 brings to your work area the tools you need–and *only* the tools you need–to complete what you're trying to create, analyze, or illustrate in your worksheet (see Figure 5-1).

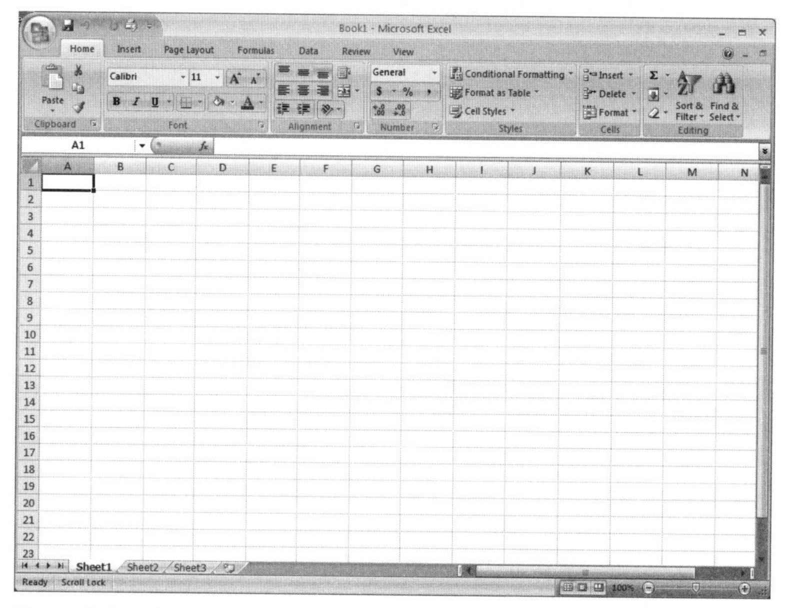

Figure 5-1 The new design of the Office Excel 2007 window.

Consistent with other major Microsoft Office system applications, the user interface is designed to help you be more productive by offering a series of command tabs, as well as command sets and contextual commands related to specific objects in your worksheet. Here's a list of the command tabs you'll find in Office Excel 2007:

- The **Home** tab includes the commands you need to work with the Clipboard; choose and change fonts; control the alignment of cell content; select number formats; choose cell style and format; and edit, sort, and search your data.
- The **Insert** tab houses the commands for the objects you add to your worksheets; for example, tables, charts, illustrations, links, and various kinds of text items, such as column or row labels.
- The **Page Layout** tab offers all things related to setting up the worksheet, including choosing themes, selecting page setup options, controlling the scaling of individual objects, selecting worksheet options, and arranging items on the sheet.

- The **Formulas** tab includes the Function Wizard, the Function Library, the commands you need for creating and working with named cells, commands for formula auditing, and calculation options.
- The **Data** tab offers commands for getting external data; managing the connections to external links; sorting and filtering your data; removing duplicates, validating and consolidating your data; and grouping and ungrouping cells.
- The **Review** tab includes what you need to proof, comment on, and share and protect the sheet.
- The **View** tab provides commands for choosing different workbook views, hiding and redisplaying worksheet elements (gridlines, the ruler, the formula bar, and more), magnifying or reducing the display, and working with the worksheet window.

Tip To find out more about the new elements in the Microsoft Office system user interface—including the new command sets, contextual tools, live preview, galleries, and more—refer to Chapter 2, "A New Look."

Page Layout: A New View for Better Printing

Printing worksheets–getting the margins just right and including everything you want on the page–can be a bit of a challenge (and time-consuming!) for both new and experienced Office Excel users. Office Excel 2007 includes a new view, called Page Layout view, which gives you the ability to see how your worksheet is shaping up while you're working on it. Display the worksheet in Page Layout view by clicking the View tab and selecting Page Layout View (see Figure 5-2).

Page Layout view makes printing easier by taking away the guesswork. Rulers along the top and left side of the work area enable you to plan for specific content areas on the page. Because everything in Page Layout view is fully editable, you can make data changes, select new formatting options, and save and print in this view. You can also view multiple pages in Page Layout view by reducing the size of the pages using the Zoom control.

Tip Make changes that relate to the appearance of the overall document—for example, adjusting margins, changing orientation, or filtering data—while you're working in Page Layout view. This enables you to get the best "big picture" sense of how the changes will affect your worksheet when printed.

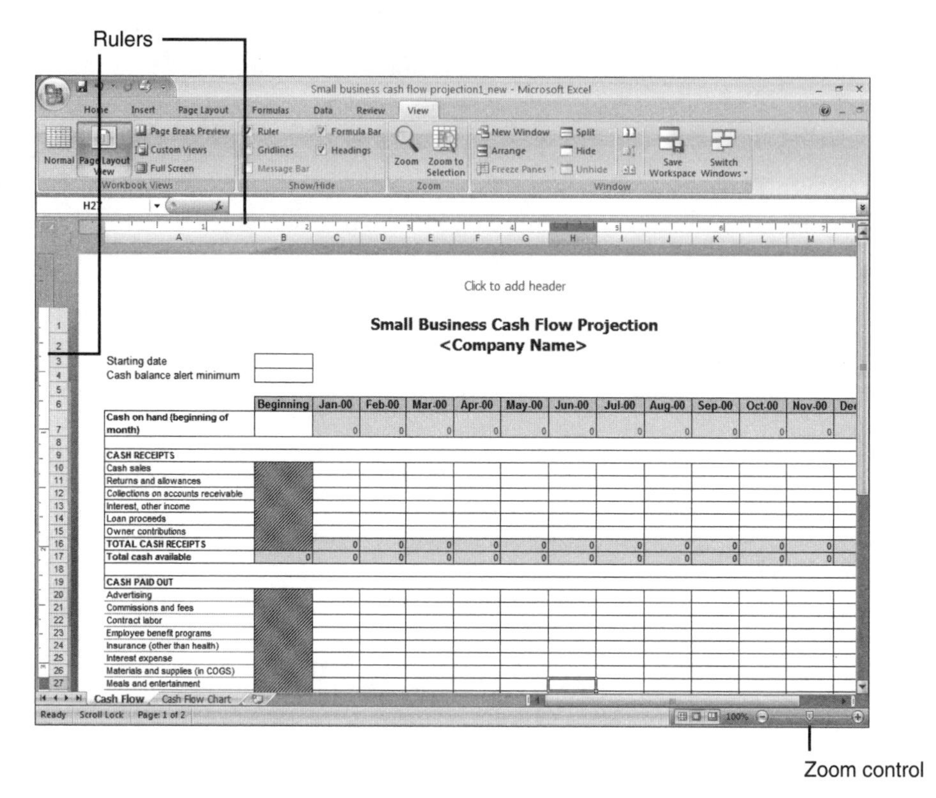

Figure 5-2 Page Layout view displays your worksheet as it will appear when printed.

Page Layout view is also available in the view controls in the lower-right corner of the Office Excel 2007 window. The three views displayed in the control (to the left of the Zoom control) are Normal view, Page Layout view, and Page Break preview.

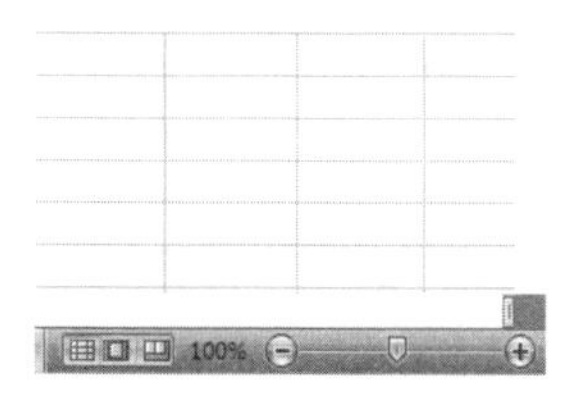

Tip The Custom Views feature in Office Excel 2007 is now available in the Page Layout tab of the user interface. Set the display features the way you want them, click Custom Views, and then click Add to create a view you can apply to other worksheets as well.

More Room, More Speed, More Choices

Some of the changes in Office Excel 2007 will be most important for power users who create, update, modify, and report on mega worksheets that demand the utmost in processing power and speed. Here's an overview of some of the changes that affect the way Office Excel 2007 manages and supports large, complex worksheets.

If you were maxxing out the row and column limits of Office Excel 2003, you'll be glad to know that the Office Excel 2007 worksheet has been greatly enlarged. According to David Gainer, Group Program Manager for Microsoft Office Excel, "Specifically, the Excel 12 grid will be 1,048,576 rows by 16,384 columns. That's 1,500 percent more rows and 6,30 percent more columns than in Excel 2003, and for those of you that are curious, columns now end at XFD instead of IV."[1]

And even on huge, formula-intensive worksheets you will experience faster calculations because Office Excel 2007 now supports dual processors and multithreaded chipsets, which enable Office Excel 2007 to take full advantage of your system's processing power and dramatically reduce your wait time. Another speed booster: The memory management in Office Excel 2007 has been increased from 1 GB to 2 GB, giving you more room to work with complex, sophisticated spreadsheets that previously maxxed out your system resources.

Additionally, Office Excel 2007 moves the bar on some of the limits in the earlier version; for example, now you can set unlimited formatting in the same workbook (this used to be capped at 4,000 format types). The color palette of Office Excel 2007 has grown to support the full 16 million colors, and now you can create as many cell references to a single cell as your computer's memory will allow (this used to be limited to 8,000 references per cell).

Create Better Spreadsheets, Faster

Most professionally created worksheets today–if they are shared with an audience out of house–include a least a little bit of design. The titles are formatted to stand out; rules or shading might be used to call attention to special areas of interest. Worksheets, when they are included in financial reports, business plans, or presentations, often are given the same look and feel as the surrounding material, so the font, color, and arrangement of the information becomes important.

Office Excel 2007 makes it easier to create better looking documents by providing a number of easy-to-apply formatting options. And if you're working in Page Layout view, you can see how those design changes look when you print them.

---

1. For more information about the changes in Office Excel 2007, see David Gainer's blog at *blogs.msdn.com/excel/archive/2005/09/23/473185.aspx*.

Easier Access to New Templates

When you start a new worksheet in Office Excel 2007 by choosing New from the File menu, the New Workbook window opens, immediately offering you a list of template categories from which you can choose. This greatly simplifies connecting to Microsoft Office Online (which Office Excel 2007 does automatically when you choose a template type) and searching for the template categories you might want to try.

Click the template category you want to see (for example, Business), and if the category includes subcategories, click the one you want (such as Accounting). Office Excel 2007 connects to Microsoft Office Online and displays a collection of templates available in that category. The selected template appears in a preview pane on the right side of the window (see Figure 5-3). If that's the template you want, click Download to download it to your system.

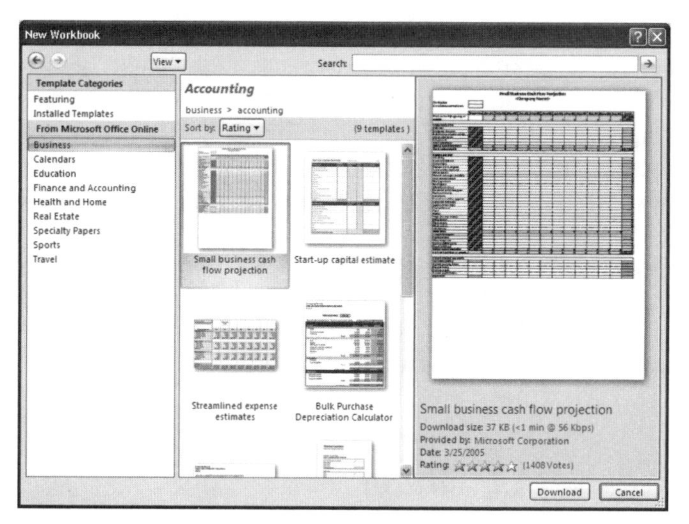

Figure 5-3 Office Excel 2007 comes with dozens of new templates you can use to create worksheets.

Three Things to Try

Mark Dodge and Craig Stinson, authors of *Microsoft Office Excel 2007 Inside Out*, recommend these as their favorite new features:

1. Use Page Layout view to see how your worksheet will be distributed between pages, to switch quickly between portrait and landscape modes, and to enter headers and footers directly on the worksheet.
2. Use Table Styles in conjunction with Themes to give your workbooks a consistent, professional appearance.
3. Use the new conditional formatting features to highlight dates that meet dynamic conditions, such as yesterday, today, last week, next week, or next month.

Choosing Themes and Setting Cell Styles

The way in which you can find, try out, and apply cell styles and themes in Office Excel 2007 is a huge improvement over the text-based, buried-in-the-menu options available in Office Excel 2003. Now you can highlight an area of your worksheet; click Themes in the Page Layout tab of the user interface; and sample a gallery of theme styles that change the color, font, and spacing of the selected cells (see Figure 5-4).

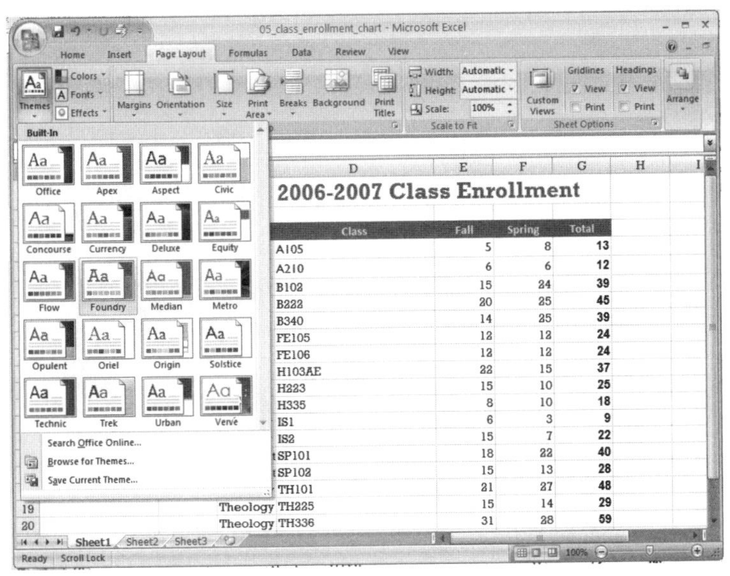

Figure 5-4 The built-in themes enable you to apply a professional new look to your worksheet.

Tip As you can see, choosing a different theme changes a collection of format elements. Several characteristics are included in each theme: the colors used, the fonts, and the effects. The three tools to the right of the Themes command enable you to set each one of these items separately, if you prefer.

Setting the format of a cell used to be something that required up-front thought and effort; now you can apply predesigned formats to cells and ranges by simply clicking the Cell Styles command and choosing the format from the gallery that appears (see Figure 5-5). You'll find the Cell Styles command in the Home tab; just click the command to view and select an available format.

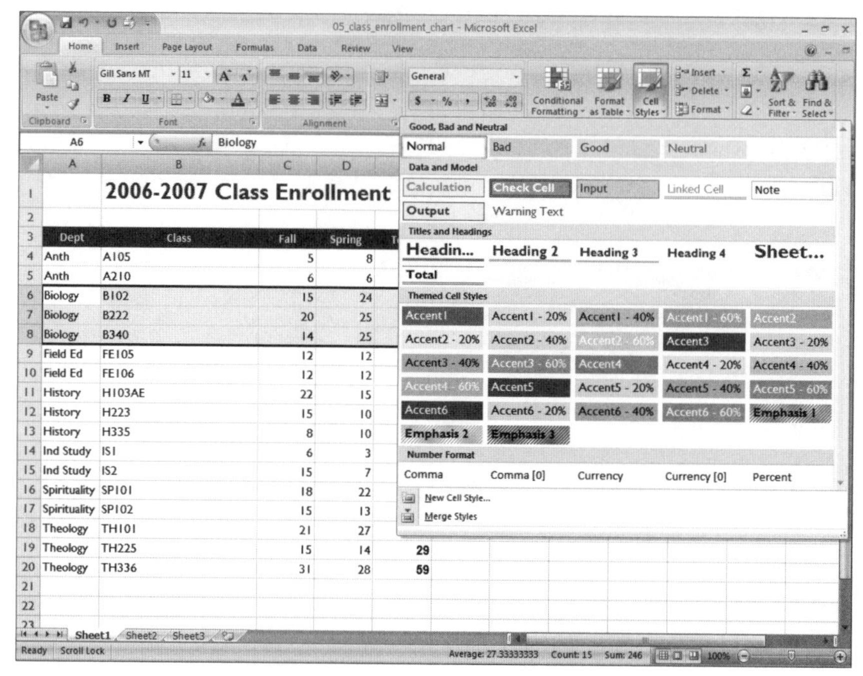

Figure 5-5 Apply cell styles to call attention to specific cells or their functions on your worksheet.

> **Tip** You can create formats for your own cell styles and add them to the gallery. Start by applying the format you want to a specific cell. Then click Cell Styles in the Sheet command tab and choose New Cell Style in the Cell Styles gallery. Review the information in the Style dialog box and click Format if you need to make any changes, type a name for the style in the Style Name field, and then click OK to save the style. The new style you created appears at the top of the gallery in the Custom category.

Click-and-Type Headers and Footers

If you ever had a problem trying to get headers and footers to print correctly on your worksheets in the past, you will appreciate the simplified way of adding and editing headers and footers in your Office Excel 2007 worksheets. Now you can simply click the Insert command tab and click Header & Footer in the Text command set. The worksheet is displayed in Page Layout view, and the user interface changes to offer a collection of header and footer tools (see Figure 5-6). A header box opens on the worksheet; you can simply click and type your header and use the elements shown to add items you need; for example, the page number, date, time, and worksheet name.

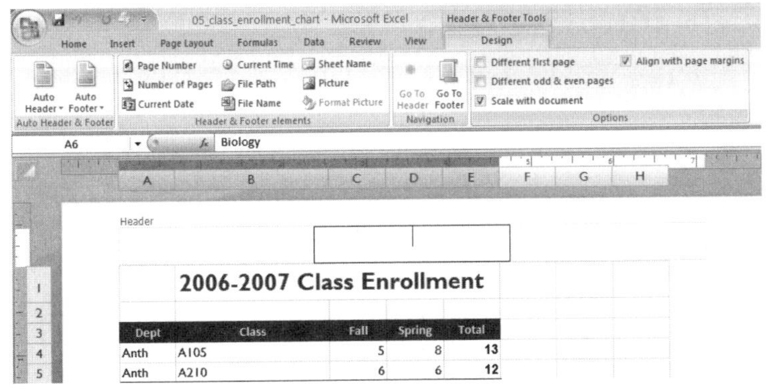

Figure 5-6 Click Header & Footer in the Insert tab to display the header and footer tools.

Tip The Auto Header and Auto Footer commands on the left side of the header and footer tools give you a collection of ready-made headers and footers you can apply to your worksheet. Simply click the command and click the selection to add it automatically to your worksheet.

The Benefits of Microsoft Office Open XML

The applications in the Microsoft Office system now use Microsoft Office Open XML format as the default file format. Open XML offers users several major benefits that relate directly to issues that Office Excel 2007 users care about:

- Open XML enables you to save huge worksheet files by using just a fraction of the space required by the previous format required.
- Open XML saves data independent of the format or schema, used to display the data in a particular way. This means the content can be preserved and used–independent of its particular form–in an almost unlimited number of ways. The information you create and share in your Office Excel 2007 worksheet, chart, or report can be incorporated in other worksheets or documents you create at a later time, saving you time and reducing the margin for error involved in rekeying important data.

Major Charting Enhancements

Charts provide you with a way to communicate–visually and quickly–the numeric story your worksheet is telling. Charts help others understand how you are interpreting your data, enabling you to show trends and comparisons quickly and colorfully. Office Excel 2007 includes a huge array of chart improvements with galleries of predesigned formats you can apply instantly, great new 3-D options, and a full set of contextual tools that you can use to communicate your message in just the right way.

Begin the process by selecting the data range(s) you want to chart. Then click the Insert tab and choose the chart type you want to create (see Figure 5-7).

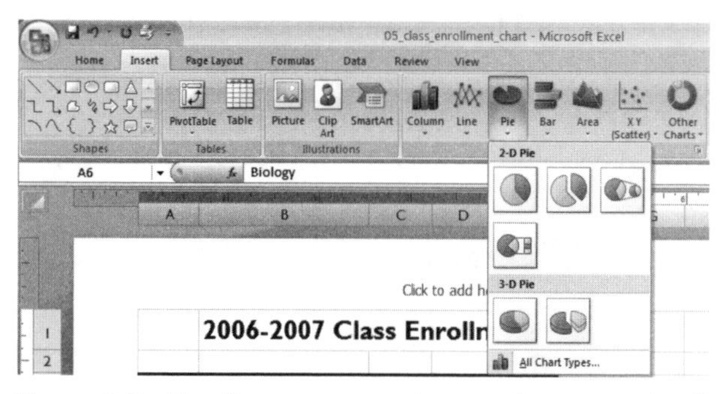

Figure 5-7 The Charts command set on the Insert tab offers the basic chart types to get you started.

The chart appears on your worksheet, and the Chart Tools contextual tab offers three full sets of options for customizing your charts:

- The Design tab gives you choices for selecting the chart type, data source and arrangement, Quick Layout, Quick Styles, and the Move Chart command (see Figure 5-8).
- The Layout tab in Chart Tools enables you to enter chart properties, choose Office Shapes, add or edit chart elements, and make choices related to 3-D charts.
- The Format tab provides you the means to select different chart elements, add styles to the chart shape, including 3-D edges, shadows, bevel, and more (see Figure 5-9).

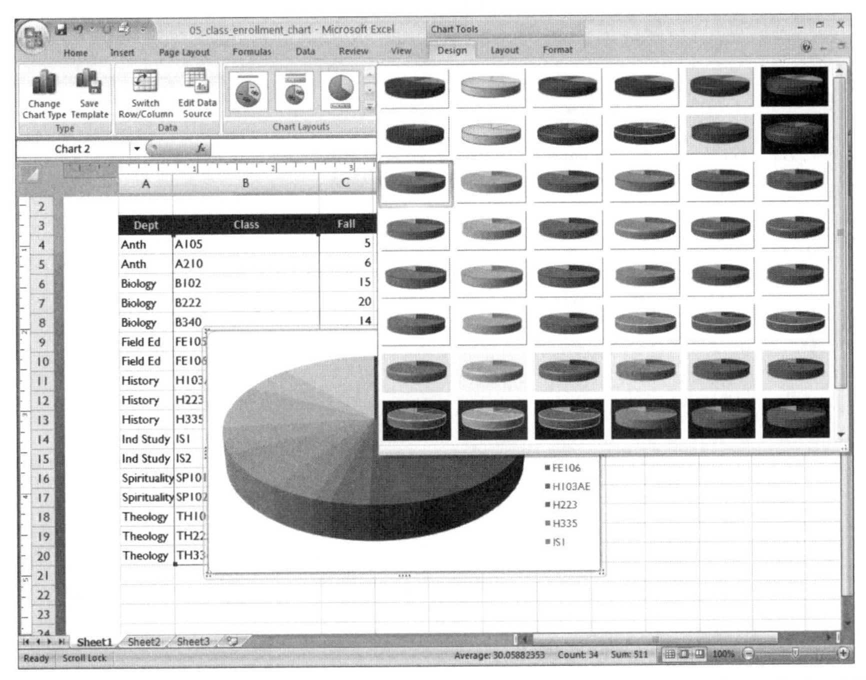

Figure 5-8 A huge array of charting options enables you to find just the right look for the data you want to display.

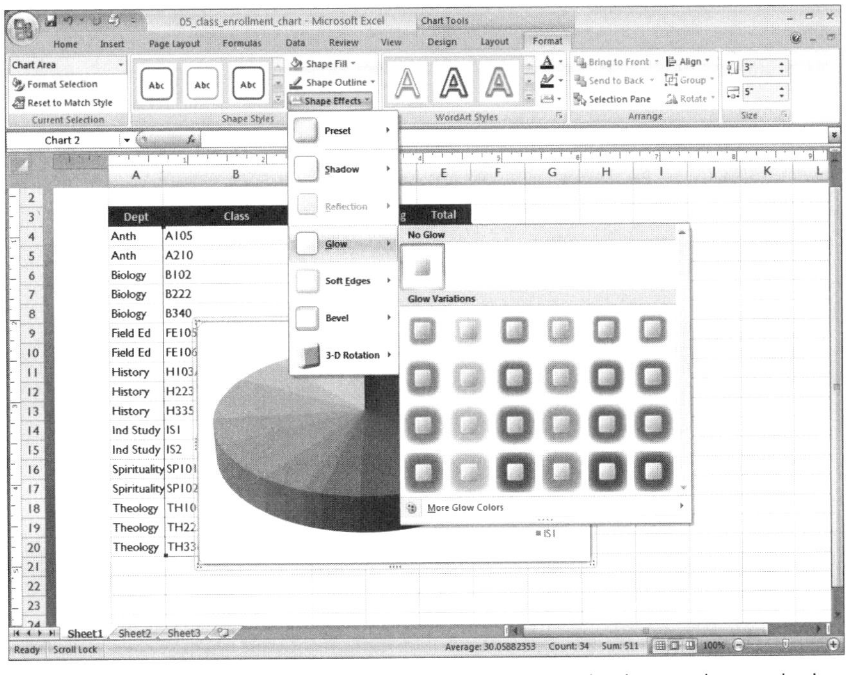

Figure 5-9 Change the Shape Effects to give your chart background a new look.

New Office Shapes and WordArt

Office Shapes—the lines, rectangles, block arrows, and more—that used to be buried in the Drawing toolbar now have their own space on the Insert toolbar. To see the expanded collection of shapes, click the Shapes tool. You'll find more choices and new categories, including new Equation Shapes.

WordArt also has been improved and made more accessible, now housed in the Text command set of the Insert menu. When you choose the WordArt command, a gallery of styles appears. Click the one you want and the WordArt item is placed on your worksheet; click the item to replace it with your own text.

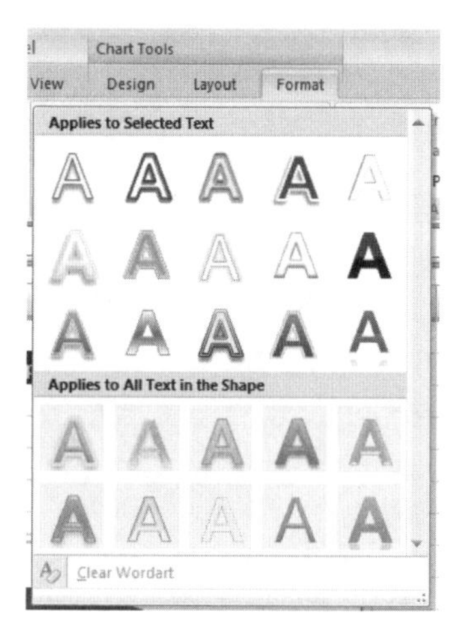

Tip Office Excel 2007 includes the SmartArt option for those times when you want to add a sophisticated diagram to your worksheet. To create SmartArt graphics, choose the Insert tab, click SmartArt in the Illustrations command tab, select the diagram type you want to create, choose the style you prefer, and click OK.

Conditional Formatting and Data Visualizations

Conditional formatting is a great feature that enables you to apply specific formatting to cells according to the value of a cell or the value of a formula. This feature helps you to easily point out certain values or trends in your worksheet—which enables others to grasp what you want them to see. Some conditional formatting was available in Office Excel 2003, but in Office Excel 2007 it's easier to find and use, and you can set up conditional formatting without writing formulas at all.

Begin by selecting the range of cells to which you will apply the conditional formatting. Then in the Sheet tab, click Conditional Formatting. The menu that appears offers two different sets of rules—Highlight Cell Rules and Top/Bottom Rules—that you can apply to your data simply by choosing the rule you want to apply. For example, to find quickly the top 15 percent of the values in your selected range, choose Top/Bottom Rules and click Top N %. In the window that appears, increase the percentage to 15 and choose the condition you want to apply (the default is Red Fill With Dark Red Text. The change is previewed in the worksheet as soon as you make the selection; click OK to save the change.

In addition to these predesigned rules, Office Excel 2007 includes new data visualizations that help you understand and illustrate trends and comparisons in your data. Here are the three new data visualizations:

Data bars show you immediately, in the form of value bars, how the values of selected cells compare to each other and to the whole (see Figure 5-10).

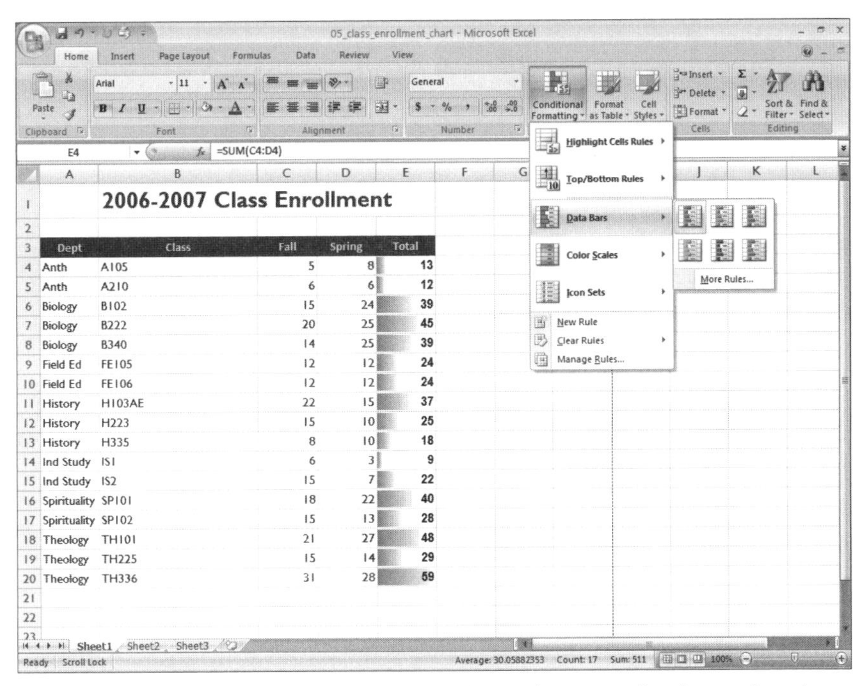

2006-2007 Class Enrollment

Dept	Class	Fall	Spring	Total
Anth	A105	5	8	13
Anth	A210	6	6	12
Biology	B102	15	24	39
Biology	B222	20	25	45
Biology	B340	14	25	39
Field Ed	FE105	12	12	24
Field Ed	FE106	12	12	24
History	H103AE	22	15	37
History	H223	15	10	25
History	H335	8	10	18
Ind Study	IS1	6	3	9
Ind Study	IS2	15	7	22
Spirituality	SP101	18	22	40
Spirituality	SP102	15	13	28
Theology	TH101	21	27	48
Theology	TH225	15	14	29
Theology	TH336	31	28	59

Figure 5-10 Data bars show quickly how values relate to each other and to the selected range.

Color scales apply coloring schemes you select to a specific range of values so that individual cells display in a particular color based on their value.

Icon sets provide you with a set of individual characters you can apply within the cell to show trends in a variety of ways.

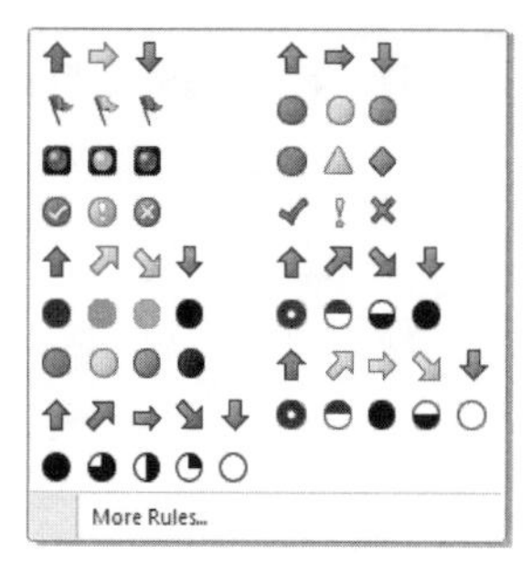

Creating Conditional Formatting Rules

You can design your own rules to tailor the visualizations to your own worksheets. When you choose New Rule from the Conditional Formatting menu, the New Formatting Rule dialog box opens. (If you have applied a conditional formatting rule to the selected range previously, the settings for that rule are displayed by default.) Choose a rule type (for example, Format Only Cells That Contain) and edit the rule description so that the format you want displays when the new rule is applied. Click OK to save and apply the new rule to the selected cells.

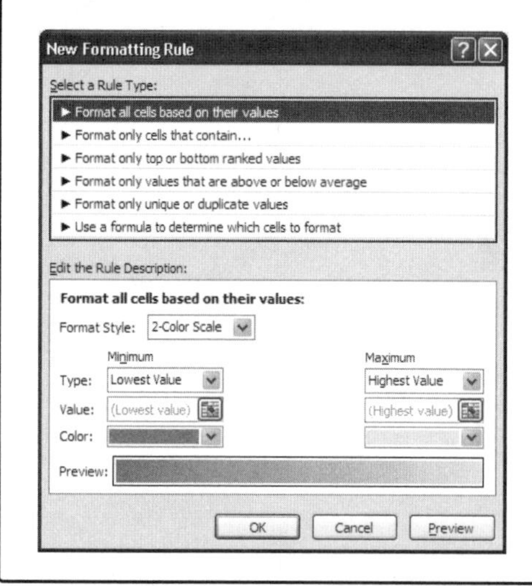

Share Workbooks and Manage Information with Excel Services

Excel Services is a new feature in Office Excel 2007 that enables you to save your workbook to a server that is running Microsoft® Office SharePoint® Server 2007 (and also supports Office Excel Web Access).

Here are some of the biggest benefits of using Office Excel 2007 with Excel Services:

- Share and manage collaborative worksheets more securely
- Display only those worksheet areas users have permissions to see; hide confidential data, formulas, and macros
- Create, sort, filter, and modify PivotTable views using any Web browser

To set permissions for the worksheet to enable the worksheets or ranges you want to make available to the users you specify, open the File menu, point to Save As, and click Excel Services.

The Save As dialog box provides an Excel Services Options button that enables you to control which sheets are visible in the user's browser. After you make your selections and click OK, enter the name of the shared folder in the Save In field and click Save. The file is stored on Office SharePoint Server 2007, and your team members will be able to access the worksheets via the Web.

Quick Facts about Office SharePoint Server 2007 and Office Excel 2007

- You can save sensitive or critical spreadsheets to Office SharePoint Server 2007 and indicate permissions for which elements (specific worksheets, tables, charts, ranges, and so on) will be available to other team members.
- Office SharePoint Server 2007 includes the Report Center to help users create and work with "trusted" Data Connections so they can safely connect with external data sources.
- Use Office SharePoint Server 2007 to centrally store important spreadsheets to control the distribution of multiple versions and ensure that business members and partners are working with the most recent files.

For more information on Office SharePoint Server 2007, go to *www.microsoft.com/office/preview/servers/sharepointserver/highlights.mspx*.

PivotTables Views—More Support, Better Insight

If part of your work involves making sense of large amounts of data and displaying it in a format that is both flexible and understandable for others, you will be relieved that Office Excel 2007 makes PivotTables easier to understand and use. Sometimes the simple things make a great difference–such as adding an Undo function for most operations, using the familiar plus and minus indicators for drilling down, and allowing sorting and filtering of data.

More PivotTable Support

Begin the process of creating a PivotTable by selecting the range of data you want to use in your report; then click PivotTable on the Insert command tab. The Create PivotTable dialog box will ask you to confirm the range you selected and choose whether to create the PivotTable report in a new worksheet or on the existing worksheet. Make your choice and click OK.

The PivotTable Field List is displayed in a panel along the right side of the work area, and the PivotTable Tools contextual tab appears above the user interface (see Figure 5-11). The Design tab enables you to choose the layout of the PivotTable, add Quick Style features such as column and row headers, and choose a design from the PivotTable Quick Styles gallery.

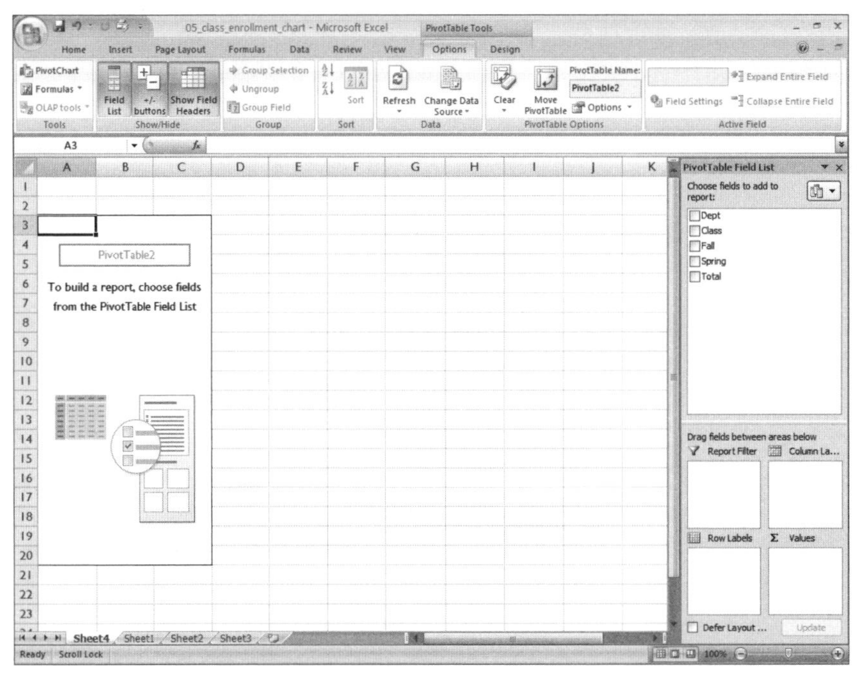

Figure 5-11 The new PivotTable features include an improved Field List, the ability to undo operations, and a greatly expanded tool set.

Improved PivotCharts

When you are happy with the PivotTable you created, you can put those numbers in a visual format by creating a PivotChart to illustrate your data. The expanded features for PivotCharts parallel those found in the charting enhancements throughout Office Excel 2007; when you create a PivotChart, both the Chart Tools and PivotChart Tools are at your disposal, giving you a huge range of choices for analyzing, displaying, sorting, editing, and saving your information (see Figure 5-12).

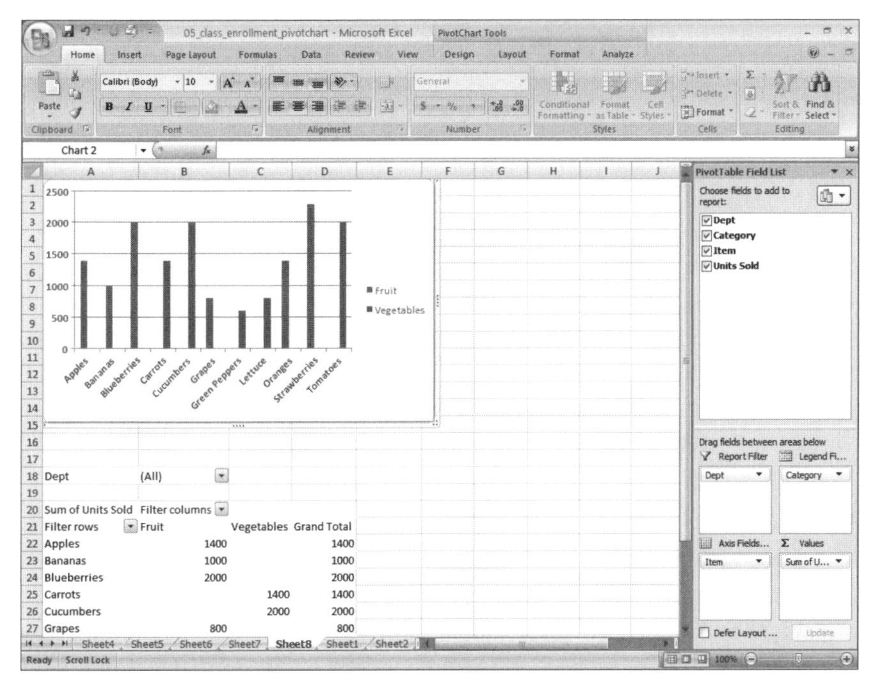

Figure 5-12 Additional controls for PivotCharts display your data in many different ways.

Microsoft Office System Behind-the-Scenes Interview

Mor Hezi, Senior Program Manager, 2007 Microsoft Office system

Do you have a favorite new Office Excel 2007 feature? If so, what is it? I have two favorite features. The first one is to convert a range of cells into a table and then use quick formatting. Personally, as an Office Excel user, I used to spend a lot of time formatting tables–making the headers stick out, separating rows, changing cell colors, etc. Now it is amazing how Office Excel 2007 recognizes a table, even if you click on only one cell within the range. The gallery of table styles is quick, simple, and makes my spreadsheet look great, even if I want to paste it in a Microsoft® Office PowerPoint® 2007 slide. My second favorite feature is the new PivotTable™ tools. I have always been "afraid" of PivotTable views. I thought they were for geeks. Now, not only are PivotTable views easy to use with drag-and-drop tools but it is also easy to understand why and when I should be using PivotTable to analyze my information. It is also fun to toggle between fields and see how the table gives me different results, which provide me with different insights.

In what ways does this version of Office Excel 2007 connect with what business users have been asking for? First of all, most customers tell us that business users barely use 10 percent of the features in Office Excel 2003. Even if we do not expect every user to use all the features available, we have made significant investments to make sure users will find the features they need, when they need them. We also wanted to lower the bar with some other features that today are reserved for "power users." Other big challenges our customers have today have to do with sharing spreadsheets with others and keeping one version of the "truth." They get lost in multiple versions, and it is hard to gain control over the information. The integration with Excel Services to save spreadsheets on the server providing Office Excel Web Access will make many customers happy.

This release has a number of great features that give us more ways to visually represent our data: icon sets, data bars, chart improvements, and more. What do you know about the average user that led to the inclusion of these features? How do you think they will be received? So far, these have been the features that got the most applause in product demos. Data bars, icon sets, heat maps, and the other conditional formatting capabilities are easy to understand and are easy to use. The bigger the data set you are analyzing, the harder it is to identify trends, gaps, or red flags on which to make business decisions. I do think that users will start overusing these capabilities at the beginning, mainly because it brings color to the spreadsheet, but with time, I do believe it will make a big difference for decision making. Charts are very commonly used to communicate the analysis to others. They are pasted in Office Word documents and Office PowerPoint slide decks. People love presenting good-looking reports. It makes them look more professional and helps them communicate results. Our new charts with 3-D and shadowing effects are customer-ready quality and the colors automatically update according to the document theme.

What's it been like for you to be so involved with this major release? I am extremely proud and happy to be a part of the Microsoft Office system 2007 release. The biggest advantage is to be able to use it ahead of everyone else. Office Excel 2007 in particular is probably one of the most-used software products in the world. Working with the program management and the developer team is very rewarding. You learn something new every day and the customer reactions are very rewarding.

Coming Next

This chapter showed off some of the biggest changes in Office Excel 2007. The next chapter builds on the great visual enhancements theme running throughout Microsoft Office system by taking you into the presenting realm of Office PowerPoint 2007.

Chapter 6

Produce Attention-Getting Presentations with Office PowerPoint 2007

What you'll find in this chapter:

- A tour of the Office PowerPoint 2007 Window
- New design choices and tools
- Improvements for your text
- Expanded graphics capabilities
- Creating slide libraries
- Improvements for team presentations

Getting–and keeping–your audience interested is more than half the battle when you are presenting your ideas to a group, whether you are pitching a new product, training employees, presenting to stakeholders, or giving potential customers an overview of your company's services. Microsoft® Office PowerPoint® 2007 includes a number of great new features–in a new easy-to-navigate user interface–to help you produce, share, save, and even reuse professional-quality slides you create.

A Tour of the Office PowerPoint 2007 Window

Office PowerPoint 2007 shares the new features of the 2007 Microsoft® Office system look and feel–from the user interface to command sets to contextual command tabs, the Office PowerPoint 2007 window offers the tools you need as they relate to the task you're trying to accomplish. As you see in Figure 6-1, the command tabs in the user interface correspond to the usual sequence of steps in the presentation-creation process:

- The **Home** tab contains commands you are likely to use when you are creating and working with slides; for example, you'll find commands for adding and deleting slides, choosing slide layouts, making font and paragraph selections, adding WordArt, and searching for text on a particular slide.
- The **Insert** tab enables you to add a number of items to your slides–tables, pictures, diagrams, charts, Office shapes, links, text objects, and media clips.

- The **Design** tab is all about the look of your presentation. Use the commands in this tab to set the page orientation, choose a presentation theme, design the slide background, and arrange objects on the slide.
- The **Animations** tab gives you what you need to choose animations and add sound, transitions, and timing selections.
- The **Slide Show** tab contains the commands for setting up, rehearsing, and displaying a slide show. This tab also includes the commands for recording narration, setting up dual monitors, and changing display resolution.
- The **Review** tab offers the spelling checker and thesaurus, and provides translation and research tools; additionally you'll find commands for adding, reviewing, and working with comments in the document.
- The **View** tab provides a number of different options for the way in which you view your presentation. Choose among the traditional PowerPoint views, add gridlines and the ruler, make color and grayscale changes, and work with presentation windows.

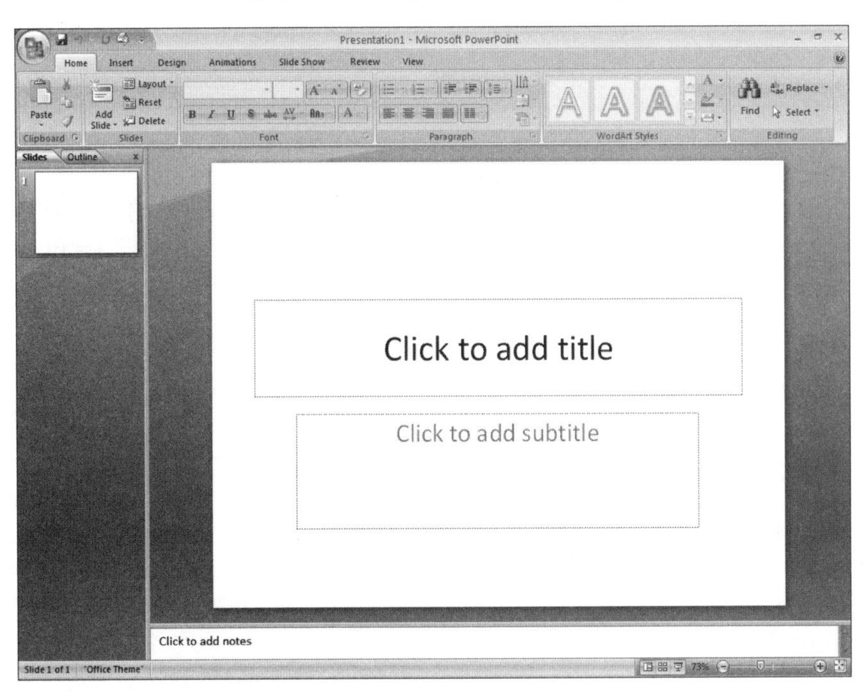

Figure 6-1 The Office PowerPoint 2007 window

> **Tip** The Zoom slider in the bottom-right corner of the window is a helpful tool when you want to zoom in or out on a specific item in your presentation. In Normal view, use the Fit Slide To Current Window tool, to the right of the Zoom slider, to maximize the current slide within the size of the display window.

Starting a New Presentation

Now when you begin a new presentation in Office PowerPoint 2007, a number of resources appear automatically (see Figure 6-2). Instead of requiring you to click around in the New Presentation task pane (as you did with Office PowerPoint 2003), the New Presentation window offers you several choices:

- Display a collection of templates in the center panel by clicking a template category on the left
- Create a new presentation from scratch by clicking Blank Presentation
- Choose one of your own customized templates by clicking My Templates
- Build a new presentation based on one you already have by clicking New From Existing
- Get tips, ideas, and additional presentation templates from Microsoft Office Online

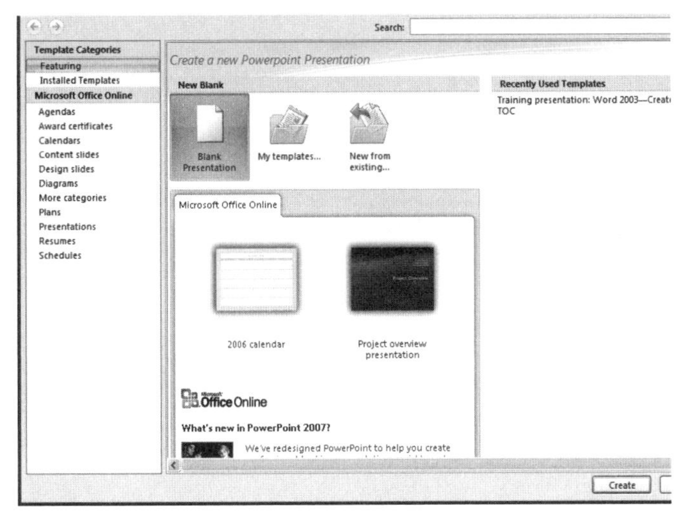

Figure 6-2 The new Presentation window in Office PowerPoint 2007.

> **Tip** Because Office PowerPoint 2007 uses the Microsoft Office Open XML file format, the file you create will not be readable in previous versions of PowerPoint. This is true for Microsoft® Office Word 2007 and Microsoft® Office Excel® 2007 as well. To share Office PowerPoint 2007 files with users working with PowerPoint 2003, for example, you can save your presentation in the PowerPoint 97–2003 format. Additionally, users of the older versions of Office Word, Office Excel, and Office PowerPoint can download a free file converter that enables them to open files created in the 2007 release versions of those applications.

New Design Choices and Tools

The new design choices in Office PowerPoint 2007 make it easier than ever to create sophisticated and effective presentations. Whether you start with a predesigned template or create a new presentation from scratch, you can rely on the new themes and styles to help you communicate your message in an engaging way.

Simplify Your Design Process with Office PowerPoint 2007 Themes

If you create presentations as a regular part of your work, you might find yourself stuck in the rut of using the same four or five backgrounds for the majority of your presentations. The new themes available in the Design tab of Office PowerPoint 2007 give you additional choices and enable you to preview them quickly by simply pointing to the one you like in the Themes gallery (see Figure 6-3).

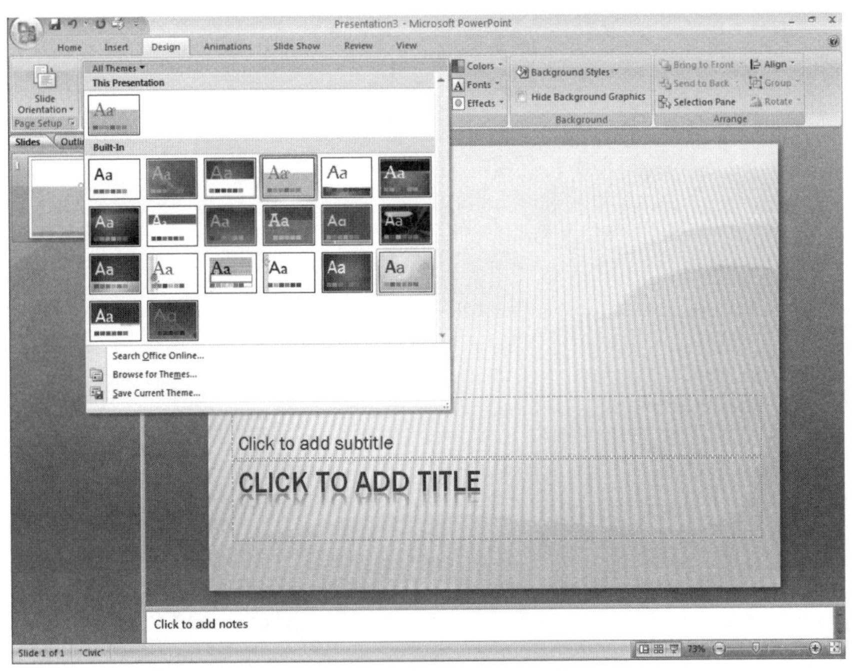

Figure 6-3 Previewing a choice in the full Themes gallery

You can easily modify themes and save them to the Themes gallery for later reuse, which is helpful if you have a specific corporate color or design used in your business presentations. Simply modify the slide to fit your corporate design (or open an existing presentation with that existing theme) and click the Save Current Theme command in the bottom of the Themes gallery.

> **Tip** You can apply a selected theme to selected slides or set a theme as your default presentation theme after you right-click in the Themes gallery.

Choosing a New Color Scheme

Making color choices is difficult for many people. Knowing which colors work well together is often a hit-or-miss proposition for nondesigners. Office PowerPoint 2007 helps you take the guesswork out of color choices by providing a large palette of color groups. You can choose an existing color group—or create a new one—that overrides the existing colors in the selected theme. When you select a color theme in Office PowerPoint 2007, the selection changes the background, all tables, text, and objects to match a consistent, coordinated, and cohesive set of colors.

The Colors command is in the Themes command set in the Design tab. Click the Colors down arrow to display the gallery of choices (see Figure 6-4). Point to a new color selection to see how it will look in the presentation; when you find one you want to use, click it to apply it to the presentation.

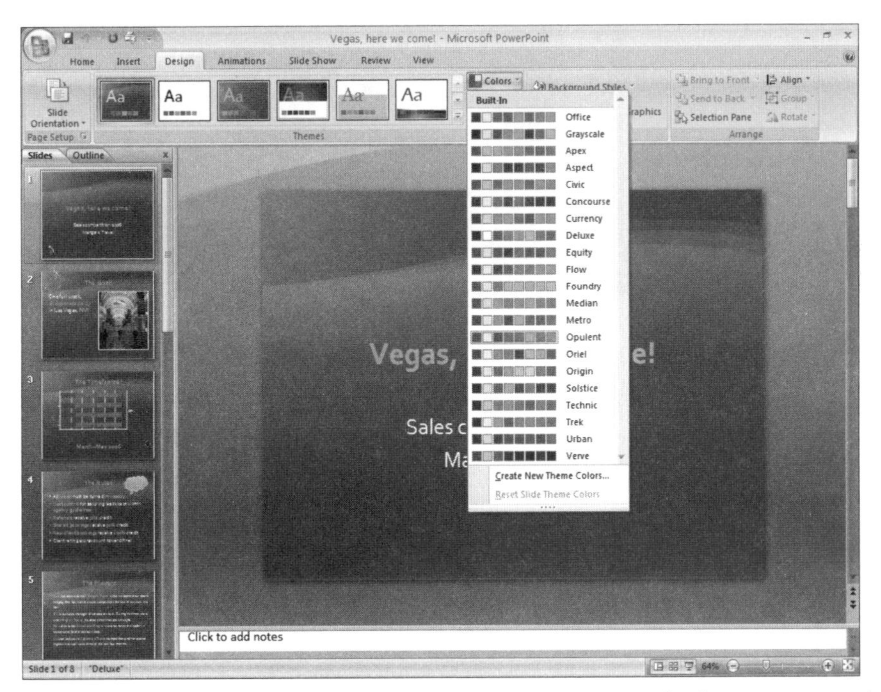

Figure 6-4 The Colors gallery provides you with a collection of colors you can apply to the selected theme.

Making Design Changes with Background Styles

Quick Styles is a feature common to all core Microsoft Office system applications, offering you different selections you can preview and then apply to your slides with a click of the mouse. The Quick Styles that are available depend on the object you select. When you are working in the Design tab, the Background Styles command provides a collection of background styles you can apply to the current slide or to all slides in your presentation.

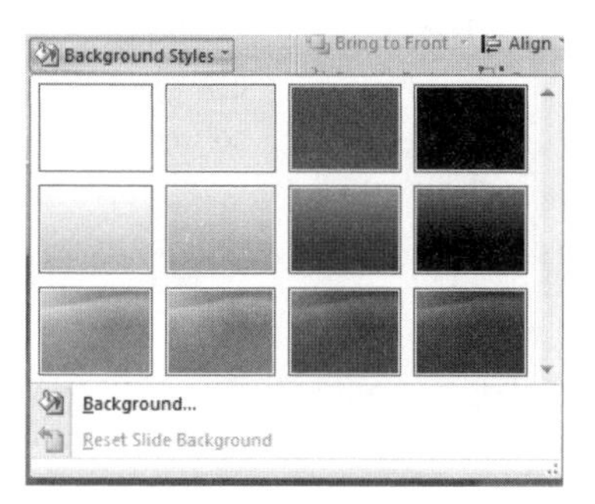

You can make additional choices for the background of your slides by clicking the Background command in the Background Styles gallery. The Format Background dialog box that appears enables you to choose a picture or texture for the background (see Figure 6-5). You can also make changes to background colors by choosing a new color scheme.

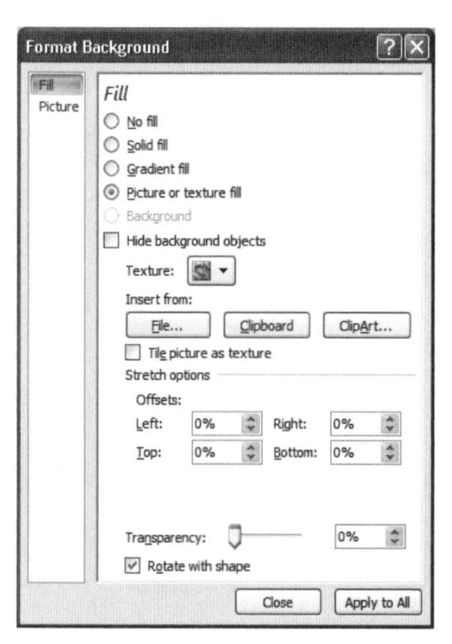

Figure 6-5 Customize the look of the slide background using the options in the Format Background dialog box.

Custom Slide Master Layouts

In Office PowerPoint 2007, you can create your own slide layouts to better fit the type of information you want to present. In previous versions, creating your own layout meant modifying an existing slide layout, which sometimes added text boxes or object frames you didn't want. (Not to mention making formatting choices you had to accommodate or undo.)

Now your custom slide master layouts can include many different elements–media objects, text boxes, and more–and you insert those elements using Insert Placeholder in the Master Layout command tab of the Slide Master tab.

Note The Insert Placeholder command becomes available when you select the Slide Master command in the View tab.

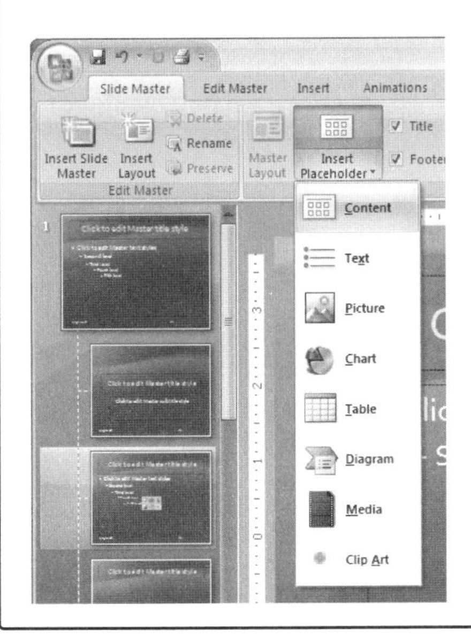

Improvements for Your Text

The words you choose and the way you communicate them makes a huge difference in the way your message is received. The text on your Office PowerPoint 2007 slides does more than simply flash a few headings or lists of bullet points; the text supports what you're saying with quick reminders for your audience members that increases their understanding and gives them phrases they can remember easily later.

Office PowerPoint 2007 includes a number of text enhancements that give you more flexibility in the way you present your text–whether you want to pull out all the stops with 3-D effects, glow, and animation, or keep it simple and profound with clear, crisp fonts and effective images.

Rich Text Capabilities

The text on your slides represents more than just characters on a screen; the text helps to convey the personality of your presentation–showing that your business is responsible and steady, high-energy and creative, or open-hearted and people-oriented. New text features in Office PowerPoint 2007 improve the readability and flexibility of text. Now you can do the following:

- Use rulers within individual paragraphs to take the guesswork out of text alignment
- Create vertical text for special effects in charts and along the edges of slides
- Wrap text within shapes to create interesting effects in graphics

Improved WordArt

WordArt is one of those features that can move your text from ho-hum to visually interesting. Used for special items, WordArt invites people to look a little closer at your presentation and helps you call attention to an important point you want to make.

The new WordArt Styles gallery enables you to preview and select a collection of specialty text styles for your presentations. You can apply WordArt to existing text or add a new WordArt object to your slide. Click the Home tab and then the More button in the lower right corner of the WordArt gallery to see the available styles. After you select a style, the Drawing Tools contextual tab becomes available (see Figure 6-6). Use the Text Fill, Text Outline, and Text Effects commands to customize the look of your WordArt.

Three Things to Try

Nancy C. Muir, author of *PowerPoint 2007 Plain & Simple*, recommends these three features to try:

1. New SmartArt Graphics enable you to turn a bulleted list into the elements of a diagram, instantly becoming, for example, the text labels on the boxes of a workflow diagram.
2. When you rest your mouse cursor on an image preview in a gallery, such as Themes, the effect is previewed on your slide.
3. Presenter View offers a separate view of your presentation when you have two monitors available so you can easily display your speaker notes as you give your presentation.

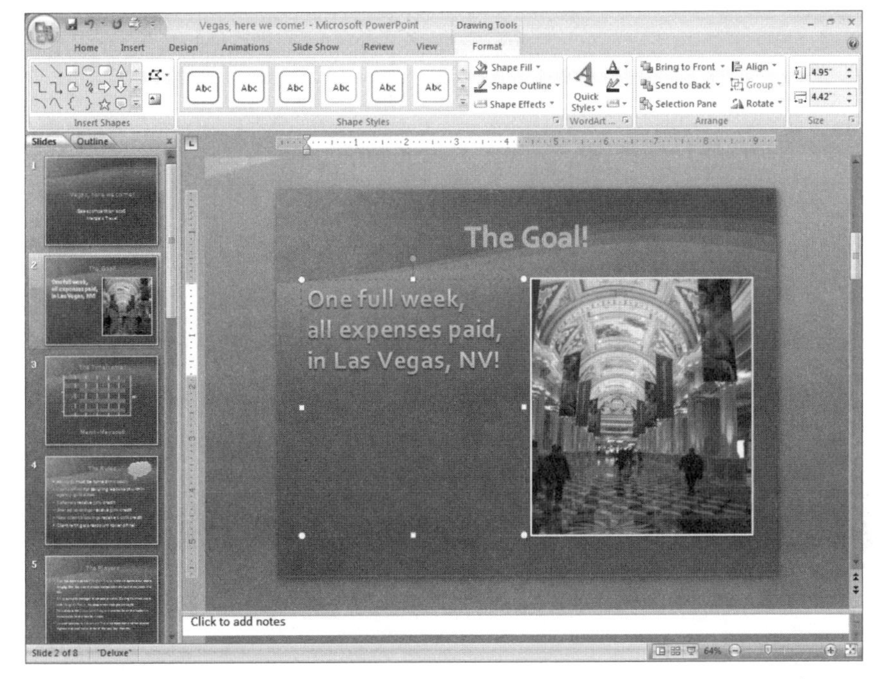

Figure 6-6 Use selections on the Drawing Tools tab to customize your WordArt.

Expanded Graphics Capabilities

Everything about the 2007 release is more visual. The new interface is designed to reduce the time you spend looking for tools by bringing them to you when you need them. The emphasis on design and function flows through to the capabilities in Office PowerPoint 2007 as well; style galleries and special effects enable you to create graphics that rival designs you would hire a graphics design firm to create.

Improved Office Shapes

Office Shapes offer a set of ready-made shapes you can add to your Office PowerPoint 2007 presentations to help add special emphasis to items. Office PowerPoint 2007 increases the number of Office Shapes and makes them available in a place that's easier to find while you work: in the Illustrations command set of the Insert tab (see Figure 6-7).

After you draw a shape, the Drawing Tools contextual tab appears above the user interface. The Format tab is selected, showing a number of tools that enable you to work with the selected shape (see Figure 6-8). The Shape Quick Styles enable you to choose the lighting, color, style, and shadow of the object; and the WordArt Quick Styles (covered in the previous section) provide choices for the look of the text you add to the shape. The Arrange and Size command sets give you options for the size and position of the object.

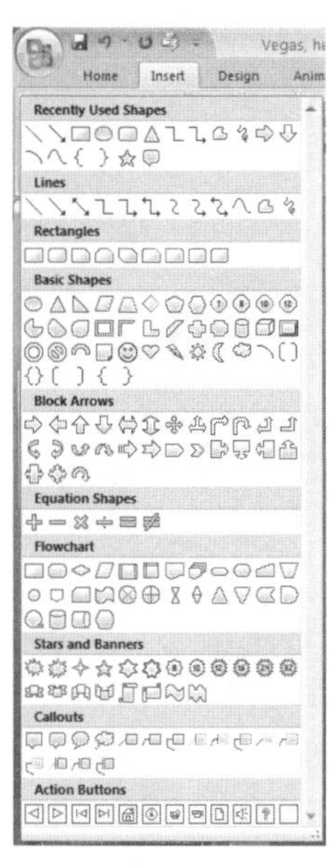

Figure 6-7 Choose a shape from the Office Shapes gallery; then draw the shape on the slide.

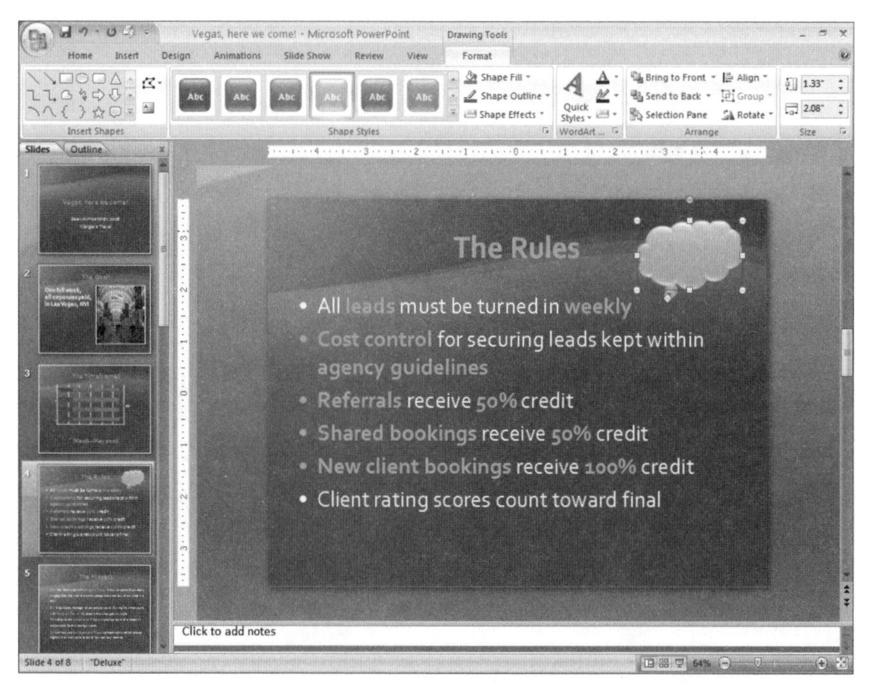

Figure 6-8 The Drawing Tools contextual tab brings you options for working with Office Shapes.

Enhanced Diagram Tools

Like Office Word 2007 and Office Excel 2007, Office PowerPoint 2007 also benefits from the addition of a new high-quality SmartArt diagramming tool that enables you to create flexible, customizable diagrams that can present your information in many different ways. You can add diagrams to your slides (by clicking the Insert tab and choosing SmartArt, and you can also easily convert the text on individual slides into a diagram (see Figure 6-9).

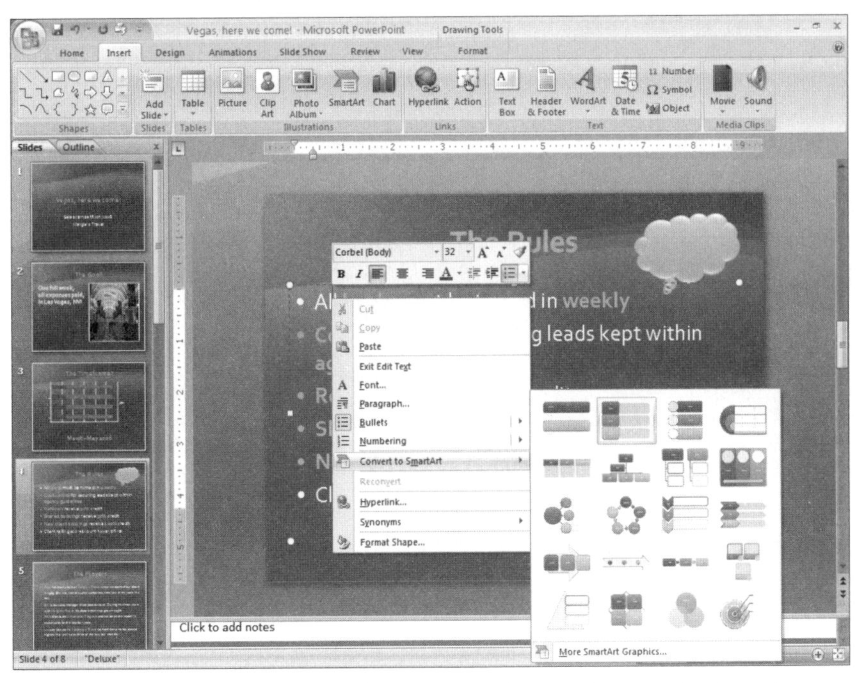

Figure 6-9 You can diagram text in your presentation with two simple clicks.

Creating Slide Libraries

After you put time and energy (and teamwork) into creating an effective presentation, why not leverage that work so that you can use the information as content in other presentations? Now you can save slides to a Slide Library and add them–in the new presentation's style–to the presentation you're working on.

> **Tip** Create slides with information you use repeatedly in business communications—for example, your mission statement, organizational chart, contact information, or hiring policy—and save them to a Slide Library so you can easily insert them in future presentations.

To save a presentation as a Slide Library so that you can easily reuse the slides later, open the File menu, point to Publish, and choose Publish Slides (see Figure 6-10). In the Publish Slides dialog box, click the checkbox of the slides you want to save to the library, click Browse to select the folder in which you want to save the slides, and click Publish (see Figure 6-11).

Figure 6-10 Choose the Publish command in the File menu to begin the process of creating a slide library.

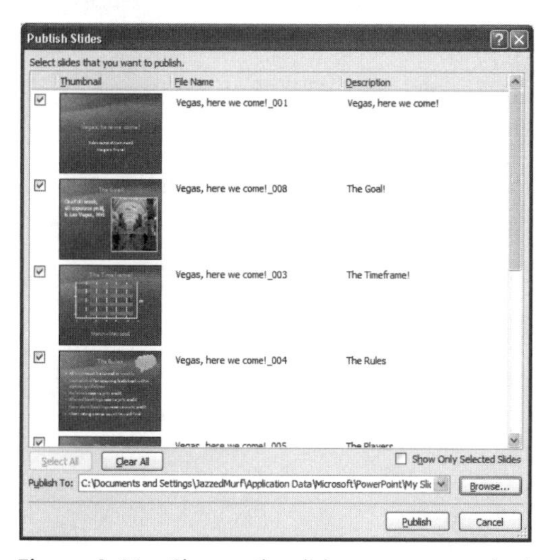

Figure 6-11 Choose the slides you want to include in the library by selecting them in the Publish Slides dialog box.

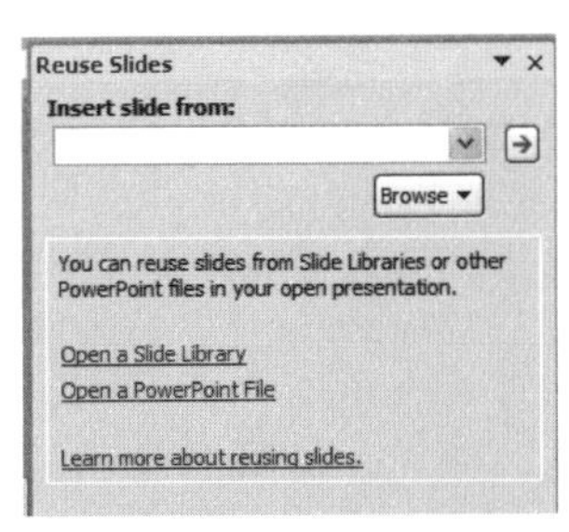

Figure 6-12 Use the Reuse Slides task pane to locate and select the slides you want to add to your presentation.

Benefits of XML

The Microsoft Office system uses Microsoft Office Open XML format as the default format for all applications. Files saved in Office PowerPoint 2007 are assigned the .pptx file extension. Saving a file in XML offers a number of benefits for users. First, XML enables you to separate data and formatting so that information you create in one application can easily be used in other forms. Secondly, XML files are much smaller than traditional files–especially when it comes to the graphics-intensive files that Office PowerPoint creates–so the new Office PowerPoint 2007 files are much smaller, easier to download, manage, and share.

Improvements for Team Presentations

Today's workforce is becoming increasingly mobile. We're no longer tied to our desks (or, at least, not for long!) when we need to finish a project or finalize a presentation for review. Office PowerPoint 2007 offers several different ways you and your team members can continue to work on presentations, whether you are all working in the same office or on different continents.

Enhancements in Shared Workspace Technology

The previous version of Office PowerPoint included support for shared documents–so if your company is using Microsoft Office SharePoint technologies, you can create a shared document workspace where your presentations can be stored and shared among coworkers. Microsoft® Office SharePoint® Server 2007 is supported in Office PowerPoint 2007, which gives you access to new features, including the project workflow and approval process. If you are routing your presentation for review to a number of members on your team, you can use the workflow process to create a task list for team members with automatic alerts to let them know when the presentation has been updated in the server space and is ready for review.

2007 Microsoft Office System Behind-the-Scenes Interview

Mary Sobcyzk, Office PowerPoint 2007

What do you feel are going to be the home run new features in Office PowerPoint 2007? The new results-oriented user interface, Themes, Quick Styles, 3-D effects, the new text effects, custom slide layouts that can contain multiple masters, SmartArt Graphics, and slide libraries.

Do you have a sense of who a "typical" Office PowerPoint 2007 user is? I'm always amazed at the creativity shown by our customers and the plethora of uses of our products. I think of Office PowerPoint 2007 customers as running the gamut from students and teachers to small business owners to large corporations (where the customer is both the person giving the presentation and the people listening to it.) In large companies, including Microsoft, often a team of people will create very sophisticated presentations for executives, but you'll also see presentations created by individuals for small team meetings.

Animations is given its own menu in Office PowerPoint 2007. Why is this? (User feedback, new features, or something else?) One of the design principles of the results-oriented user interface is to "bubble up" or expose existing features. Animations are something that a lot of people want to add to their presentation, but in previous versions you had to hunt for the feature and the options. By creating one tab and putting all the animation options on it, we made it easy for everyone to quickly animate their presentations. You can think of each of the tabs as a step you take in the process of creating and making a presentation. And adding animation to your presentation is often a key part of creating a presentation.

Are Office PowerPoint 2007 users likely to be working in teams? What new or improved features support that? One feature that I think people in teams will really like is the new slide libraries. Slide libraries let you easily share, repurpose, and reuse existing slides by storing all your slides in a common storage area, which removes the need to re-create existing content or manage lots of presentation files. Note that the full functionality of slide libraries requires Office SharePoint Server 2007, but you can also use this feature if you have multiple presentations stored locally or on a network share that you want to reuse.

Another new feature is the Compatibility Checker that tells you what (if any) loss of functionality you'll lose when you save your presentation into an earlier version file format of Office PowerPoint 2007. Our customer research has shown that many large companies have departments on different versions of Office because not everyone is upgraded at once. And, of course, the new Microsoft Office Open XML file format reduces file size, which makes it easier to share presentations.

Do you have any stories about working on the development of the new Office PowerPoint 2007 you think readers would find interesting? One of the coolest parts about working on Microsoft Office products is the chance to work on new features and see the evolution of the feature from idea to implementation. Three years ago, Matthew Kotler, the lead PM for SmartArt gave what's come to be known internally as the "candy presentation." Inspired by a candy widely consumed throughout Microsoft in large quantities, Matt walked us through a presentation that showed colorful, dancing, circular candies. He then announced that "Office 12" would have a new feature that would do in less than two minutes (and fewer than five mouse clicks) what took him about two hours to do before. And when I look how easy it is to create and customize a SmartArt graphic today, I realize that Matt and the rest of the Office PowerPoint 2007 and Graphics team have done a fantastic job.

Coming Next

This chapter gave you a glimpse of the new features of Office PowerPoint 2007—changes that make designing, producing, and sharing high-quality, engaging presentations easier than ever. The next chapter continues the theme of heightened design and enhanced productivity by showing you the new features and enhancements in Microsoft® Office Publisher 2007.

Chapter 7

Produce Professional Business Materials with Office Publisher 2007

What you'll find in this chapter:

- What's new in Office Publisher 2007
- Working with Publisher Tasks
- Make Office Publisher 2007 templates your own
- Create and apply reusable content
- Finalize your publications with Design Checker
- Prepare your materials for commercial printing
- Create, send, and track mailings

Microsoft® Office Publisher 2007 gives you everything you need to create and publish high-quality, cost-effective marketing communications, whether you want to produce e-mail newsletters for your user group, design postcards to announce the opening of your small business, or publish a Web catalog for your online store. Designing and producing publications, both printed and online, that look good and read well is an important part of sharing what you do with others–and Office Publisher 2007 includes a collection of professionally designed, customizable templates to help you do just that.

No matter what the size of your organization or what type of publication you are trying to produce, here are a few of the ways Office Publisher 2007 helps you improve the way you publish your business materials:

- Produce your publications in-house so they are finished on your schedule and within your budget.
- Customize professional templates to reflect your own brand elements–color scheme, fonts, logo, and more.
- Cut down on time you spend re-creating similar materials by saving repeating elements (text descriptions, logos, mottos, and more) to the Content Library.

- Easily complete mail merge projects by using data lists from other sources–including Microsoft® Office Excel® 2007 lists or data from your Microsoft® Office Access 2007 database–and filtering, sorting, and customizing publications for specific customer groups.

What's New in Office Publisher 2007?

One of the first things you might notice about Office Publisher 2007 is that it does not have the same sweeping visual changes that some of the other applications display. Office Publisher 2007 includes the same menu system used in the 2003 version, so if you used Office Publisher previously, you'll still know the basic lay of the land.

But appearances can be deceiving. If you look a little closer, you'll see that Office Publisher 2007 includes major changes that simplify powerful procedures, expand your range of choices, and enable you to work smarter by creating reusable data and cutting down on repetitive tasks.

An Overview of Office Publisher 2007 Changes

Throughout this chapter, you'll take a closer look at the additions and enhancements you'll find in Office Publisher 2007. Specifically, the changes in this version include the following:

- The Publisher Tasks task pane serves as a guide to walk you through creating, distributing, and following up on your publications.
- Improved templates are easier than ever to customize to reflect your own brand choices.
- The Content Library enables you to store publication elements–text, images, logos, and more–that you can reuse in other materials;
- Improvements in the Design Checker help you evaluate your publication for problems that would be apparent in the specific type of output you're creating, such as a printed piece or a Web site.
- Expanded support for commercial printing (including Pantone colors) simplifies the process of preparing your materials for professional printing.
- The ability to save files in XML Paper Specification (XPS) format makes it possible for you to post your publications on the Web and share your finished materials with a wider audience (whether they use Office Publisher 2007 or not).
- The simplified and streamlined mail merge process makes it easier than ever to create, customize, distribute, and track mailings to your entire customer list (or to selected subsets of that list).

Changes in the Office Publisher 2007 Window

Although the Office Publisher 2007 window doesn't reflect the new visual elements that some of the other applications share, you will find some changes in the Publisher window. When you start Office Publisher 2007, the Getting Started window, shown in Figure 7-1, immediately offers you choices for publication types or access to your recent publications–so you can get started right away.

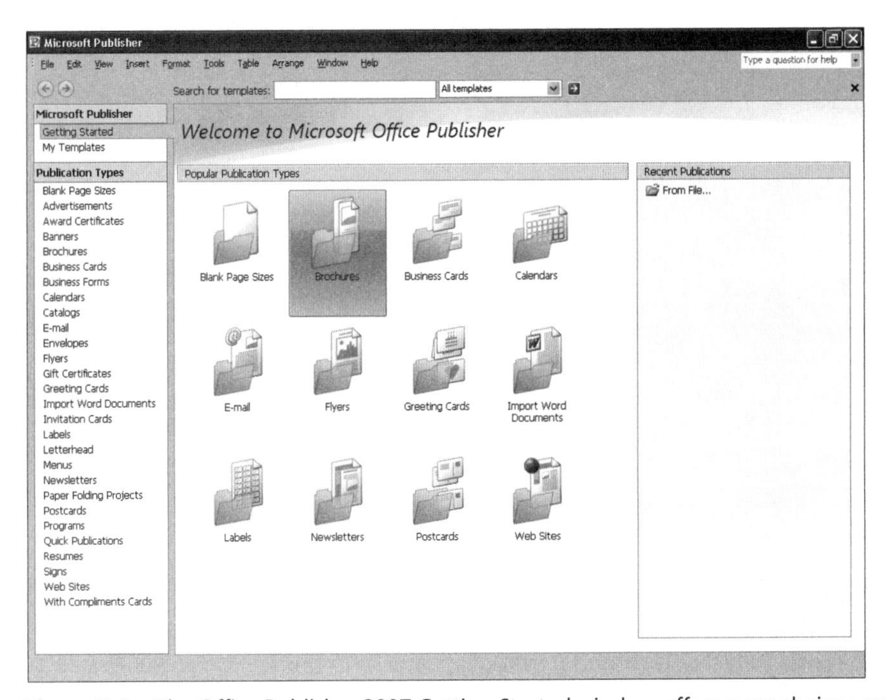

Figure 7-1 The Office Publisher 2007 Getting Started window offers more choices, more templates, and recently used publications.

When you select a publication type in the first column, the second column changes to show templates for the type you selected. At the top of the second column, you see a listing of template categories–for example, Newer Designs, Classic Designs, and Blank Sizes, shown in Figure 7-2. Directly beneath the categories you see a link that takes you to templates available on Microsoft Office Online.

Figure 7-2 Choose the template category for the type of publication you want to create.

The third panel displays a preview of the selected template, as well as a Customize box and an Options box. Customize enables you to choose the colors and fonts for your publication, as well as enter information about your business that can be used in multiple publications.

Tip For more about the new customizable template features in Office Publisher 2007, see "Make Office Publisher 2007 Templates Your Own," later in this chapter.

Working with Publisher Tasks

Business users creating publications in Office Publisher 2007 often have a variety of roles to fill. They create a worksheet or finalize a report in the morning; draft a presentation, attend a meeting or workshop in the afternoon; and work on a new publication when they have a few spare moments between other tasks. If this sounds like the hectic pace of your workday, you'll be glad to have the Publisher Tasks task pane to walk you through the steps for creating publications that you might work on sporadically or infrequently.

Display the Publisher Tasks task pane by clicking the Publisher Tasks button on the Publisher Tasks toolbar. You can also click the down arrow in the upper right of any task pane title bar and choose the Publisher Tasks task pane from the list. The Publisher Tasks task pane shows a list of links that you can use as sequential steps as you create, prepare, distribute, and evaluate the results of your publication (see Figure 7-3).

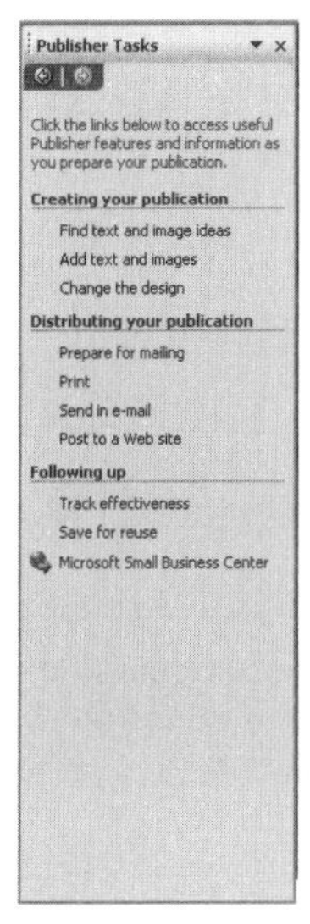

Figure 7-3 The Publisher Tasks task pane provides links to tips and specific steps you can follow to complete your publication.

Make Office Publisher 2007 Templates Your Own

Office Publisher 2007 includes a range of coordinated templates that reflect different types, color schemes, and personalities. The template styles are coordinated so that you can choose a style for your newsletter (the Arrows style, for example) and choose the same style (Arrows) for your business cards.

> **Tip** What does your business marketing packet include? Including a copy of your business newsletter, a coordinated product list, and a business card—all produced with the same basic design—sends readers a message that your company is consistent, thorough, and professional.

Customizing Your Brand Elements

When you select a template you want to work with in the Getting Started window, the panel on the right displays a preview of the selected template as well as the Customize and Options boxes (see Figure 7-4). You'll use these two items to tailor the template to reflect your brand elements.

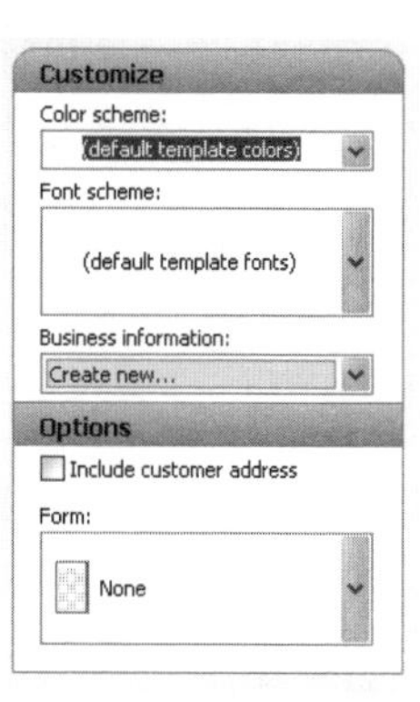

Figure 7-4 Use the Customize and Options boxes to customize the template before you open it.

> **Tip** The color scheme and font choices you make in the Customize box appear in the preview of the publication in the third column of the display. Check the preview to see whether those are the choices that work for you before you click Create to apply the changes to the template. If they're not—choose again.

What's in a Brand?

The message and values your business communicates–what sticks most in your customers' and prospective customers' minds–are your brand. You might have a well-known product name that communicates dependability, integrity, and trust. You might have established your organization as the one that "puts people first"–and so your brand communicates caring and respect of staff and customers.

The way in which you communicate your brand has a lot to do with how your customers remember it. Even small items–such as the font you choose, the subtle color of blue you always use, or the company motto you've had since the '60s–all reinforce your brand message.

Choosing colors, fonts and phrasing that reinforce the brand you want your customers to remember is an important part of telling the story of your business or organization. If you choose well and use your items consistently, your publications can go a long way toward helping your customers understand who you are and what you offer–which can mean increased customer loyalty and greater visibility down the road.

Selecting the Color Scheme

Office Publisher 2007 includes dozens of professionally designed color schemes for your publications. This saves you the trouble of trying to determine what colors match as you prepare your business materials. To make a color scheme the default for the publications you create in Publisher, click the Color Scheme down arrow in the Customize box and select your choice (see Figure 7-5).

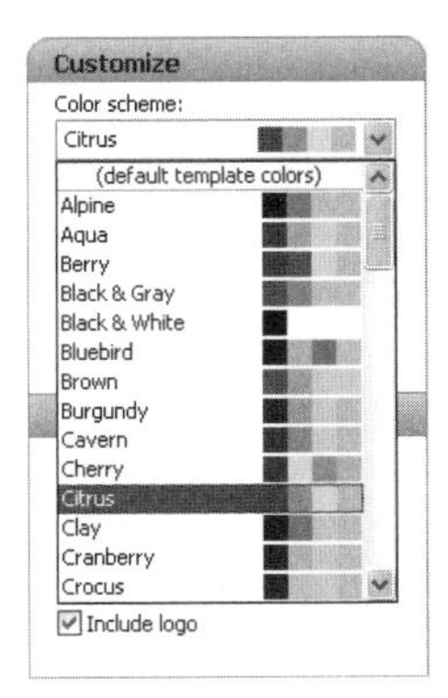

Figure 7-5 The color scheme you choose is applied to the current template as soon as you select it.

Choosing a Font Scheme

The font scheme you select for your publication includes not simply one font in a particular style and size but instead two complementary styles–one for headings and one for the body text of your materials. Each scheme has its own name (such as Deckle, Dictation, and Economy, as shown in Figure 7-6). To choose a font scheme, click the Font Scheme down arrow and scroll through the list to find and click the one you like.

Figure 7-6 A font scheme is a coordinated pair of font choices you apply to headings and body text in your publications.

Using Your Business Information

Office Publisher 2007 provides several ways to add your business information, such as the firm's telephone number or motto, to your customized template so that you don't have to retype it each time you create a new document. In the Business Information section of the Customize dialog box, you can add and display the information easily. Begin the process by clicking the Business Information down arrow and choosing Create New (see Figure 7-7).

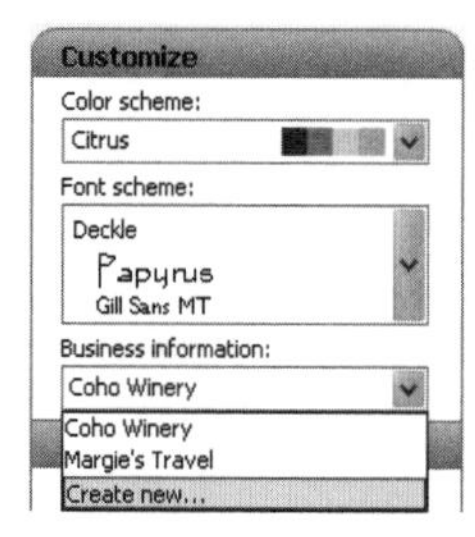

Figure 7-7 Create a new business information set.

The Create New Business Information Set dialog box (see Figure 7-8) gathers the information so that it can be applied automatically in your publications. Fill in the information and name the set by clicking in the Business Information Set Name (the name you enter will be available in the Business Information list in the Customize box).

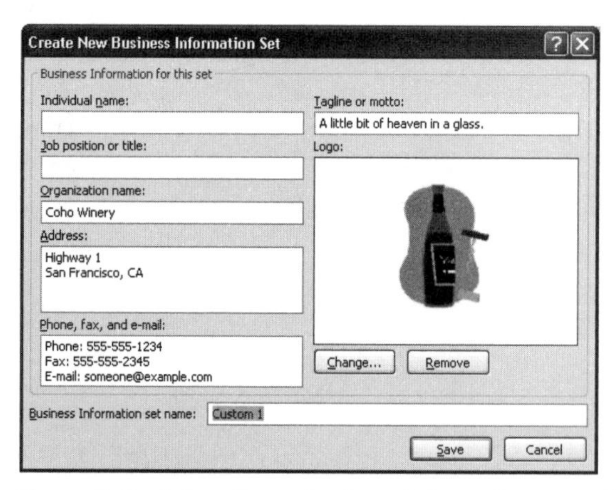

Figure 7-8 Enter all your business information, as well as your company motto and logo, in the Create New Business Information Set dialog box.

Applying Business Information

Your business information will be applied automatically to a new publication you create whenever you choose the information set in the Business Information list. The information is plugged into any business address fields (for example, in a return address text block on your company newsletter). You can also add specific items from your business information set by displaying the Business Information task pane (choose Business Information from the Insert menu or click the task pane title bar down arrow and choose Business Information).

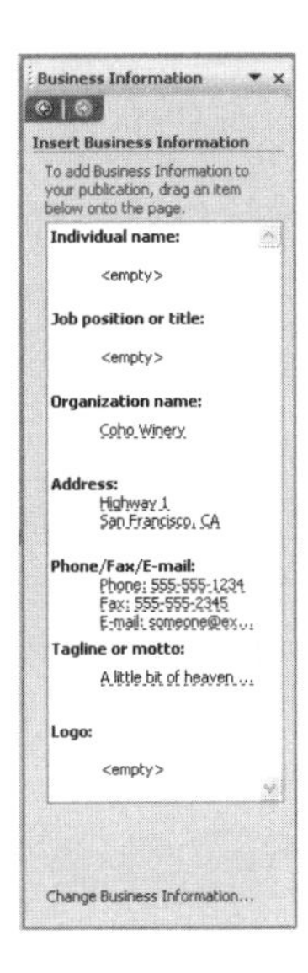

You can edit the business information you've entered for a specific set by choosing Business Information from the Edit menu (or click the Change Business Information link in the bottom of the Business Information task pane). The Business Information dialog box enables you to choose the set of information you want to edit and then make modifications, delete, or update the data as needed.

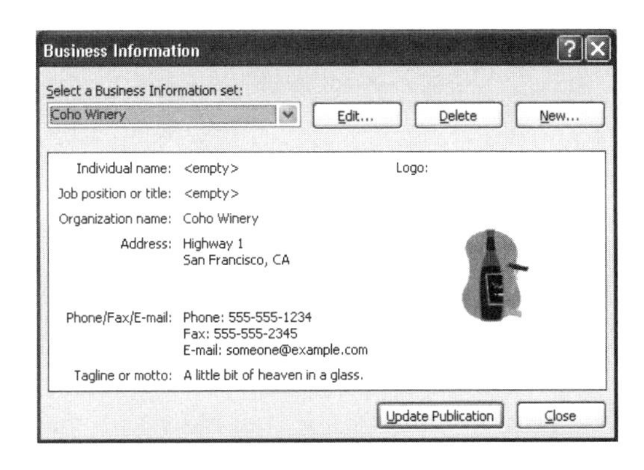

Save and Categorize Your Customized Template

After you choose the Customize and Options settings for the new template and click Create, the new publication is displayed in the Office Publisher 2007 window. This is a good time to save the publication as a template if you know you will be working with this publication type regularly.

You can easily create your own template based on your current choices by choosing Save As from the File menu. In the Save As dialog box, click the Save As Type down arrow in the Save As dialog box and choose Publisher Template. Assign a category to the template (for example, **Brochure**) by clicking the Change button and typing a word or phrase for the category and clicking OK.

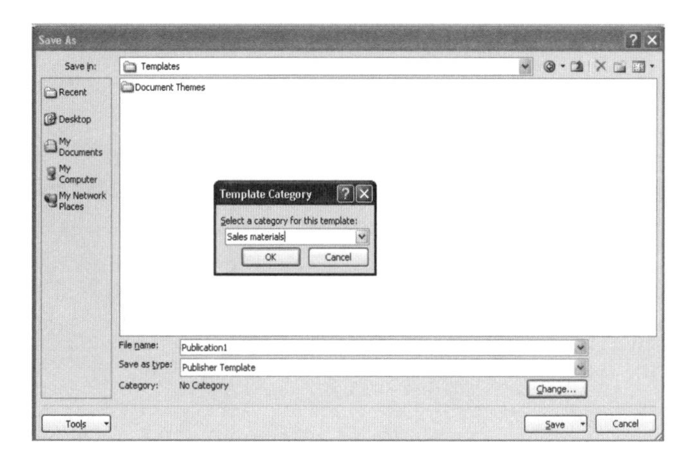

Now you can use the saved template when you begin a new publication by clicking the My Templates item in the Office Publisher 2007 opening window.

Create and Apply Reusable Content

Most businesses use some kind of repeating elements in their publications–for example, a company description, a mission statement, or a product summary. With Office Publisher 2007, you can save those items to the Content Library and add them to other publications easily. The whole process is very simple:

- You can add an item to the Content Library by right-clicking it (see Figure 7-9) and choosing Add To Content Library.
- You can insert an item from the Content Library into your current publication by displaying the Content Library task pane, choosing the item, and clicking Insert (see Figure 7-10).

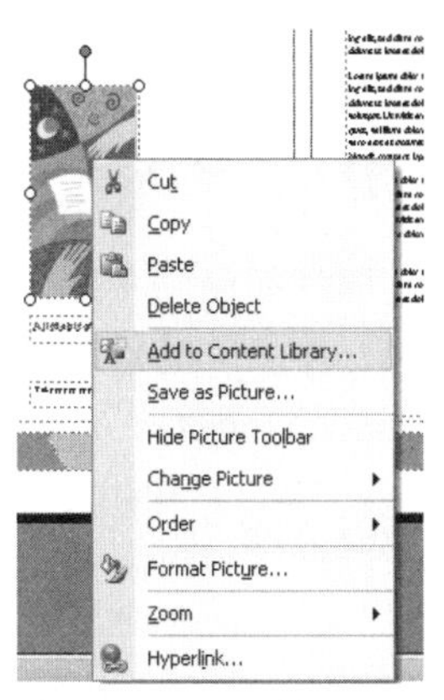

Figure 7-9 Add an item to the Content Library easily by right-clicking it.

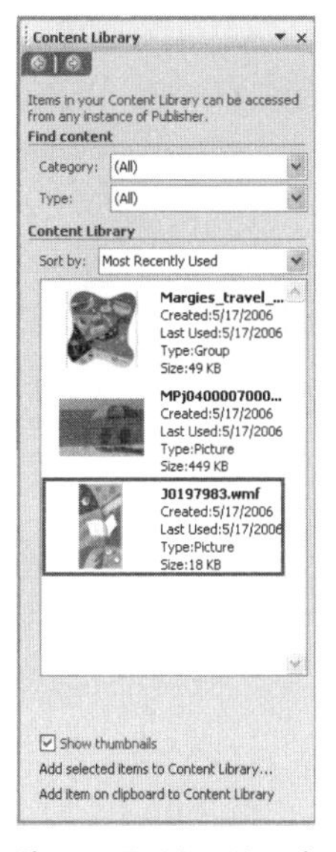

Figure 7-10 Use the Content Library task pane to insert an item in your publication.

Tip You can add keywords and categories to your content items so that you can search for them easily using the Category and Type controls in the Content Library task pane. Additionally, you can add new items and copy content from the Clipboard to the Content Library by clicking the links in the bottom of the Content Library task pane.

You can save text, images, logos, mottos, WordArt, and even entire sections and pages to the Content Library. Not only does this save you considerable time in creating and formatting content but it also ensures that your materials are worded and presented consistently, helping to reinforce your brand.

Finalize Your Publication with Design Checker

Design Checker was available in Publisher 2003, but the tool has been substantially improved in Office Publisher 2007. Now you can choose to have the program perform a number of specific checks and walk you through the process of correcting any errors that are found.

The Design Checker enables you to do four different types of checks (see Figure 7-11): you can run a general design check, check to make sure the publication is ready for a commercial printer, evaluate the file for publication as a Web site, or determine whether the file is ready to send as an e-mail message. In each case, the Design Checker looks for different potential problems–for example, the following:

- When you run the commercial printing check, one item the Design Checker evaluates is which color mode the publication is using (RGB, the default mode, is best for desktop print, not commercial printing).
- When you choose the Web site check, the Design Checker ensures that all images in your publication include alternative text (text that appears in place of the image if graphic display is turned off).
- When you choose the e-mail check, the Design Checker looks for inconsistent spacing, broken hyperlinks, misplaced graphics, and more.

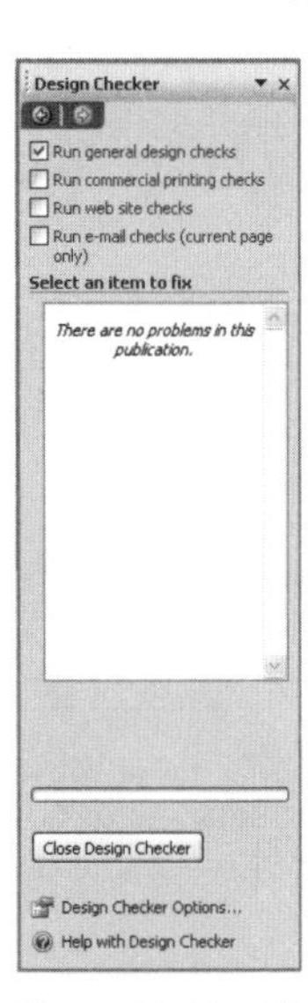

Figure 7-11 The Design Checker can perform several different checks to help you finalize your publication.

If the Design Checker finds problems in your document, the issues are listed in the list box in the middle of the Design Checker task pane. You can then click an item to display a menu of options that will correct the problem. For some errors, there may be an automatic fix Office Publisher 2007 can apply for you; in other cases, you need to correct the problem manually.

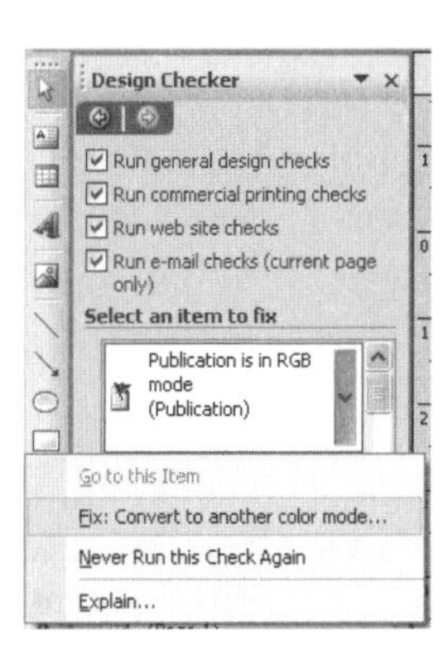

Tip If you aren't sure why the Design Checker is identifying an issue as a problem, you can click the item and choose the Explain option to find out more about it.

Prepare Your Materials For Commercial Printing

You can design, create, and proof your publication on a desktop system, but when you're ready to print a professional marketing piece, chances are that you will send the final document to a commercial printer for printing. Although this process is improving, preparing a publication for a commercial printer can seem like a cumbersome task. Office Publisher 2007 makes the process easier by including a number of features to walk you through the steps required for preparing a file for commercial printing.

Tip Getting the colors right in a professional publication can be a challenge if you use specific hues in your logo or other brand elements. Office Publisher 2007 now takes the guesswork out of color matching by providing Pantone color support. Pantone is a method of identifying colors for commercial printing so that the color is consistent among all your publications. For example, if you use a royal blue as part of the color in your brand, you want that royal blue to be the same on all your publications—not lighter on one and darker on another, or more green in yet another. In the Pantone system, the royal blue you select will have a number that will indicate a specific mix of inks that are required to create that exact color each time it is used.

Click Print in the Publisher Tasks pane to begin the process and then click Print at a commercial printer. Office Publisher 2007 gives you several links that enable you to run the Design Checker, make changes in page size or orientation; preview and print a sample; and then package the publication for the printer.

Create, Send, and Track Mailings

If you are responsible for managing a mailing list, you know that there's a real art involved in creating a publication, choosing the recipients, adding the merge fields, and sending a mailing that gets great results. Office Publisher 2007 can help you create, sort, and send a mailing–and even track the results so you can learn from the response you get and fine tune your future mailing projects.

The changes in the mail merge feature of Office Publisher 2007 simplify the merge process by enabling you to focus specifically on the type of project you want to create. Whether you are personalizing a newsletter, sending a sales e-mail message, or customizing and mailing a catalog, you'll find that turning the created publication into a mail merge document requires only three steps:

1. Create, add, or import the recipient list.
2. Add merge fields to your publication.
3. Merge the publications with the recipient list.

Choose Your Mailing Type

Office Publisher 2007 now includes three separate merge choices to enable you to choose the one that fits the type of project you're creating. You can view the merge options by choosing Mailings And Catalogs from the Tools menu (see Figure 7-12) or by choosing the Mail Merge, E-mail Merge, or Catalog Merge task panes.

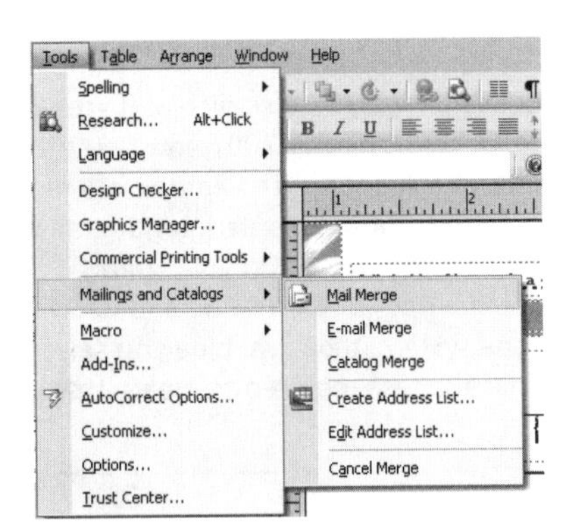

Figure 7-12 Choose one of the three merge types.

The task pane for the type of project you selected then prompts you to make the choices needed to complete the process. As you add merge fields to the publication, you can dynamically preview the merge by clicking outside the field text box. You can also position the mouse pointer on a merge field to display a Smart Tag; when you click the Smart Tag, you see a menu of options related to that particular item (see Figure 7-13). You can use this feature to change data as you work (for example, if you find that you need to change the spelling of one name) and to preview the way the customer data will appear as you create the merge.

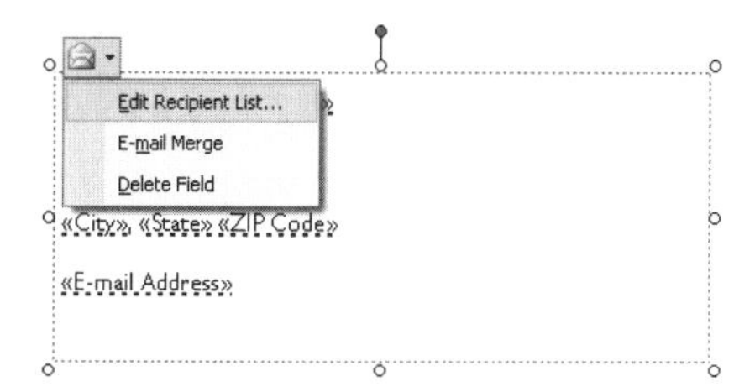

Figure 7-13 You have access to data options while you create the merge fields.

As you prepare to finalize the merge operation, you are given options for sending the merged publication (see Figure 7-14). In addition to these final choices, you can determine how you want to follow up on the merge print. The follow-up options for an e-mail merge are as follows:

- Print Recipient List displays the Print List dialog box so that you can choose the fields you want to include in the report, select the records you want to include, and choose the orientation and page size (see Figure 7-15).
- Save A Shortcut To Recipient List opens the File Save dialog box so that you can choose a location for the shortcut file. The list used in your current merge operation is then saved as a data set you can use in future mailings.
- Export Recipient List To New File displays the Save As dialog box so that you can specify a file name and folder for the list. You can choose whether to save only the contacts included in the current merge or include all records in the data list.
- Track Through Business Contact Manager is available if you have installed Microsoft® Office Outlook® 2007 with Business Contact Manager, and clicking it opens a Marketing Campaign window so that you can launch and track a marketing campaign using the publication you created in Office Publisher 2007 (see Figure 7-16). You can fill in the necessary information and click Save & Close to save your information.

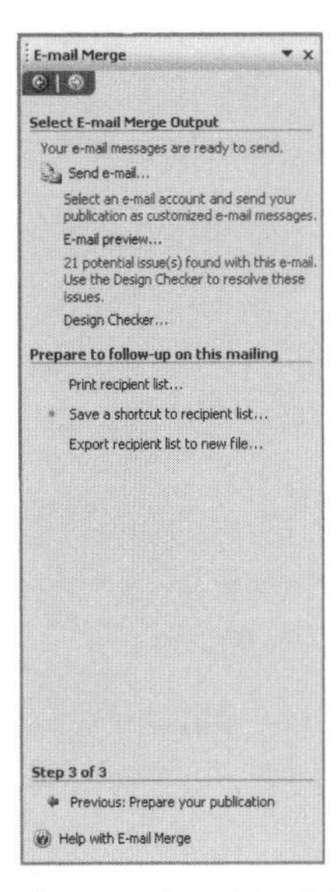

Figure 7-14 Finalizing your merge project involves choosing how it will be sent.

> **Tip** You can now manage your e-mail lists with Office Outlook 2007, Office Excel 2007, Office Access 2007, Office Publisher 2007, Microsoft List Builder, and Office Outlook 2007 with Business Contact Manager. You also can add contacts, filter and sort lists, revise entries add special text messages, or create new lists—all within Publisher.

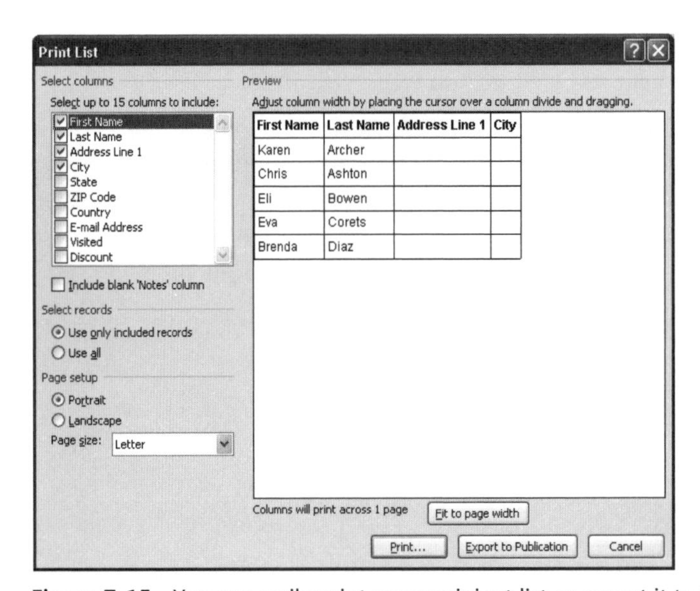

Figure 7-15 You can easily print your recipient list or export it to be used in other applications.

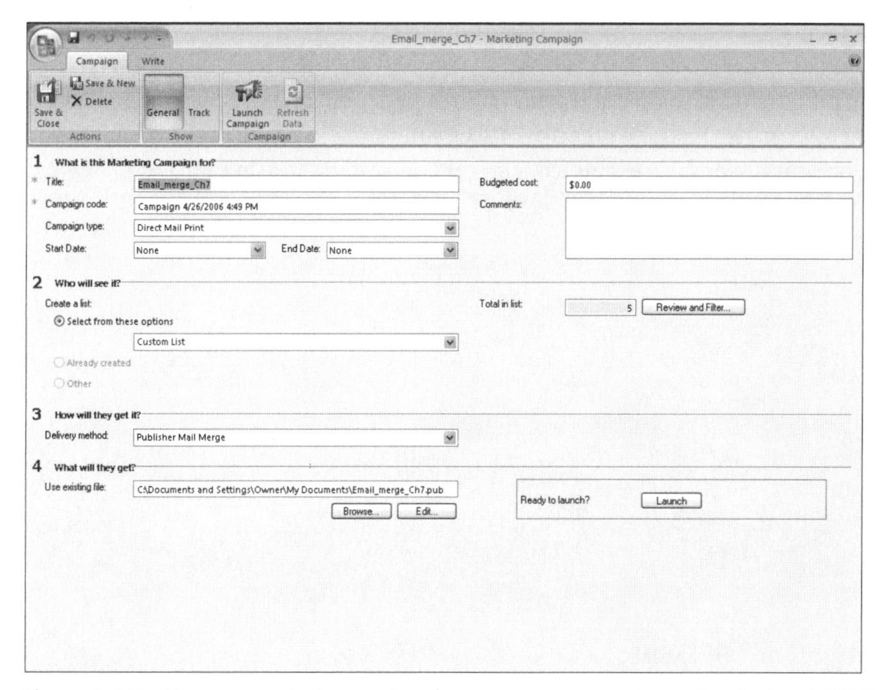

Figure 7-16 You can track the results of your merge campaign using Outlook 2007 with Business Contact Manager.

Coming Next

This chapter provided a look at the new and expanded features available in Office Publisher 2007. The next chapter introduces you to the seamless ways in which you can gather, organize, search, use, and share notes and resources using Microsoft® Office OneNote® 2007.

Coming Next

This chapter provided a look at the new and expanded features available in Office Publisher 2007. The next chapter introduces you to the seamless ways in which you can gather, organize, search, use, and share notes and resources using Microsoft® Office OneNote® 2007.

Chapter 8

Gather, Find, and Share Information with Office OneNote 2007

What you'll find in this chapter:

- The new look of Office OneNote 2007
- Working with multiple notebooks
- Collecting your notes and information
- Using drawing tools and tables
- Flagging notes for follow up
- Finding notes quickly with improved search capabilities

In today's information-rich world, finding what you need isn't the problem—managing it is. Chances are that you are inundated with information from the time you get up in the morning to the time you go to bed at night. Your cell phone connects you to family members, friends, and work associates; your PDA keeps your schedule; your MP3 player downloads your favorite podcasts; e-mail brings you news, action items, and meeting invitations; and Web pages fill you in on everything else.

Microsoft® Office OneNote® 2007 is the program to use when you want to reverse the effects of information overload by organizing, managing, gathering, and using the information you receive in a more effective way. Designed to help you gather, organize, find, and use the information you collect, Office OneNote 2007 includes a huge array of features to help you quickly collect (on a desktop PC, laptop, Tablet PC, Microsoft® Windows® Mobile powered device—or all of the above) digital information of all kinds (text, pictures, Web pages, e-mail messages, as well as audio, and video recordings) and have it at your fingertips when you need it.

The New Look of Office OneNote 2007

When you first open Office OneNote 2007, the program opens to the OneNote Guide, a sample notebook you can use to try out different tasks as you learn to use Office OneNote 2007. The opening page includes a tutorial showing you how to get starting using the various features in the program (see Figure 8-1). The tutorial suggests that you click anywhere on the opening page and type your name to get a sense of the way you can add notes anywhere and in any form that feels comfortable for you.

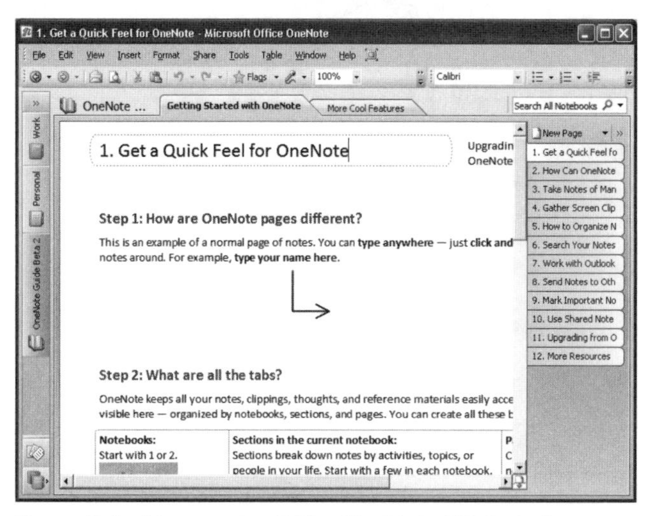

Figure 8-1 The opening Office OneNote 2007 window

Figure 8-2 shows the layout of the Office OneNote 2007 window. The names of open notebooks (in this example, OneNote Guide Beta 2, Personal, and Work) appear in the navigation tab on the left, section tabs for the selected notebook appear at the top of the window, and page tabs appear along the right side of the notes area, making it easy for you to choose the notebook, section, and page you want to work with at any time (see Figure 8-2).

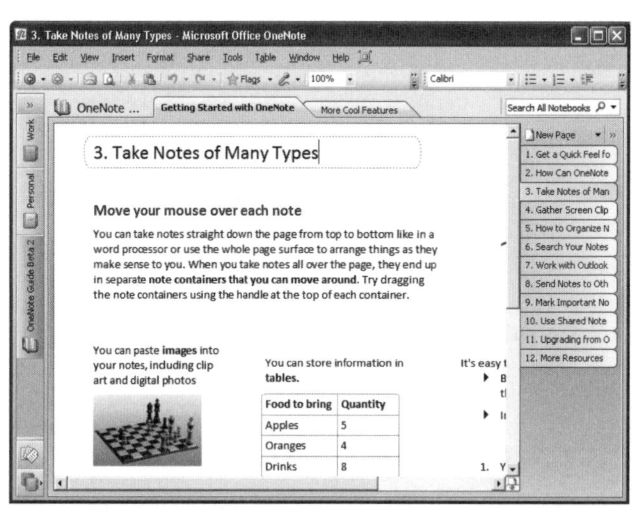

Figure 8-2 You can choose the notebook, section, and page you want to work with by clicking the item tab on the left, top, or right side of the notes area.

> **Tip** One of the new features of Office OneNote 2007 is the ability to work with multiple notebooks. Now you can open several notebooks at once and move information from one notebook to another by dragging and dropping it into the new location.

You can click the double arrows in the right side of the navigation bar to expand it and display a listing of open notebooks and sections in your current work session (see Figure 8-3). You can move to any item in the listing by simply clicking it; you can also move sections from one notebook to another (or reorder items) by dragging and dropping the section name to another point in the list.

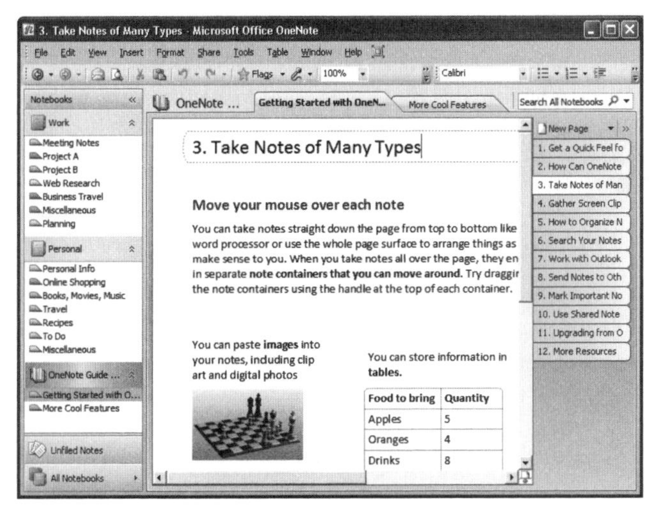

Figure 8-3 Expand and collapse the navigation pane by clicking the double arrows in the top right corner.

Two new menus are available in Office OneNote 2007 that spotlight important program capabilities. The Share menu enables you to create shared notebooks and host live note-sharing sessions; and the Table menu contains the commands you need to insert and work with tables on your notes pages.

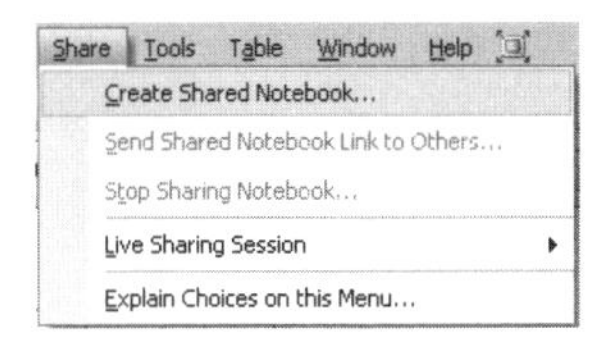

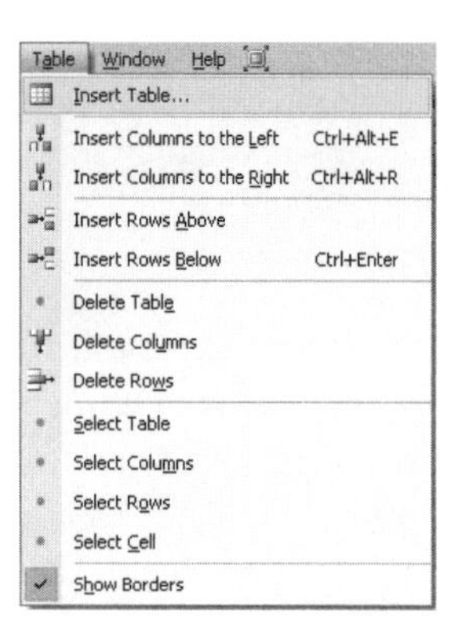

Tip For more about working with shared notebooks and hosting live sharing sessions, see "Sharing Your Notes with Others," later in this chapter. To learn more about the new table features, see the "Use Drawing Tools and Tables" section.

Using Templates to Customize Your Notes

Office OneNote 2007 now includes dozens of page templates you can use to organize your notes. Whether you begin with a blank page and then add a template or start with a template right off the bat, you can choose from a number of different styles to find the one that best matches the type of data you are capturing.

To choose a page template, click the New Page down arrow and choose More Template Choices and Options at the bottom of the displayed list. Five categories (Planners, Decorative, Business, Blank, and Academic) offer you a variety of ready-made templates you can use as the basis for your notetaking. Click a category to expand the choices in the list; click one to display the note page in that particular view.

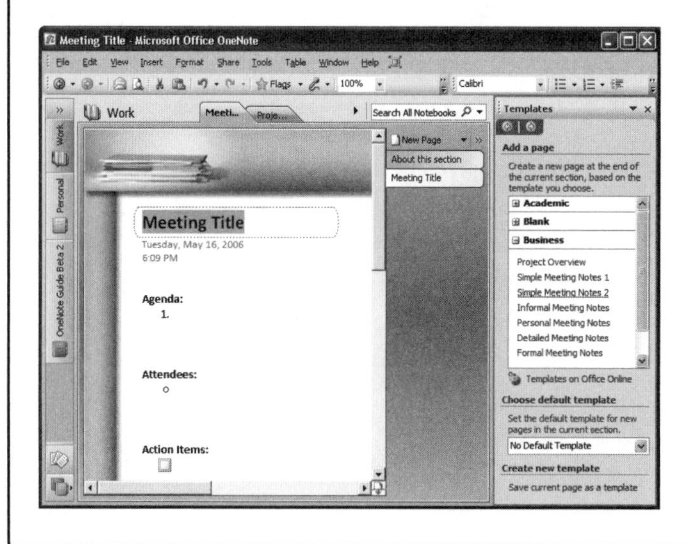

Working with Multiple Notebooks

In Office OneNote 2007 you can open, work with, and share information among multiple notebooks in a single work session. It's not usual to be working with information that relates to more than one project you're working on. As you prepare a marketing plan for a new product launch, you might work with one notebook containing information about the product and another notebook you created as you work on the launch event.

The new look of the Office OneNote 2007 window makes it easy for you to easily move from one notebook to another; click the tab of the notebook you want to use on the left side of the window. You can also copy and paste information among notebooks and share information easily by simply selecting, dragging, and dropping information in one notebook to the tab of another notebook.

Setting Notebook Properties

Now that you can have multiple notebooks open in the work area during a single Office OneNote 2007 work session, you need a way of distinguishing one notebook from another when more than one is open in the work area. You can name a notebook and assign a color to it by choosing Notebook Properties from the File menu. In the Notebook Properties dialog box, enter the display name you want to use for the notebook and select a color for the notebook tab. Click OK to save the settings; and then new color and name are applied to the notebook tab in the navigation bar.

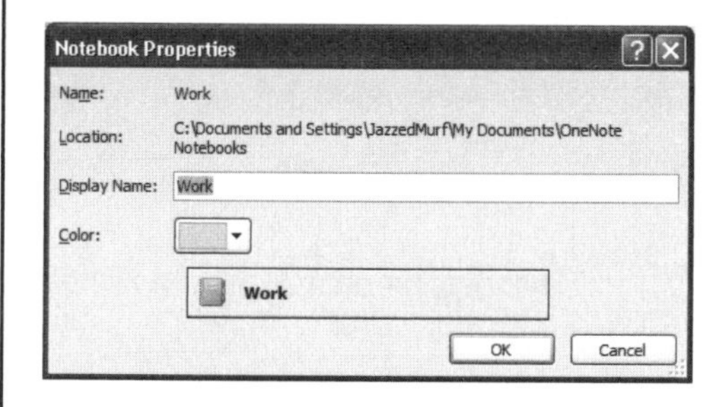

Collecting Your Notes and Information

Where you find your information has a lot to do with *how* you record it. If you are in a business meeting, you can click and type notes in your Office OneNote 2007 notebook. If you are researching a topic online, you can clip and save Web addresses, quotes, statistics, or more from the Web pages you visit. If you are assembling information you've used in reports, worksheets, or business correspondence, adding those existing files to Office OneNote 2007 is one way to pull together the information you want to work with. This section shows you various ways of incorporating notes and information in your Office OneNote 2007 notebooks.

Start a New Notebook

You can use the New Notebook Wizard in Office OneNote 2007 to create a new notebook from scratch or to base it on template. Start the notebook by opening the File menu and choosing New Notebook. In the New Notebook Wizard (see Figure 8-4, enter a name for the workbook, choose a color (to distinguish it from other open notebooks), and, if applicable, click a template; then click Next.

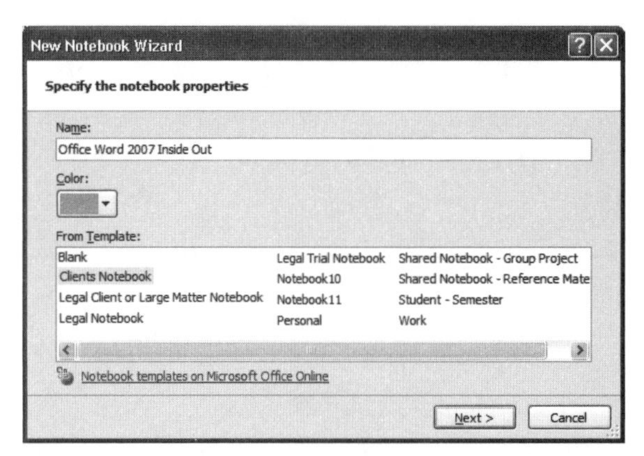

Figure 8-4 The New Notebook Wizard enables you to enter a title and choose a color and template for the new notebook.

The New Notebook Wizard asks you where you will use the notebook and where you want the notebook to be stored before creating the notebook. After you click Create, the new notebook is displayed. Several tabs are added by default as section placeholders, and tips and suggestions are displayed in the notes area.

Type Anywhere on the Page

When you jot notes on a scrap of paper, you probably just put the pen on the page and start writing. You can add notes to your Office OneNote 2007 page with the same ease–just click anywhere on the page and start typing. Clicking and typing creates a "container" that stores the note wherever you add it.

You can easily group similar items by dragging one container to another; you can also move containers in the notebook by clicking the note in the Outline and dragging it to a new location. The notes you create are even more flexible than the handwritten notes you scribble on the back of an envelope–as electronic information, you can move, reorganize, edit, use, copy, and flag the notes in your notebook for use in an unlimited number of projects.

Blog This!

An exciting new feature in Office OneNote 2007 enables you to blog about a feature, idea, or product you have included in your notes. When you're working with an object on a notes page, right-click the object and choose Blog This. The feature works with Office Word 2007 to enable you to get the message out quickly, easily, and with a minimum of effort.

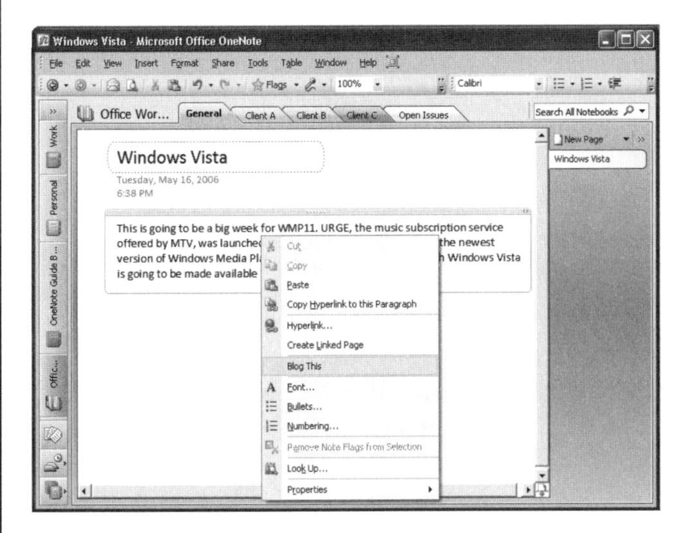

The blogging feature that has been added to the 2007 release is a late-breaking feature that the developers are saying "is still hot." It's very much a beta release (with some great functionality and huge potential), but you may run into some glitches during beta 2. Here's a workaround that Office OneNote 2007 program manager Chris Prately posted on his blog (blogs.msdn.com/chris_pratley/archive/2006/05/12/596010.aspx) to get the blogging feature working smoothly in Office OneNote 2007:

"*FYI ... to get the OneNote 2007 feature to work you will need to perform a little workaround: Copy Blog.dotx from C:\Program Files\Microsoft Office\Templates\1033 to C:\Documents and Settings\%username%\Application Data\Microsoft\Templates.*"

Insert File Attachments

The types of files you use in your note gathering are likely to extend beyond the scanned images and picture files you could insert with the previous version of OneNote. In Office OneNote 2007, you can add files of all types directly to your notes pages by simply dragging and dropping a file onto the page–or by choosing Files from the Insert menu and selecting the file(s) you want to add. The files are added as shortcuts, as shown in Figure 8-5. You (or those who share the notebook) can view the files by double-clicking the file icon.

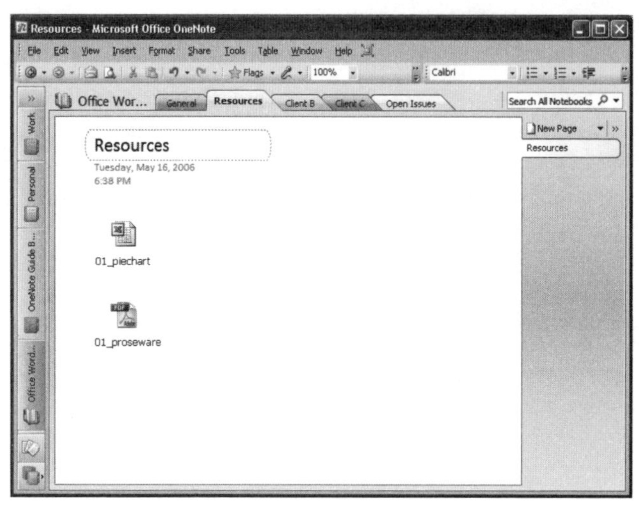

Figure 8-5 Bring together files of all types as part of your research.

Collecting Web Research

When you're using Internet Explorer, you can gather information from Web pages by clicking the Send To OneNote button in the Standard toolbar. Doing so saves the content of the page to your current note page.

Office OneNote 2007 also includes a new Side Note feature that makes saving and incorporating information from the Web a simple two-step process. When you are browsing a site from which you want to clip information, right-click the OneNote icon in the system tray and choose Open New Side Note. A small note window then opens on top of the current display. Type your note and click the close box, and the item is added as a new page in the current notebook.

Printing Information to Your Notebook

A new import feature enables you to print other files directly into your Office OneNote 2007 notebook so that you can review, mark up, and share the document with others. Simply go to print a document or worksheet as usual (by choosing Print from the File menu). In the Print dialog box, click the Name down arrow and choose Microsoft OneNote Import. Click OK, and the file is printed to an electronic file and incorporated directly as a graphic image on your notes page (see Figure 8-6).

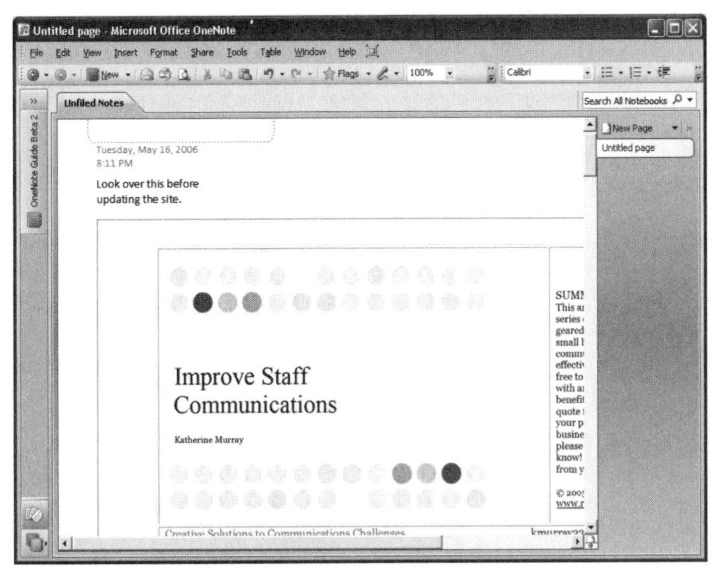

Figure 8-6 Now you can print your files directly into your Office OneNote 2007 notebook.

Using Drawing Tools and Tables

Office OneNote 2007 continues the tradition of supporting ink–enabling you to add handwritten notes directly onto your note pages. But now you can also draw on the page using a full set of drawing tools; you can better control the writing tool or pen mode you want to work with, add tables to your pages, and insert files directly onto your notes pages.

Using the Drawing Tools

Office OneNote 2007 now includes a complete set of Drawing Tools you can display along the bottom edge of the notes window (see Figure 8-7) by choosing Drawing Toolbar in the View menu. The tools on the toolbar give you what you need to add freeform shapes, autoshapes, and diagram connectors to your pages. You can also choose line color and thickness settings, and even duplicate and rotate selected objects on the page.

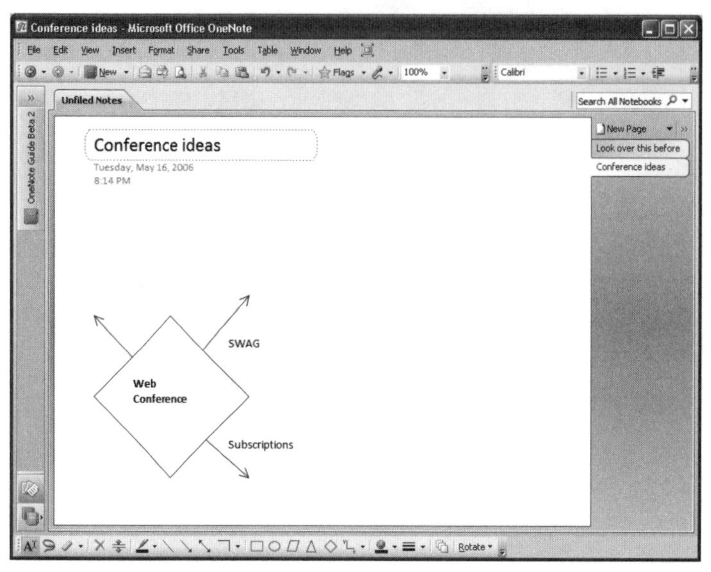

Figure 8-7 New drawing tools enable you to add shapes, connectors, and freeform drawings to your notes pages.

Working with Writing Tools and Pen Modes

Office OneNote 2007 expands the capability of the writing and drawing features by breaking each out into its own separate function. Now you can use the Pen mode to choose whether you want the pen to be used for writing or drawing, or writing *and* drawing. The Writing Tools option (in the Tools menu) enables you to choose the style of pen or eraser you want to use to write freehand on your notes pages. You can also use the Type/Selection Tool to switch from Pen mode to Typing mode easily.

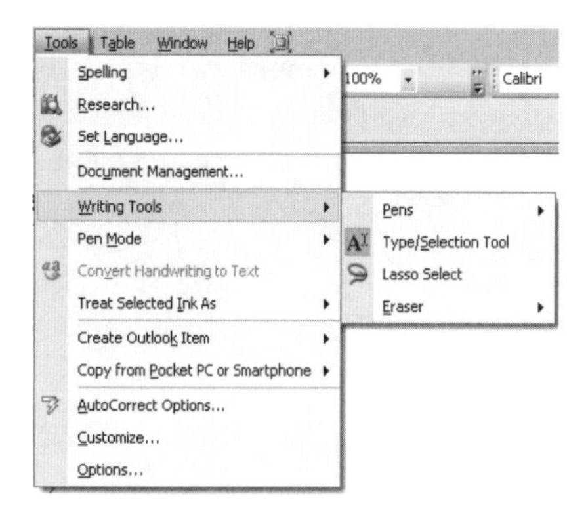

Additionally, the new Lasso tool enables you to select, freeform, any object on a page you want to copy, save, or drag to your notes pages. This is great for capturing an ink note you've added on another page or document; now you can use the Lasso tool to grab that note and move it to your current notes page.

Adding Tables to Your Notes Pages

Adding tables to your notes pages in Office OneNote 2007 is as simple as choosing Insert Table from the Table menu, entering the number of columns and rows you want to include, and then clicking OK. Using the commands in the Table menu, you can modify the table by adding or deleting rows or columns and displaying or hiding borders (see Figure 8-8).

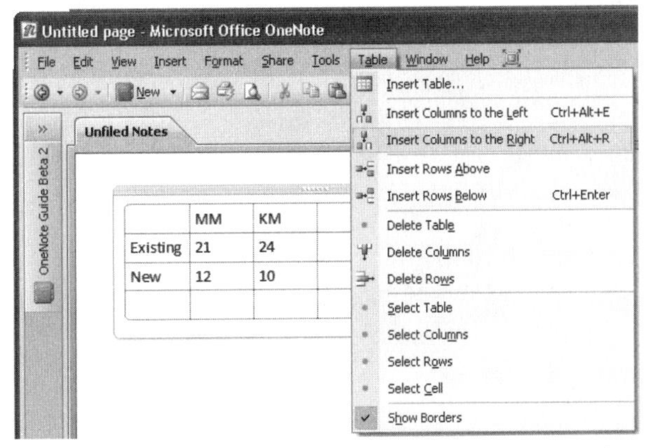

Figure 8-8 Use the Table menu to add and work with tables in your notes.

Tip Because of improved integration with other Microsoft Office 2007 system applications, you can copy and paste a table from Office Word 2007 directly onto your Office OneNote 2007 page—or simply drag and drop selected text or images onto your notebook page

Using the Calculator to Do Simple Calculations

Here's a great new feature in Office OneNote 2007: quick calculations. How many times in the course of a day do you need to stop and quickly open the Calculator accessory to do some simple math? Maybe you need to figure out the total number of lunches you need to order for an upcoming workshop; or you might need to reserve the larger conference room for the sales meeting next week (but you need a total to be sure).

In Office OneNote 2007, you can now simply type your calculation on a note page, and when you type the equal symbol (=) and press the spacebar, Office OneNote 2007 performs the calculation and enters the result automatically for you. This simple feature saves you the time and trouble of stopping what you're doing, opening another application, entering the calculation, and pasting it back into your notes.

Flagging Notes for Follow Up

Whether you are working individually with Office OneNote 2007 or plan to share your notes with your team, flagging items for follow up is an important part of prioritizing and acting on important tasks. Office OneNote 2007 includes a huge set of Note Flags you can add to your notes or customize to suit the needs of your project (see Figure 8-9). You can add your own images, choose new colors, and more.

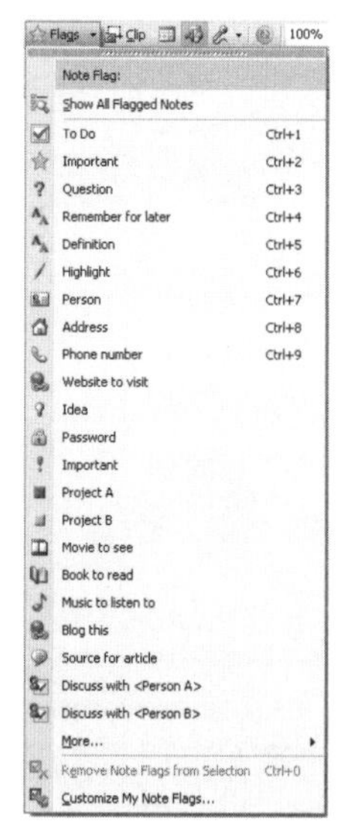

Figure 8-9 Use the Office OneNote 2007 Note Flags to make sure you follow up on specific items.

You can use the Note Flags Summary Task pane to see at a glance all the Note Flags you've added to your notebook (see Figure 8-10). In addition, you can use the Note Flags Summary Task pane to navigate to specific notes–just clicking a flag takes you directly to that note in your notebook.

Tip Any item you flag with a To Do flag in Office OneNote 2007 automatically appears as a task in your Microsoft® Office Outlook® 2007 To-Do Bar.

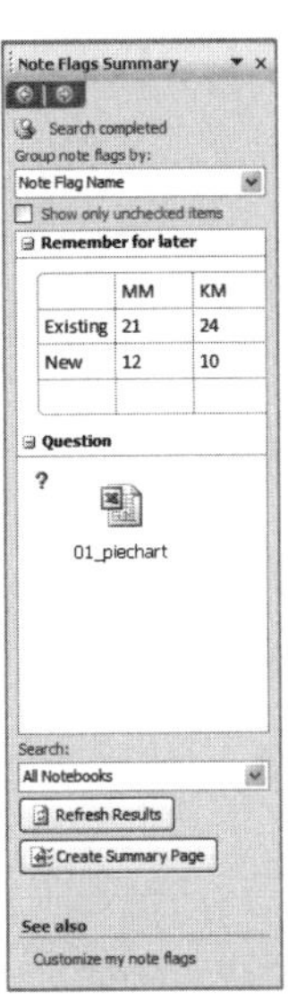

Figure 8-10 The Note Flags Summary Task Pane enables you to see quickly all the items you've flagged for follow-up in a notebook section or an entire notebook.

Customizing Flags

You can easily customize the flags in Office OneNote 2007 by clicking the Flags down arrow in the Standard toolbar and choosing Customize My Note Flags. The Customize My Note Flags task pane appears so that you can click the flag type you want to change and click the Modify button. In the Modify Note Flag dialog box, specify a name for the flag and choose a new symbol, font color, and highlight color. Click OK to save your changes.

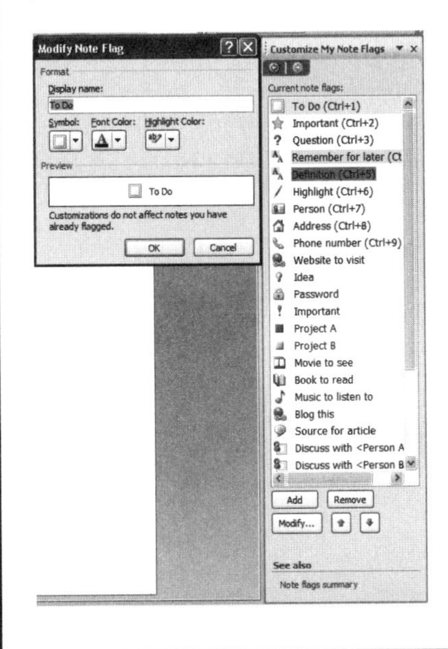

Finding Notes Quickly with Improved Search Capabilities

The expanded and improved search capability in Office OneNote 2007 enables you to find–quickly–all items you've gathered that are related to a specific topic. OneNote uses the Windows Desktop Search engine to constantly build an index of your notes in the background, delivering fast search results when you need them.

Simply type a search word or phrase in the Find box in the top-right area of the Office OneNote 2007 window and click Go (see Figure 8-11). If you want to limit the search by looking only in specific folders, click the search down arrow and choose the notebook, section, or group you want to limit the search to.

Figure 8-11 Enter the search word or phrase in the Find box, choose where you want to search, and click Go.

The program finds all occurrences of that item–in text, audio segments, e-mail messages, and even images–and displays them in a Note Search Results list in the Page List task pane on the right side of the window. You can move directly to one of the notes in the results list by clicking the note title.

When a note is stored in Office OneNote 2007, the program uses optical character recognition (OCR) to recognize text in individual images (such as Web pages, business cards, and diagrams) and relies on speech-to-text tools to locate the spoken words in audio and video files you have saved on your computer.

Tip Another search technique will help you target your search and find just what you're looking for quickly. You can now use NEAR (in all capital letters) to indicate the proximity of two words in a phrase. For example, if you want to find all information about the product review meeting that will meet in August as opposed to the one that meets in June, you can enter **product review NEAR August** to have Office OneNote 2007 find all references that have those two phrases in close proximity to each other.

Sharing Your Notes with Others

The shared notebooks feature is a great new addition to Office OneNote 2007. Now you have several different choices for the way in which you share the notebooks you create–in fact, you can even host a live sharing session that can serve as a kind of online meeting, complete with whiteboard, file sharing, and more. This section introduces you to the way in which you can share your notebooks with others.

Sharing Notebooks

The Share menu houses the commands you use to create a shared notebook or make changes to the way in which you share your notes.

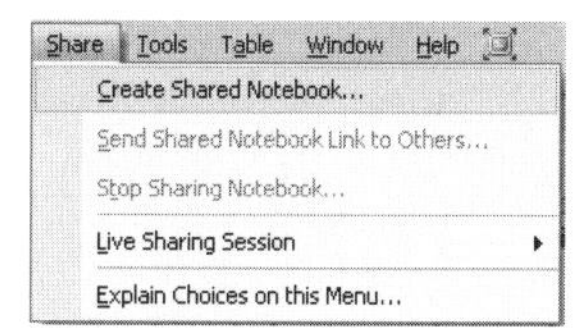

When you click Create Shared Notebook, the New Notebook Wizard launches, asking first for the name of the new notebook, and then offering you sharing options (see Figure 8-12). You can choose whether you want to create the shared notebook on a server or in a shared folder on your current system. When you make your choice and click Next, the wizard enables you to specify the shared location and click Create.

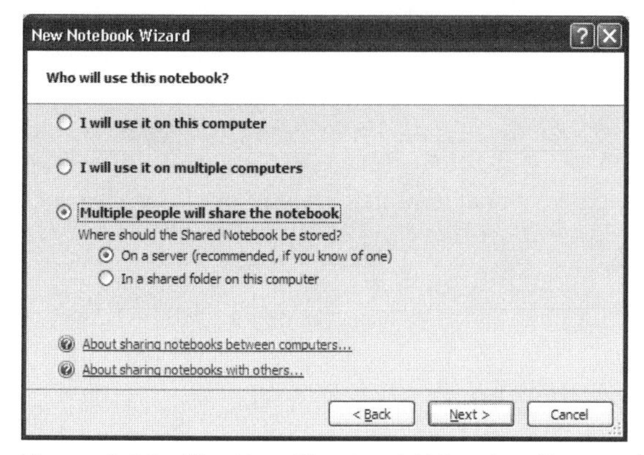

Figure 8-12 The New Notebook Wizard walks you through the process of setting up a shared notebook.

The program automatically walks you through the process of setting up the shared program and determining the necessary permission settings for users you want to give access to the shared folder or server space. Additionally, an e-mail message is automatically prepared to send team members the necessary file link so they can access the shared notebook (see Figure 8-13).

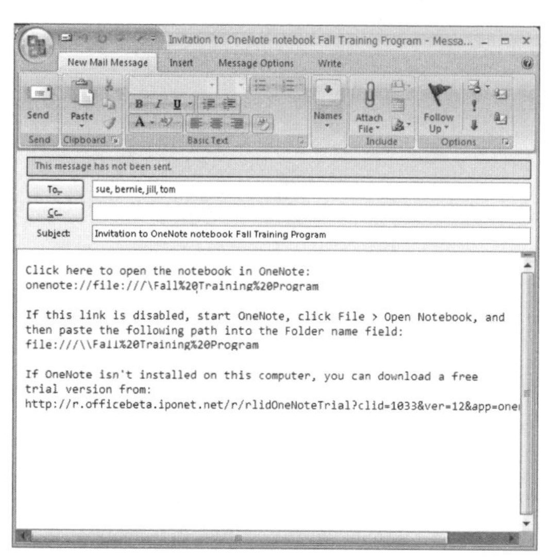

Figure 8-13 Office OneNote 2007 prepares an e-mail message to provide team members access to the shared folder.

When others make changes to the notebook, Office OneNote 2007 automatically synchronizes the changes so that the most recent changes are reflected in all versions of the file.

> **Tip** All programs in the 2007 Microsoft Office System include the capability of saving files in XPS format, and Office OneNote 2007 is no exception. When you save your notebook in XML Paper Specification (XPS) format, you save a final formatted version of the file that others can view (but not modify) whether they have Office OneNote 2007 or not.

Sharing Notes Live

Another way you can share notebooks with others and review items together online is by inviting others to join a live note-taking session. When you choose Live Sharing Session and then Start Sharing Current Section from the Share menu, the Start Live Session Task Pane opens (see Figure 8-14).

You can enter the necessary information, choose the pages you want to share, and start the session. When you include Invite Participates on the second page of the Start Live Session Task Pane, an e-mail message is displayed with an invitation to the sharing session. You simply add your team members to the To line and send the message. Others can then join the session simply by opening the attachment, and you can review the notes, add text and drawings, and invite feedback during the shared session. When you end the session, the notes are saved on each participant's computer automatically.

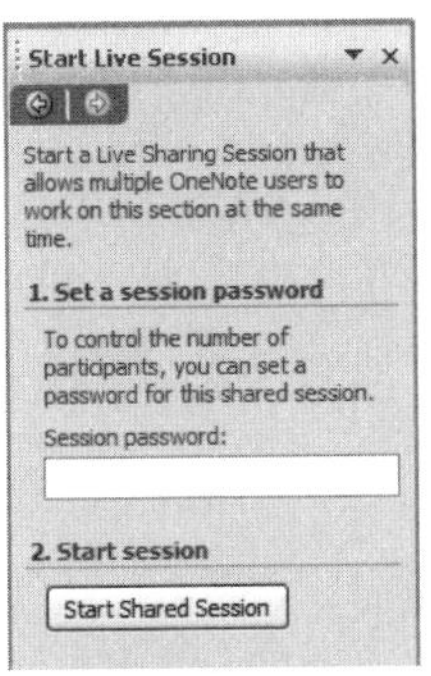

Figure 8-14 Starting a live note-taking session is as simple as clicking a button and sending an e-mail message.

Sending Notes by E-Mail

Gathering information with Office OneNote 2007 is so easy and intuitive that you are likely to gather a collection of notes, files, Web clippings, and more in a very short time. You can share what you learn with other team members to ensure that everyone is using the same information and that no one is duplicating the effort you've already put in. One way to share your notebook is by sending selected pages to others as e-mail attachments.

If you open the File menu and choose E-mail, an e-mail message window opens, and the current notes page is added as a file attachment (see Figure 8-15).You can add an introduction to the message to give the recipient more information about the page before you send it. Office OneNote 2007 users who receive the file can add the page to their own notebooks, and users who do not use Office OneNote 2007 can view the notes page as part of the e-mail message.

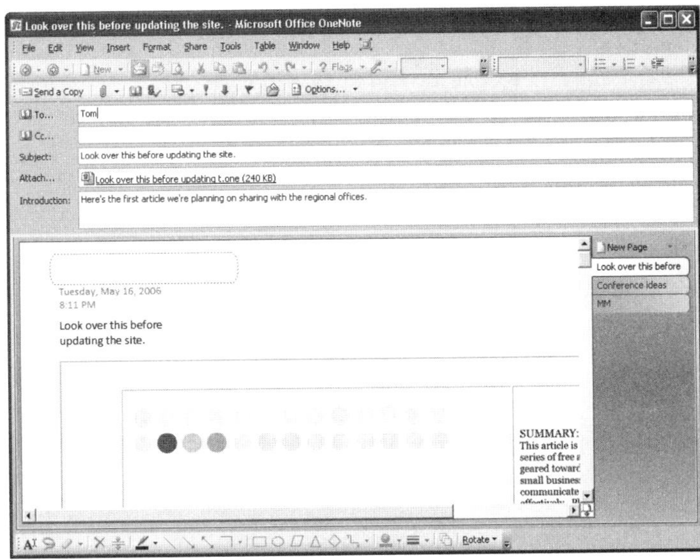

Figure 8-15 You can e-mail notes pages to team members; those who are using Office OneNote 2007 can add the page directly to their own notebooks.

Tip You can also share your notes with people who are not using Office OneNote 2007. Open the File menu, choose Send To, and select Mail Recipient to display an e-mail message window you can address to the desired recipients. The current notes page is formatted as HTML and attached to the message. When you send the message, others can view the information as a Web page.

Microsoft Office System Behind-the-Scenes Interview

Daniel Escapa, Program Manager, Office OneNote 2007

What are your favorite new features in Office OneNote 2007? This is a hard question—it is like asking which of your children is your favorite? I would have to say it is the calculator feature, which we call "napkin math." You can just type some simple equations, and Office OneNote 2007 will figure them out for you. If you want to know 7*6, just type 7*6=, and Office OneNote 2007 will solve it for you. Not something you use every day, but when you need it, it's great.

Who do you envision as your "typical" Office OneNote 2007 user? What is he or she trying to accomplish? Everyone actually [is a typical Office OneNote 2007 user]; they just don't know it yet ☺. We all have information we are keeping track of on a daily basis, but we aren't storing it effectively or finding it easily later.We keep stickies all around our desk, write on the margins of paper, and send ourselves e-mail reminders. Almost everyone has information they want to keep: frequent flyer numbers, product research, lecture notes from a class, or notes from a meeting. We tend to take notes and never look at them again; plus they are hard to find, let alone search. Office OneNote 2007 is the place to keep track of this and find it later on—think of it as an add-on pack for your brain!

Do you think there is a "home run" feature in this version of Office OneNote 2007 that everyone will be raving about? Shared notebooks. Imagine being able to have a shared notebook with your coworkers where everyone can edit and contribute. You can share information, meeting notes, brainstorming ideas, and other information that you all might need (documents, pages with annotation, embedded files, etc.). The shared notebook is much like a wiki, but better because multiple people can edit at the same time, you can take the notebook with you while you are offline, you can have a rich surface, not just a plaintext Web site—and it all just works seamlessly. You can also use this technology to sync your personal notebook with your desktop computer. The runners up would be the improved ink capabilities and Office Outlook 2007 task sync.

Do most people use Office OneNote 2007 on multiple devices—for example, a tablet PC, a desktop system, and a PDA? Or do users tend to use Office OneNote 2007 most on one favorite system? All of the above, actually; Office OneNote 2007 works on desktops, laptops, tablet PCs, and now with Windows Mobile Devices. Most of our users are mobile and working on laptops, taking Office OneNote 2007 into meetings, customer visits, classes, etc. With Office OneNote 2007, things work even better because you can easily sync your notes between all your computers. Plus with OneNote Mobile you can now take notes on a pocket PC or a Smartphone and they will sync directly into Office OneNote 2007–including camera phone photos and voice notes. You can also have notes go from Office OneNote 2007 directly to Office OneNote Mobile on your device. Now all my notes go wherever I go.

What's it been like for you to be involved with such a major release? I actually don't know any other way of working because I joined the team during this release. It has been a challenge and a great experience to be part of this team during this huge release. The team has been awesome and working hard to give our customers what they have been asking for. I must admit it is amazing when you step back and look at what we did in this release from Office OneNote 2007 all the way up to the Microsoft Office system, it truly is amazing. The new user interface, new file formats, new server integration, and more–it really is breathtaking, and I'm proud to be a part of it.

Coming Next

This chapter introduced you to the various ways you can gather, find, and share information using Office Outlook 2007. The next chapter takes you further into working with more structured data by exploring the new and enhanced features in Microsoft® Office Access® 2007.

Chapter 9

Tracking Information Quickly and Effectively with Office Access 2007

What you'll find in this chapter:

- Beginning with the Getting Started window
- Choosing a professional template
- A look at the new user interface
- Making design changes easily
- Entering, viewing, and expanding your data with flexible new features
- Using the new Report view
- Improved security features
- Collecting data via e-mail
- Take control of your Inbox

What's on your wish list for Microsoft® Office Access 2007? If you were hoping to be able to manage your data faster, more efficiently, and more easily, your wish has been granted. The totally redesigned user interface is now easy to navigate and use—designed to quickly bring you the results you need. And the addition of full-featured templates and trackable applications provides professionally designed database applications you can use right out of the box and customize to meet your own data needs—no matter what your database experience level might be.

You can use Office Access 2007 to create simple or highly sophisticated database applications—and this new release includes great new features for both (and the range of data needs in-between). If you stayed away from learning Office Access in the past because you thought it was too difficult (preferring instead to store long lists of data in Microsoft® Office Excel® or another "easier" application), this release is for you! You can organize, track, manage, update, and share your data in powerful ways—even if database programs are completely new to you. Let's start with a closer look at the changes in the Office Access 2007 user interface.

> **Note** Office Access 2007 shares all the major user interface changes—the command tab structure, command sets, contextual commands, live previews, galleries, and more—with Microsoft® Office Word 2007, Microsoft® Office Excel® 2007, and Microsoft® Office PowerPoint® 2007. This section focuses specifically on unique features in Office Access 2007. To learn more about the new features throughout the 2007 Microsoft® Office system, see Chapter 2.

Beginning with the Getting Started Window

The previous version of Office Access was straightforward and efficient, but using the program was easier if you knew what you were doing right from the start. Geared toward the person who was familiar with database applications, earlier versions of Office Access provided only limited support for someone just starting out. In the Getting Started window, Office Access 2007 provides you with a range of choices that enable you to get to work quickly, whether you are a new or experienced user (see Figure 9-1).

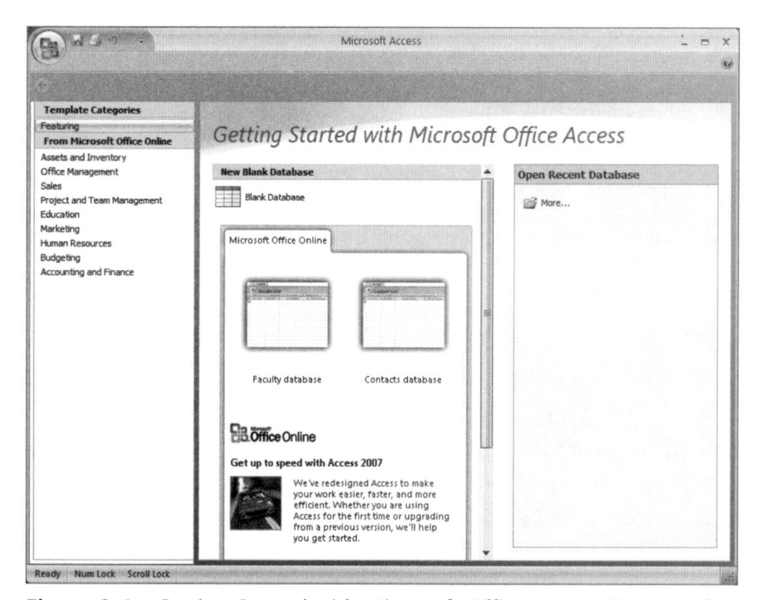

Figure 9-1 Getting Started with Microsoft Office Access 2007 window

The Template Categories pane on the left offers a number of ready-made database applications you can customize to fit your own data requirements. The center panel enables you to start a new blank database or choose an online template. The Open Recent Database pane displays any database files you've used recently and provides a More link you can use to navigate to additional files.

Tip Be sure to click the Downloads link regularly (in the bottom of the center area of the Getting Started window) to find any new downloads (add-ins, updates, converters, and more) to use with Office Access 2007.

Choosing a Professional Template

Office Access 2007 includes a collection of full-featured, professionally designed templates that you can modify to fit your own data needs. The Getting Started window displays template categories in the navigation panel on the left side of the screen. When you click one of the template styles (see Figure 9-2) in the middle pane, a description of the database, the File Name field, and the Create button appear in a panel on the right.

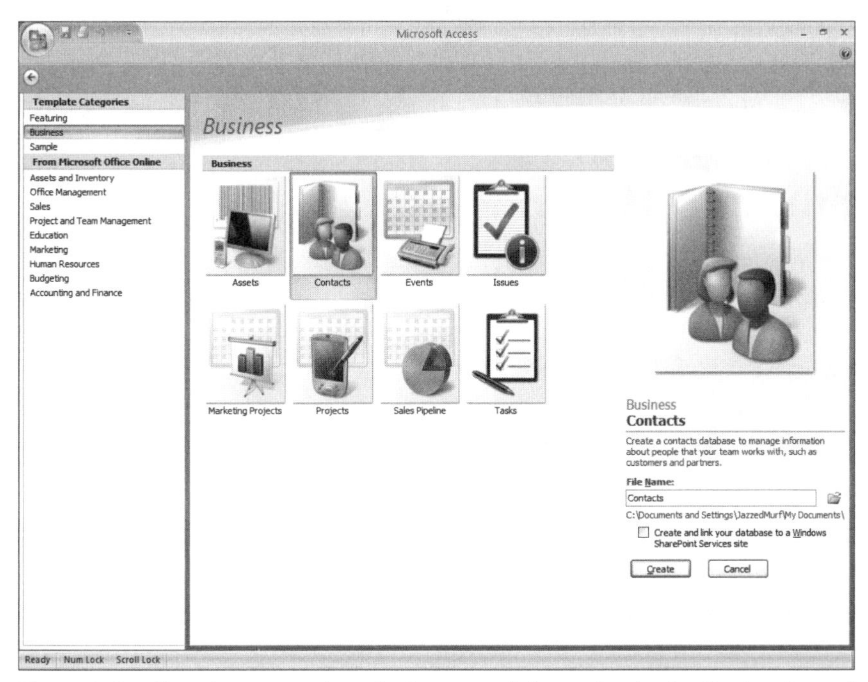

Figure 9-2 Choosing a template displays more information in the Getting Started window

Tip One new feature in Office Access 2007 is the capability to link a database to a Microsoft® Windows® SharePoint® Services Web site. If you will be sharing the new database on a SharePoint site, click the check box above the Create button before you click Create.

When you choose one of the Office Access 2007 templates, you find a usable set of data tables, queries, reports, and more that you can use as the basis for your own data management needs. For example, if you are responsible for coordinating marketing projects in your company, you can use the Marketing Projects database (in the Business template category) to set up, organize, and track the marketing projects you produce. The database template includes a number of predesigned tables (Projects, Open Projects, Common Deliverables, Deliverables, Employees, Vendors, and more); you can simply begin to create records and enter your own data to use the application as-is. These full database applications not only save you a huge amount of time you would otherwise spend designing a new database but they also help you see how professional database developers create a database system and help you ensure that you are tracking critical business information in the best possible way.

New Trackable Applications

In the past, some potential Office Access users have shied away from the program because creating a database for relatively simple data management needs seemed too complicated. Office Access 2007 now includes a number of full-featured templates that function as "trackable applications" right out of the box. Users can use these templates to track their data easily in a variety of settings.

A Look at the New User Interface

The new Office Access 2007 window is designed so that you can quickly select and work with the tables, forms, reports, and queries in your database. New design features help you get a quick sense of important data items and provide you with the tools you need to complete the task at hand.

Choosing Your View

You need a set of tools to work with information in a meaningful way. You need to be able to enter information quickly in Datasheet View; display information items in such a way that others can respond easily by using Forms View; create and modify that form for others to use (that's Design View); and set up how the information will look in a report in Layout View. Now you can switch among all those views easily when you're working with your information by clicking the View button in the Home tab (see Figure 9-3).

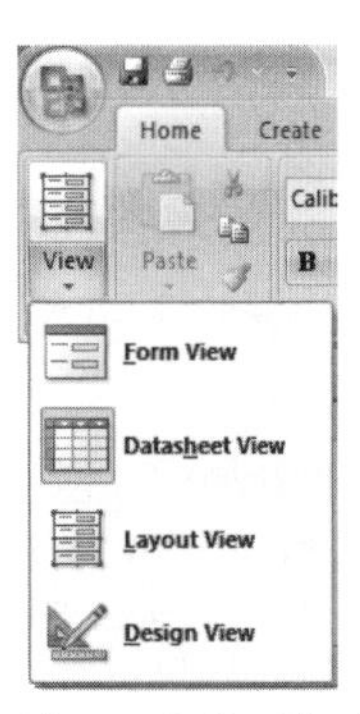

Figure 9-3 The View button in the Home tab enables you to display different views easily.

Tip You can also change the view by clicking the view control you want to use in the lower-right corner of the Office Access 2007 window.

New Command Tabs

You'll notice right away that the tabs in Office Access 2007 are new and intuitive. Now the command tabs follow a simplified progression: Home, Create, External Data, and Database Tools. Here's what you'll find in the various menus:

- The Home tab contains the command sets you will use to change views; and add, format, filter, and search records in your database.
- The Create tab gives you the tools you need to design and add tables, Office SharePoint 2007 lists, forms, reports, queries, and macros.
- The External Data tab (see Figure 9-4) provides tools for importing information from and exporting to Office Access 2007, Office Excel 2007, text files, XML files and more. You'll also find tools for saving as in XPS format, gathering information via e-mail, and synchronizing your information with Office SharePoint 2007 lists.
- The Database Tools tab contains more advanced tools for working with macros; displaying relationships and dependencies; and analyzing, managing, and synchronizing your information.

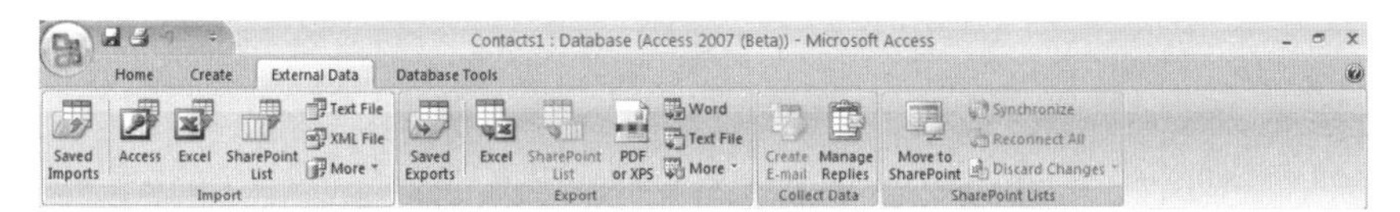

Figure 9-4 The External Data tab displays all your import, export, and data collection tools in one place.

Navigation Pane

A new Navigation Pane stretches along the left edge of the database window in all views in Office Access 2007. When you open the Navigation Pane by clicking the right arrows, it fills the left column of the database window, giving you quick access to your tables, queries, reports, and more (see Figure 9-5). The new Navigation Pane replaces the Database window and the Switchboard function in previous versions of Office Access. (Note that switchboards you created as part of custom applications in previous versions should continue to work in Office Access 2007.)

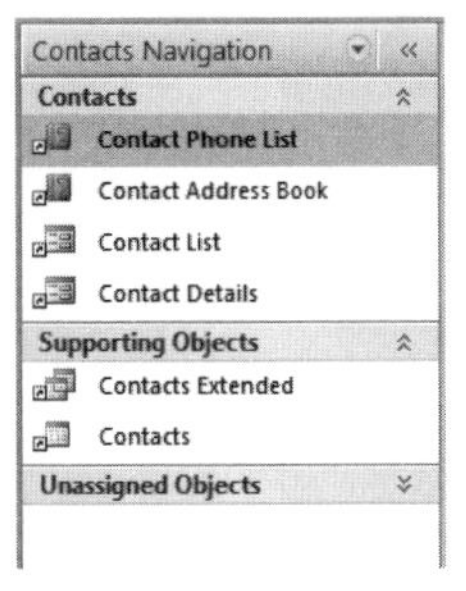

Figure 9-5 The Navigation Pane displays all the tables, forms, reports, queries, and macros you use to work with the information in your database.

The Navigation Pane groups your database objects so that you can find them easily. For example, if you have a table for your customer data and a form that enables you to add to and modify the information in that table, both items will be grouped together in the Navigation Pane.

Home Window

Depending on the template you select for your database, you might see the Home window when you open a database application. The Home window offers you quick-look information, providing a summary of the data in the current database. Charts spotlight important data trends; lists related to the content and focus of the application (such as Active Orders and Inventory to Reorder, shown in Figure 9-6) appear in the Home window.

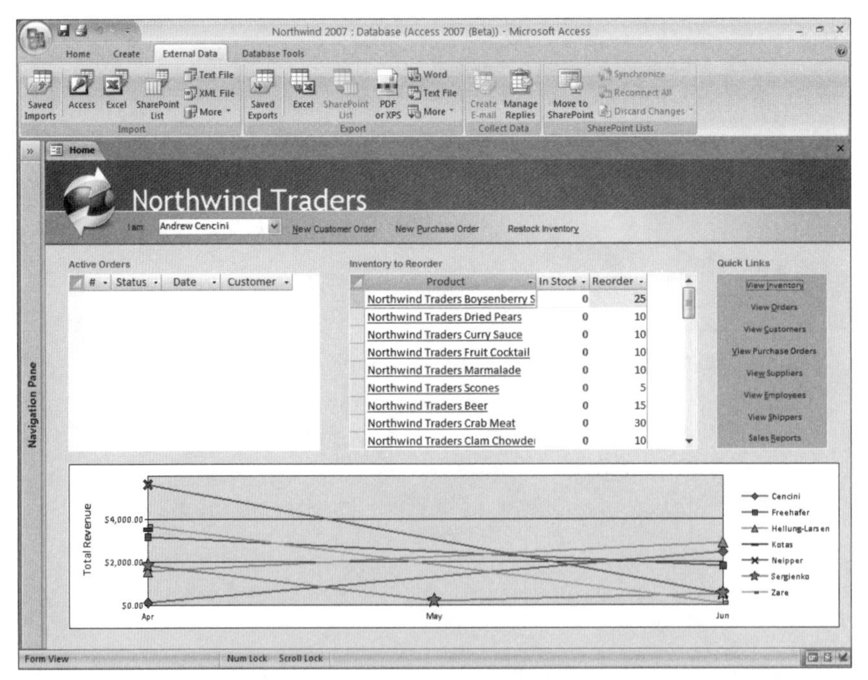

Figure 9-6 The Home page gives you a quick-look summary of data items.

Tabbed Windows

When you open tables, queries, reports, and forms by double-clicking them in the Navigation Pane, they open in the work area (see Figure 9-7). Each item you open becomes a tabbed window in the display. You can move among the different items by simply clicking the tabs. When you want to close a view, right-click a tab and choose Close.

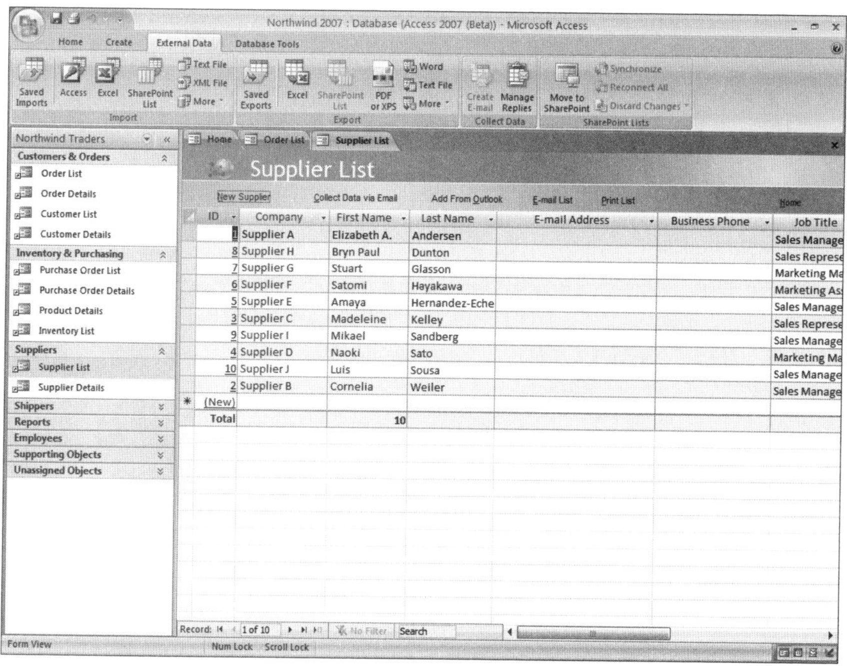

Figure 9-7 Tabbed windows enable you to display multiple elements and move among them easily.

Making Design Changes Easily

Whether you choose to create a database from scratch or customize one of the templates included with the program, you will need to add forms, tables, and more to make the database your own. The process of adding objects to your database is much easier in Office Access 2007. Click the Create tab to display options for adding tables, lists, forms, reports, queries, and macros (see Figure 9-8).

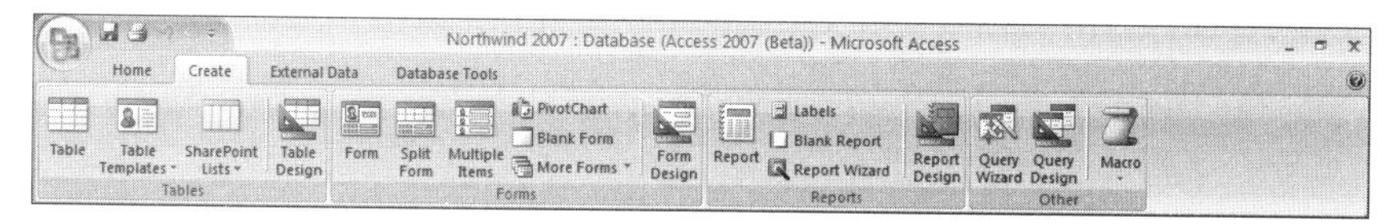

Figure 9-8 Commands in the Create tab enable you to add items to your database easily.

Three Things to Try in Office Access 2007

John L. Viescas and Jeff Conrad, authors of *Microsoft Office Access 2007 Inside Out*, offer the following three features as their favorites for you to try:

1. Explore the new Layout View in Access 2007 for fast, what you see is what you get (WYSIWYG) report generation with the use of live data.
2. Try out the new Split Form View option to display part of a data entry form in Single Form View and another part in Datasheet mode. Twice the fun and half the trouble.
3. Make yourself the hero to the accountants and data entry staff with built-in alternating row color (also called the "Greenbar" effect) for forms and reports.

All the things you ever wanted to be able to do in Access, but couldn't.

Adding and Enhancing a Form

Suppose that you want to add a data entry form to a Customers List. With the Customers List tab selected, click the Create tab and select one of the form commands (for example, click Form). The form is displayed in the work area in Layout View so that you can modify it as needed (see Figure 9-9). The Form Tools contextual command tabs are available, providing a set of tools you can use to customize the form to fit your needs.

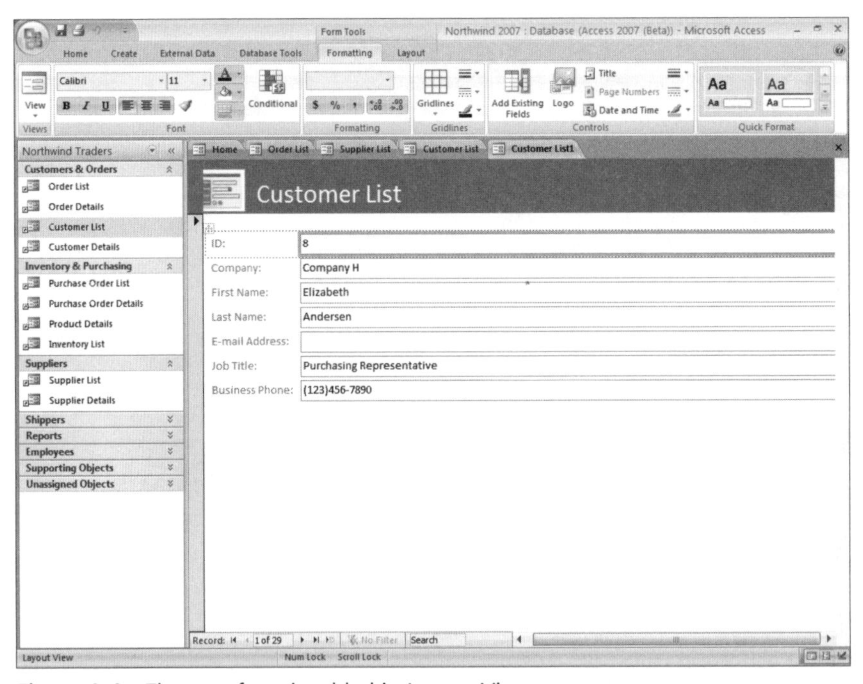

Figure 9-9 The new form is added in Layout View.

Using Layout View to See Immediate Changes

Layout View is a WYSIWYG (what you see is what you get) view that enables you to make changes to a form or report and immediately see the effects of your changes. If necessary, change to Layout View by clicking the View control and choosing Layout View. The elements in the data table or form become selectable–you can drag and drop them to new locations on the page, edit the content and placement of labels and field names, and change the format and spacing of headers, row dividers, logos, and more (see Figure 9-10).

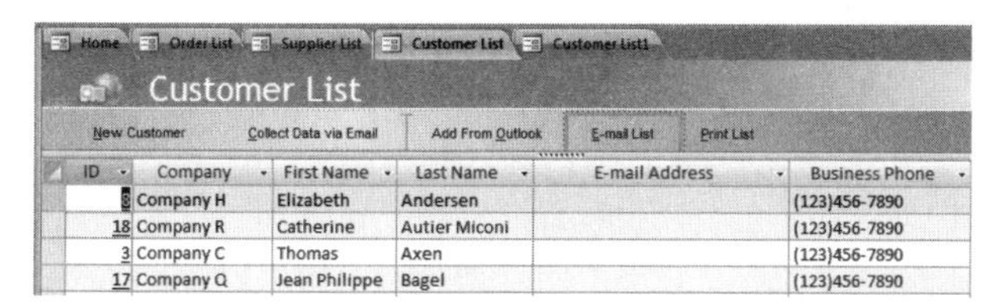

Figure 9-10 Layout View enables you to make and view changes in your report or form.

New Split Form View

Now you can work with both your data and a form open on your screen at the same time. When you click Split Form in the Insert tab, Office Access 2007 displays a form in the lower portion of Layout View. You can enter information in the form and it is automatically added to the table in the top portion of the window.

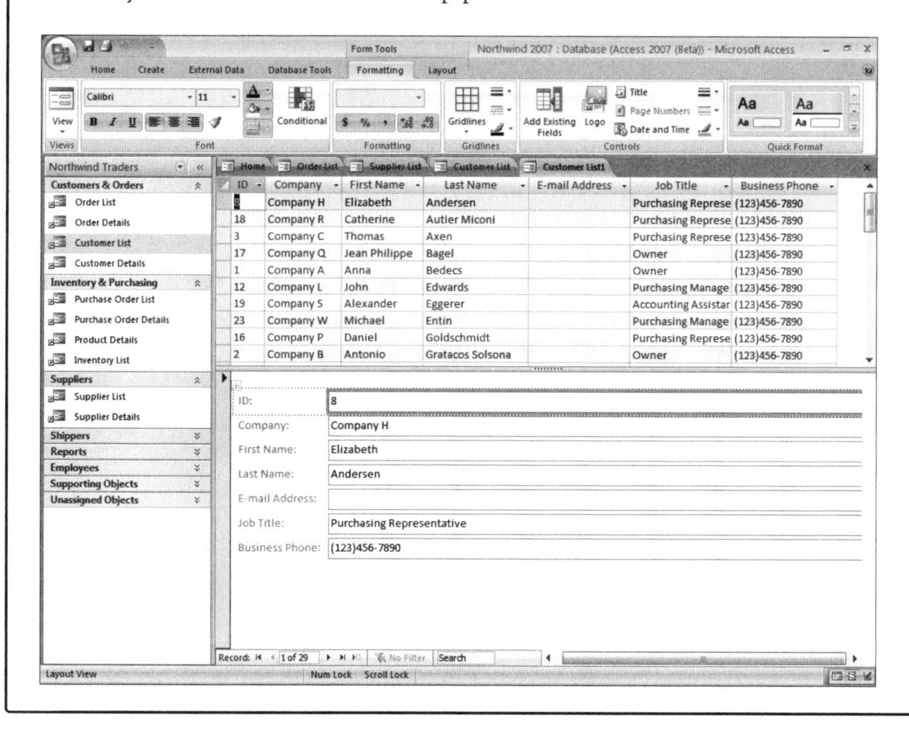

Adding Tables

Working with tables has also been simplified in Office Access 2007. Now you can create a table using the Insert tab and choose either to create your own table your way or choose a Table Template (Contacts, Tasks, Issues, Events, or Assets). A table template includes common fields you would expect for the specific table type you select. For example, if you insert a Contacts table, you will have Full name, First Name, Last Name, E-mail, Phone, and so forth.

When you click the Table command and choose Table, a new Table tab opens in Datasheet View and you can simply begin entering your information right away, without stopping to set data types as you work. Office Access 2007 reads the data type automatically.

Adding Fields

The simplest way to add a field in Office Access 2007 is simply to start typing in the last column. Double-click on the header and you can name the field.

When you want to add field templates used in other tables or table templates, you can use the Field List task pane. The Field List task pane replaces the field picker and includes fields from other tables in your database. You simply drag and drop fields from the list to your table, and Office Access 2007 creates the relationships automatically. You'll find the command for this in the Create tab, in the Form Tools contextual tab in the Controls command set. Click Add Existing Fields to display the Field List (see Figure 9-11) and add the fields you want by dragging them to the table.

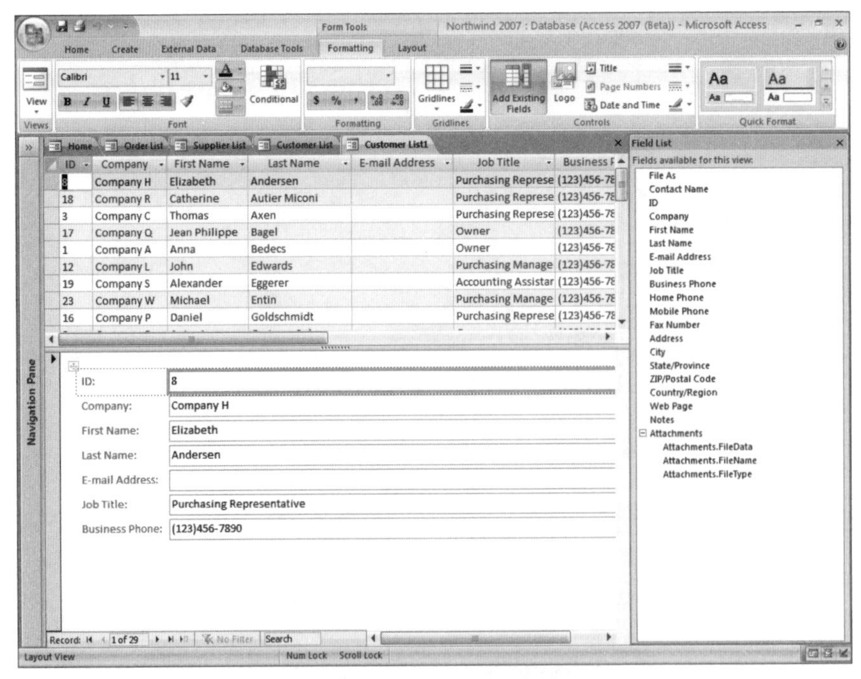

Figure 9-11 Add fields to a table using the Field List.

Applying Themes

Office Access 2007 includes 25 new professionally designed themes you can use to add a polished look to your database forms. When a form is displayed in Layout View, the Quick Format gallery appears on the far right of the user interface. Point to a theme in the Quick Format gallery to preview the theme; when you find one you like, click it to apply it to your database.

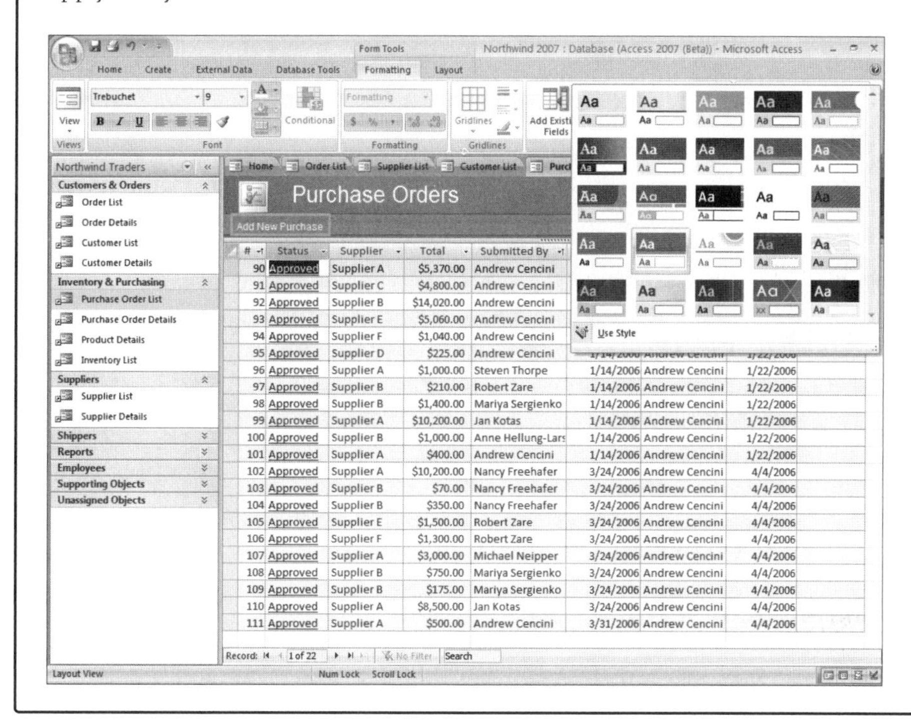

Entering, Viewing, and Expanding Your Data with Flexible New Features

The way in which you gather your data—and the data types you use to identify it—have been expanded in Office Access 2007. This section describes some of the features you can use to enter, add to, and work with the data in your database.

Choosing Your Date with the Calendar Button

Now whenever you're working with dates in an Office Access 2007 table or form, you can click the Calendar button to choose the date. Click the Calendar button, use the arrows to navigate to the month you want, and click the date. The date value is added to the form and the datasheet, as you see in Figure 9-12.

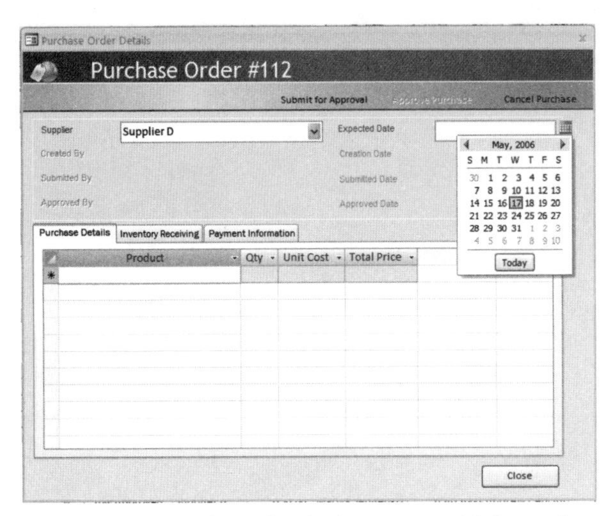

Figure 9-12 Use the Calendar button to add date values to your table or form.

Using Multivalue Fields

Some fields require a range of possibilities rather than absolute answers. For fields that need to provide a "both/and" rather than an "either/or" value, you can now use multivalue fields. You might use a multivalue field, for example, when you want to show that a customer purchased two or more items from your catalog. With a multivalue field, both items can be recorded in the field as legitimate values.

Adding File Attachments

Office Access 2007 offers a richer data gathering experience by offering a new field type for attachments. You can attach an image, document, or worksheet to a record to provide additional detail for a specific record. When you double-click an attachment field, the Attachments window opens so that you can click Add to attach the file you want to include (see Figure 9-13).

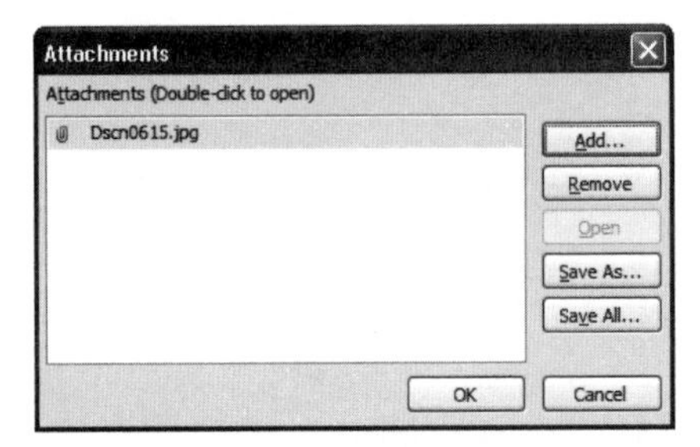

Figure 9-13 Use the new attachment data type to include other data files in your Office Access 2007 tables.

Using the New Report View

Several new features make creating reports easier in Office Access 2007. A wide selection of reporting tools helps you gather and display just the information you want to report on. Begin by clicking the Create tab and selecting the command in the Reports command set you want to use. The Report Wizard walks you through the process of creating a report; the Report command displays a simple report using the currently selected table. If you want to design your own custom report, click Blank Report.

After you create the report, the Report Tools contextual tab offers you three additional sets of tools: Formatting, Layout, and Page Setup. You can add fields; display and hide various items; format and arrange information; and set margins, alignment, and print options (see Figure 9-14).

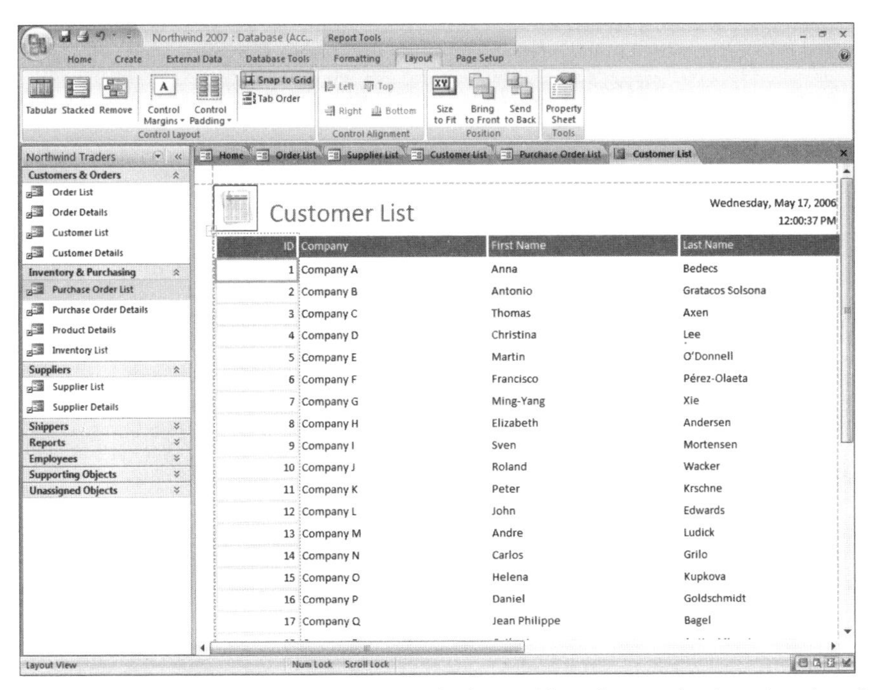

Figure 9-14 The Report Tools contextual tab provides a large selection of options for your reports.

> **Tip** Another new data type change in Office Access 2007 enables you to track changes in memo fields. Now you can set a property to tell Office Access 2007 to retain a history of all changes in a Memo field; you can then view a history of the changes that have been made.

Improved Security Features

Now when you open a database application in Office Access 2007, the program automatically checks it against a Trusted Publishers list to determine whether the file is a potential risk to your data security. If the file contains a macro, add-in, ActiveX control, or another extension that was created by a person or company not appearing on the list, Office Access 2007 disables the code and displays a Security Warning in the Document Action Bar, just above the Office Access 2007 work area (see Figure 9-15).

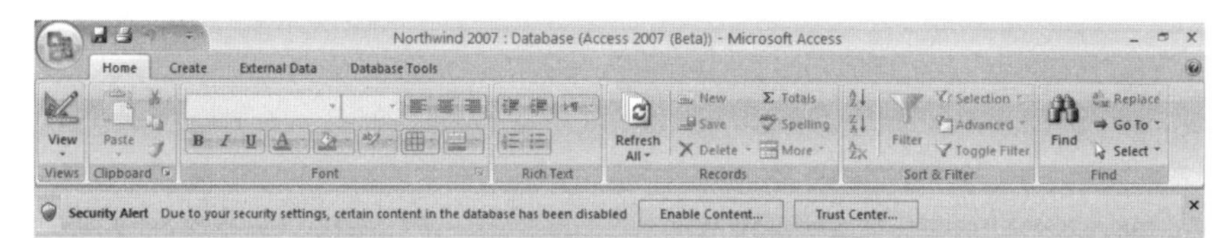

Figure 9-15 A Security Warning lets you know the file contains content created by a person or company not listed on the Trusted Publishers list.

A Security Warning lets you know the file contains content created by a person or company not listed on the Trusted Publishers list. To add someone to the Trusted Publishers list, you need to be able to show that the project has been signed by the developer with a current, valid, digital signature and that the signature was verified by a certificate authority. Click Trust Center in the Document Action Bar to display the Office 2007 Trust Center and review the Trusted Publishers list. You can also click Enable Content to display the Trust In Office dialog box (see Figure 9-16), in which you can choose to enable the content without the necessary protection if you choose.

Figure 9-16 The Trust In Office dialog box gives you the choice of enabling content from publishers not included on the Trusted Publishers list.

Collecting Data via E-mail

Gathering the data you need to compile research for a project can be a challenging task. Asking for input can be time-consuming and complicated; whether you are mailing paper questionnaires, sending file attachments via e-mail, or asking respondents to click a link and come to your site, you need to make responding as easy as possible for others to be able to take time out of their busy schedules to participate.

Office Access 2007 has a great new feature that enables you to send forms by e-mail so respondents can simply click Reply, add their answers to the form, and send them back to you. The data they enter is added to the appropriate table in your Office Access 2007 table as soon as it arrives in your Inbox, saving you a huge amount of time and cutting down on potential data-entry errors you might inadvertently introduce by entering all the responses by hand.

Begin the process by clicking the External Data tab and choosing Create E-mail. A wizard walks you through the process of creating the data collection e-mail message. To use this feature, you need to have Office Access 2007 and Office Outlook 2007. You can also choose to use Microsoft® Office InfoPath® 2007, although you have the option of using an HTML form or an InfoPath form (see Figure 9-17). To be able to access and use the form you send (if you choose the InfoPath form), your recipients will also need to have Office Outlook 2007 and Office InfoPath 2007.

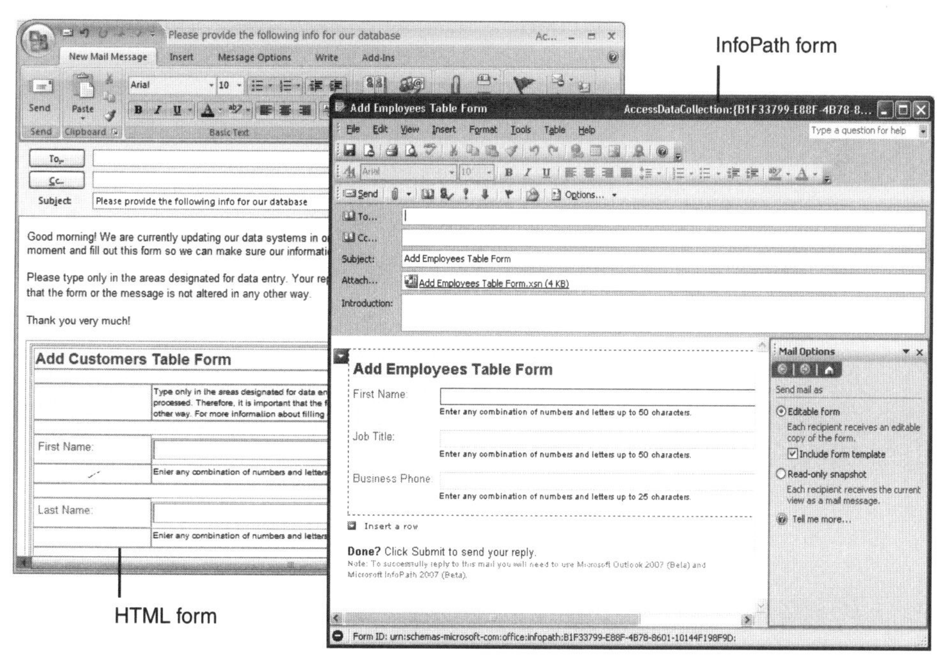

Figure 9-17 Gather information via e-mail that is then merged with your Office Access 2007 information.

Sharing Data Easily Using Windows SharePoint Services Lists

Companies that use Microsoft® Windows® SharePoint® Services (a feature of Windows Server 2003) know the value of being able to store, share, back up, and manage documents and data on their Windows SharePoint sites. Now Office Access 2007 includes SharePoint integration with Windows SharePoint Services so that you can move your data from the local data storage to Windows SharePoint Services. This enables a kind of two-way data communication: you can add/edit data directly within the Office Access 2007 client environment or use the browser interface of Windows SharePoint Services. You can also track any list in Windows SharePoint Services by opening it with Office Access 2007, on which you can create rich Office Access 2007 objects (such as forms and reports). With Office Access 2007 you can also take the Windows SharePoint data offline when you travel and sync back to the Windows SharePoint site when reconnecting to the network.

Microsoft Office System Behind-the-Scenes Interview

Mor Hezi, Senior Product Manager, Microsoft Office 2007

What are the major new changes in Office Access 2007? Office Access 2007 has been completely revised. You can just launch it and see the difference. You no longer have to be a database administrator (DBA) in order to work with Office Access 2007. The revised user interface makes it much easier to use; with the interactive design capabilities, designing forms and reports cannot be easier; and the integration with Windows SharePoint Services makes Office Access 2007 a great collaboration tool. Another very cool thing is that we are adding several prebuilt solutions, so our customers can start being productive from day 1 and get inspired by how Office Access 2007 can help them manage their overload of information in different ways.

Who do you see as a "typical" Office Access 2007 user? This is the beauty. For the first time, I expect the new "typical" Office Access 2007 users to be information workers who are quite proficient with Office Excel 2007 today–not the financial gurus, but those who keep very long lists in very large tables. I expect increased adoption by small business owners, the casual project managers (people who manage projects, but don't have Project Manager as their titles), administrative assistants, managers, and engineers. Now Office Access 2007 is truly an Office application. I am sure people will have so much fun working on it that they will run home and start using it for their personal lives as well (to track their CD/DVD collection, their wedding invitations, etc.)

Did the changes in Office Access 2007 come about as a response to user comments and suggestions? If so, in what way? Well, we have heard from our customers that on the one hand, Office Access was too hard to use (and here the current Office Access "power users" will be shocked when they find how easy it is); on the other hand, it was very hard to manage Office Access databases at the corporate level. We found a way to satisfy both requests with this release. We made the application much more user-friendly and with the integration with Windows SharePoint Services, we not only have created a collaborative environment but now the database is also more manageable because the data can reside on the server where it can be backed up, audited, managed, and shared; deleted data can be recovered, and read/write permissions easily managed.

Is there one "home run" feature in Office Access 2007 that you think will get a lot of attention? Do you have a personal favorite? This is a tough one. When I have presented the product to different audiences, peoples' eyes popped at different points of the presentation/demo. Releasing the product with several prebuilt solutions out of the box will definitely demonstrate to users why to use Office Access 2007 and help them understand the power and get productive immediately. The new report designer is a killer and the collaboration with Windows SharePoint Services is a great story. My personal favorite is to be able to collect updates into my database by e-mail. Now Access can create automatically an InfoPath form (you can also select HTML form if you don't have InfoPath) that will be sent via e-mail to collect data directly from coworkers/customers that I won't have to retype into my database. I wish I had it before in my previous job. It is awesome.

Do you have a fun or interesting story about what it was like to be part of such a major release? The most fun part is the internal "battles" about which product is the most exciting. Even internally, several coworkers have thought of Office Access as a hard-to-use database program that hadn't seen a lot of new things in a long time. When I show them Office Access 2007, I love to see the amazement on their faces. Without any doubt, from among all Microsoft Office system products, Office Access 2007 is the application that received the highest "jump." Even when I show the product to agencies or internal groups that help us write content or training material, they all want to start using it today. I am really excited about being part of the 2007 release, but even more of being part of the new Office Access 2007 launch.

Coming Next

This chapter introduced you to the new and enhanced features in Office Access 2007. The next chapter begins Part III, "Communicating and Collaborating: People and Processes," starting with a look at Office Outlook 2007.

Part III
Communicating and Collaborating: People and Process

In this part:

Chapter 10

Manage Your Time, Tasks, and E-Mail with Office Outlook 2007

What you'll find in this chapter:

- A look at Office Outlook 2007
- Manage time and organize tasks
- Share and compare calendars
- Take control of your Inbox

Many of us wish there were more hours in the day. We go into work in the morning with good intentions—determined to get caught up—but somehow when we leave at night we have the same number of items (or more!) on our To Do lists. We are inundated every day with a mountain of e-mail messages; tasks to identify, assign, and act on; meetings to schedule and attend; and calls to make and respond to. The new features in Microsoft® Office Outlook® 2007 can help you make the most of the time you have and even take you a few steps closer to being caught up. By using the task management, e-mail filtering, and calendar sharing capabilities in the 2007 release, you'll be spending more time on the tasks that really matter and less time on distracting details such as sorting through unwanted e-mail, searching for lost messages, and struggling to find meeting times for your group.

A Look at Office Outlook 2007

Office Outlook 2007 doesn't share the same new user interface that Microsoft® Office Word 2007, Microsoft® Office Excel® 2007, Microsoft® Office PowerPoint® 2007, and Microsoft® Office Access 2007 all share. The new Office Outlook 2007 at first glance looks similar to Office Outlook 2003: the menus are familiar (File, Edit, View, Go, Tools, Actions, and Help), and the navigation pane on the left looks the same (see Figure 10-1). But a closer look will show you a number of new features—specifically, you'll notice the Search box at the top of the Inbox column, the RSS Feeds folder in the Mail Folders navigation pane, and the new To-Do Bar along the right side of the window. Each of these items will be more fully discussed in the appropriate sections later in this chapter.

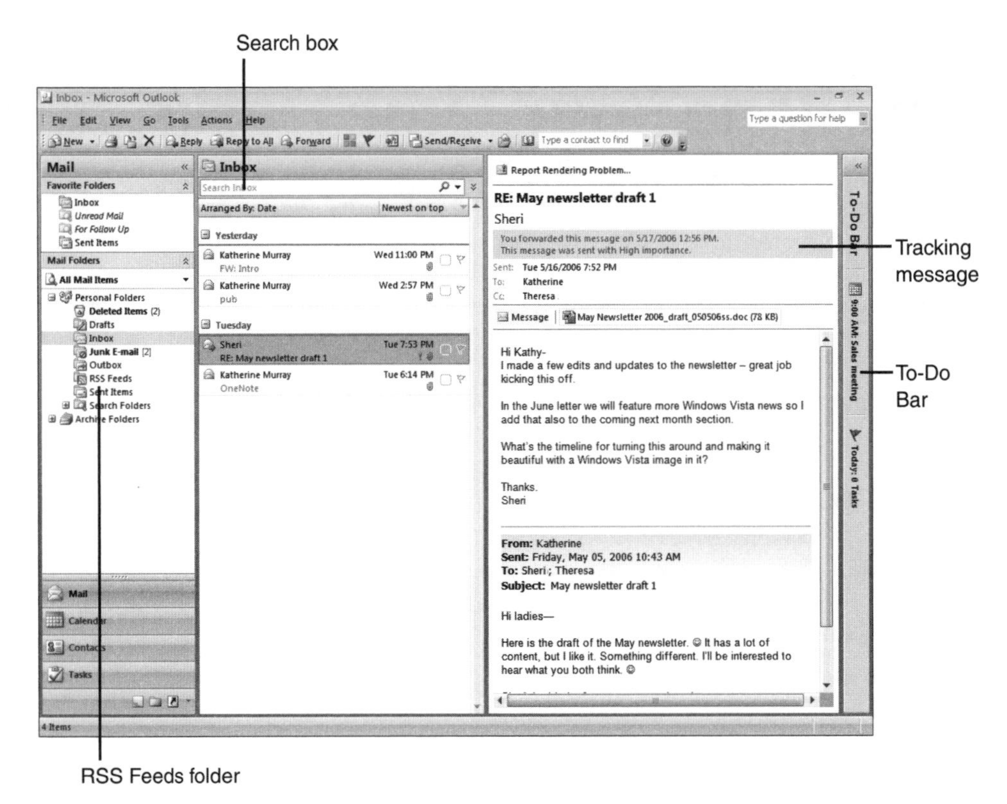

Figure 10-1 Changes in Office Outlook 2007.

Changing the Office Outlook 2007 Window

You can now “collapse” the navigation pane in Office Outlook 2007 when you want to give yourself more room to work on-screen. Your favorite folders and the icons for the primary views–Mail, Calendar, Contacts, and Tasks–are available in the collapsed bar so that you can continue to select those views as needed.

To collapse the navigation pane, click the left arrows at the top of the pane. The navigation pane is minimized to a vertical bar, stretching alongside the left edge of the Office Outlook 2007 window (see Figure 10-2). When you want to return the navigation pane to its original display, click the right arrows at the top of the bar.

Manage Time and Organize Tasks

One time-consuming aspect of managing schedules and information is switching among different capabilities within Office Outlook 2007 to keep things organized. Office Outlook 2007 greatly simplifies managing your to-do lists and keeping an eye on upcoming appointments with the new To-Do Bar, which brings all those items together in one place, displaying them along the right side of the Office Outlook 2007 window. As with the navigation pane, you can minimize the To-Do Bar to get more room onscreen for your e-mail list and reading pane. Figure 10-3 introduces the various elements in the To-Do Bar.

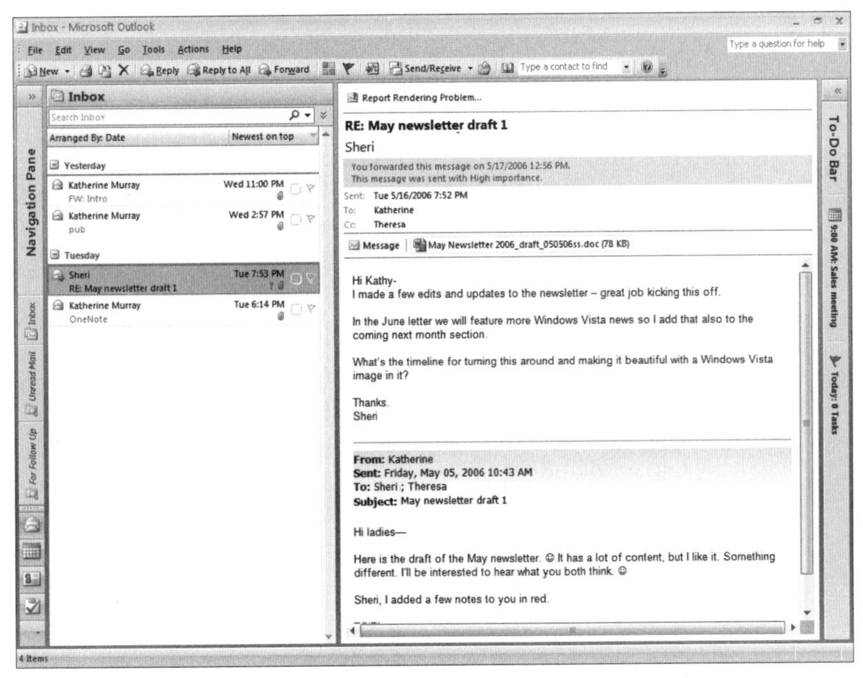

Figure 10-2 The Office Outlook 2007 navigation pane minimized.

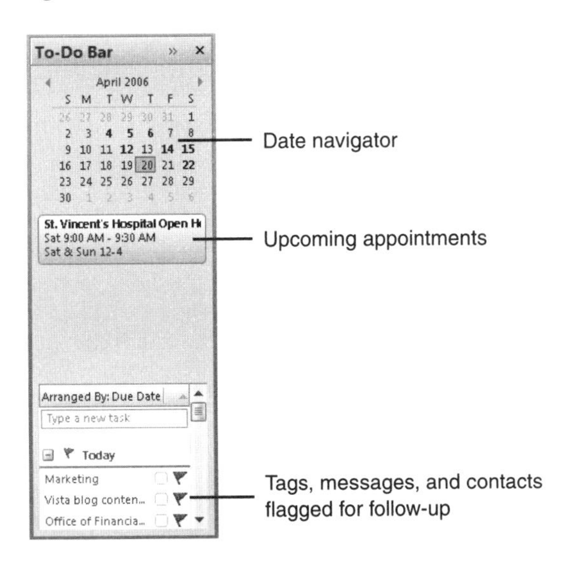

Figure 10-3 The To-Do Bar is a command center for your tasks and appointments.

The To-Do Bar is visible in all Outlook modules, so you have access to the information whether you're working in the Calendar, Tasks, Mail, or one of the other modules. And the To-Do Bar integrates more than just the tasks you create in Office Outlook 2007: your Microsoft® Office OneNote® 2007, Microsoft® Office Project 2007, and Microsoft® Office SharePoint® Server 2007 tasks can also appear in To-Do Bar, so you can see easily at a glance what you need to accomplish today.

An item is added to the To-Do Bar automatically whenever you flag an e-mail message or contact, or when you drag a message to the To-Do Bar. When you flag an e-mail message in your Inbox, an entry is added to the Today category in your To-Do Bar; when you drag an item to the To-Do Bar, it is placed in the category (Later, Next Month, Next Week, or Today) where you place it.

Tip You can change the look of the To-Do Bar by clicking anywhere in the title and choosing Customize. Select Customize to display the To-Do Bar Options dialog box. You can change the settings that control how many months and appointments are displayed in the To-Do Bar (or hide the items altogether). Enter your choices and click OK to save your changes; the To-Do Bar display then changes to reflect your choices.

Adding Tasks to Your Calendar

Here's another timesaving and organizing feature in Office Outlook 2007: Now you can actually schedule time to work on tasks by simply dragging them to the Calendar. Previously, tasks and the Calendar worked somewhat separately–to keep track of the same event or project in both views, you had to create entries for each, duplicating the effort you spent in organizing one task. Because the Daily Task List displays your tasks in the To-Do Bar according to the day on which they are due, they are already organized so that you can easily drag them to your Calendar to block off time to complete them. Using the Daily Task List, you can also modify the date of tasks by dragging them from one day to another, and the To-Do Bar will update accordingly.

Note In real life, we often don't get to everything on our list during the day. Interruptions and changes in priorities often cause us to leave for tomorrow what we meant to do today. When this happens with a task you created in Office Outlook 2007, the task is carried over to the next day automatically, without any action from you. The task will remain active on your To-Do Bar (and in your Task list and Calendar) until you mark it as completed.

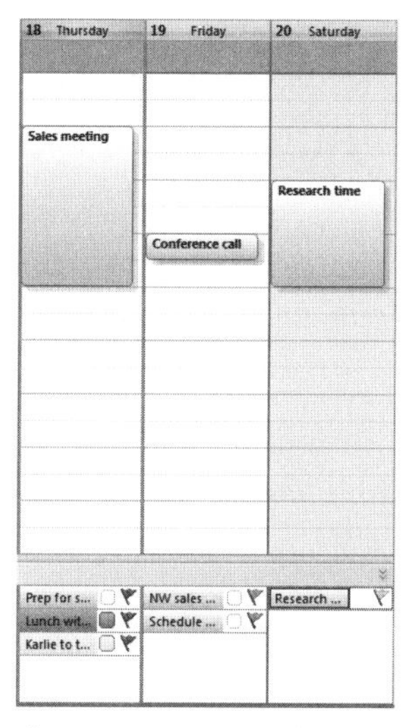

Figure 10-4 Tasks from the Daily Task List in the To-Do Bar are displayed automatically in the Calendar module.

Colorizing Tasks, Appointments, Messages, and Contacts

You can apply a color category to any item you create in Office Outlook 2007 so that it stands out visually no matter which view you are using. For example, if you want an appointment you just created to be easy to spot on your Calendar, you can assign a color to it using the Categorize control in the user interface. When the Appointment window is open, click the Categorize button and choose the color you want from the displayed list (see Figure 10-5).

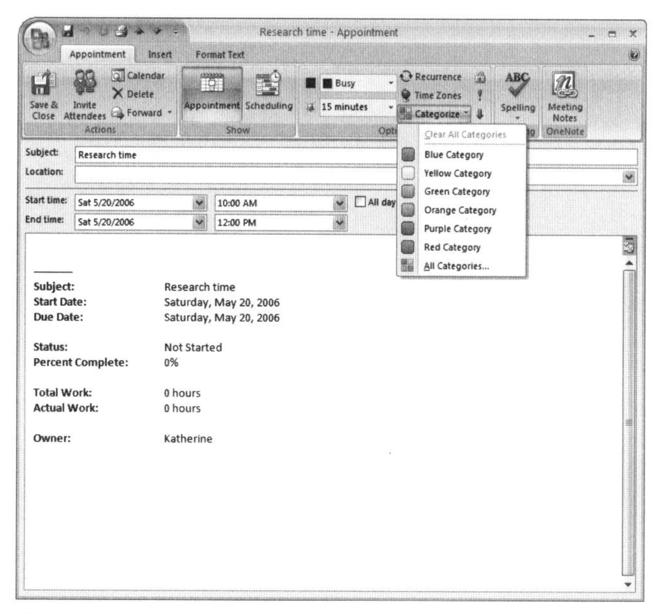

Figure 10-5 Assign a color category to an item so you know at a glance what it involves.

Color Categories in Office Outlook 2007 help you unify the way you organize and search for information. Because the categories are shared among mail, contacts, tasks, and the calendar, you have an easy way to visually distinguish all types of data relating to one project or one purpose. For example, if you're working on a business report, all mail meetings, tasks, and contacts you're working with to create the content for the report might be categories in a green color. You can then arrange and search all your information by this Color Category to gather the relevant information you need, which ultimately saves you time.

The easiest way to assign a color category is to click the Categories column in the list box in your current view. Both the Inbox and the Task List have Categories columns to the left of the flag column (see Figure 10-6). When you're working with the Calendar, as you see in Figure 10-7, the Categories column appears beneath the Calendar area (more about this in the next section). In Contacts view, the Categories column is included as part of the Contacts list (see Figure 10-8).

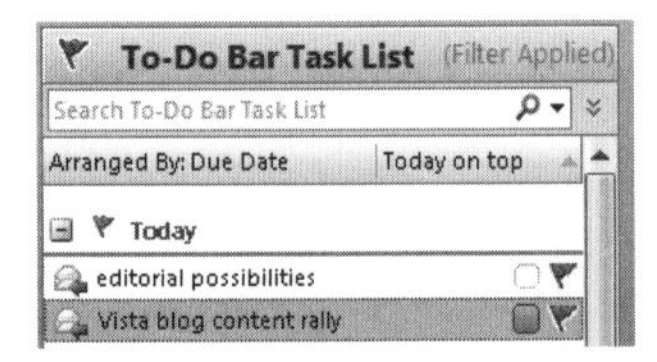

Figure 10-6 Click the Categories column in the Task List to colorize a task.

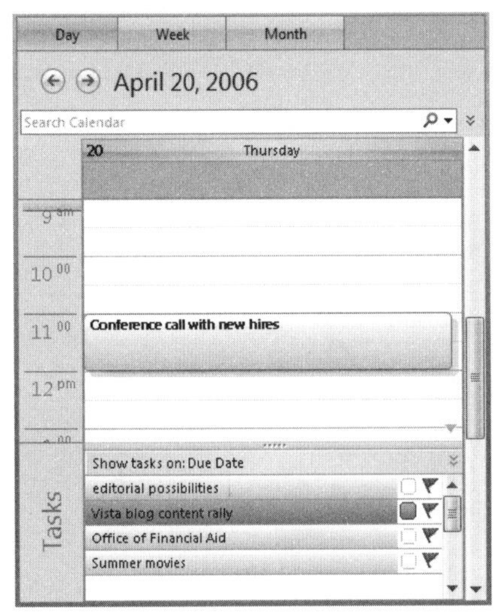

Figure 10-7 The Categories column in Calendar view appears below the appointment area.

Figure 10-8 You can assign color categories to Contacts to help you recognize people by role, company, or relationship.

Note In your Contacts list, the Categories column will appear several columns to the right—in this illustration, the Categories column was moved to the left so it would be visible in the example.

If you want to change the color of the selected category, you can do it quickly by right-clicking the item in list view or in the To-Do Bar. Whether the item is a task, appointment, message, or contact, simply right-click and choose Categorize; then choose the category you want to assign to the item (see Figure 10-9).

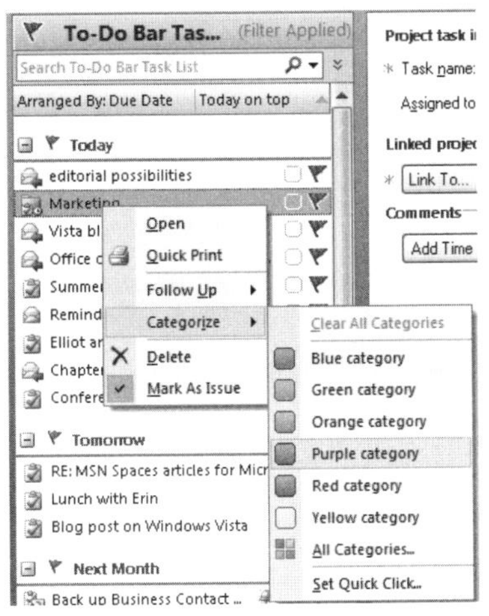

Figure 10-9 Change the color category by right-clicking the item.

Tip If you tend to use one category regularly, you can set up a Quick Click feature that enables you to make one category the default assigned whenever you click an item. Right-click the item and choose Categorize; then select Set Quick Click. Choose the color you want to use as the Quick Click category and click OK to save your settings.

Share and Compare Calendars

When you work with a team of busy people, finding a time when everyone can meet can be difficult. Using meeting invitations to contact team members by e-mail is helpful, but you still wind up coordinating all the times yourself. Office Outlook 2007 includes several new features that help take the busywork out of scheduling meetings:

- You can send a calendar snapshot to a coworker as part of an e-mail message.
- You can connect Office SharePoint 2007 calendars to Office Outlook 2007 and have a dynamically updating relationship between Office Outlook 2007 and Office SharePoint 2007.
- You can publish your calendar online using Microsoft® Office Online Hosting Services.
- You can use calendar overlay view to layer calendars easily spot open times.

Sending a Calendar via E-Mail

When you click Send A Calendar Via E-Mail in the Calendar navigation pane, Office Outlook 2007 allows you to send an HTML representation of your calendar information. This helps ensure that you can communicate your daily availability to anyone, regardless of whether they are a client working outside your company or just a friend. When you click this link, Office Outlook 2007 automatically opens a new message window and displays the Send A Calendar Via E-Mail dialog box (see Figure 10-10). Here you choose the Date Range (you can choose anywhere from the current day to the next 30 days–to your whole calendar!) and determine how much Detail you want to show (you can show only the times you are available; include limited details such as availability and the subject lines of calendar entries, or full details of all entries). Additionally, you can click the Show button in the Advanced area to choose whether to include information marked private and include any attachments for calendar entries.

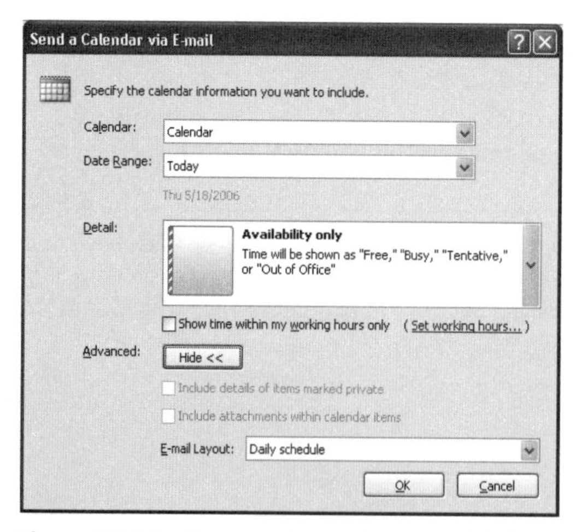

Figure 10-10 You can choose how much information you want to show when you send a calendar by e-mail to other team members.

In the Send A Calendar Via E-Mail dialog box, you can also choose the E-Mail Layout of the message you send, providing either a list of events or your daily schedule. Figure 10-11 shows an example of a message sharing a daily calendar.

Three Things to Try

Jim Boyce, author of *Microsoft Office Outlook 2007 Inside Out* and *Microsoft Office Outlook 2007 Plain & Simple*, says these are his favorite new features in Office Outlook 2007:

1. Attachment Preview enables you to preview the contents of attachments without opening them.
2. Instant Search helps you quickly and easily find messages, tasks, and other items almost instantly.
3. You can subscribe to, read, and manage Really Simple Syndication (RSS) feeds right in Office Outlook 2007.

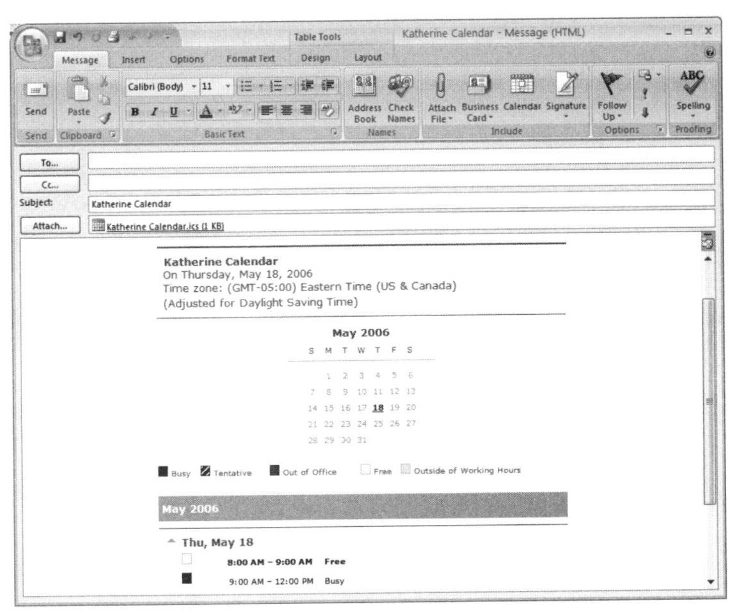

Figure 10-11 You can easily send your calendar to others by e-mail.

Publishing Your Calendar Online

If you're struggling to share long-term calendars with partners, friends, or family, you can use the new free publishing capabilities to communicate calendar information with others. For example, if you're organizing an event and want all participants to view a calendar of the activities and get the latest updates, you can create that calendar in Office Outlook 2007 and publish it to Office Online. After you invite others to see your calendar, they can view it on a Web browser or download it onto their machine and view it using Office Outlook 2007 or any other calendar tool that supports files with the .ics extension. Any updates you make to the calendar will be automatically updated on the Web version and then also synchronized with any locally stored copies.

Use the Publish My Calendar link in the Calendar navigation bar to start the process. In the Publish Calendar To Microsoft Office Online dialog box (see Figure 10-12), you specify the following items:

- Choose the time span for the calendar you want to display.
- Select the level of detail to show (Availability only, Limited details, or Full details).
- Set permissions to determine who has access to your calendar.
- Choose whether the calendar will be uploaded only once or automatically as updated.

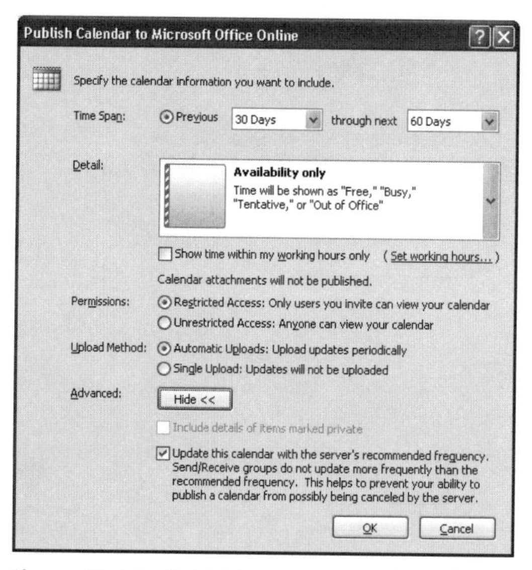

Figure 10-12 Publishing your calendar online makes it easy for those with access to view your schedule.

After you publish the calendar online, you are given the option of sharing it with others. After you enter the e-mail addresses of others you want to receive your calendar information, the Web address of your calendar is sent, along with instructions on how others can access it.

Tip Office Online includes a number of specialty Internet calendars you can download. Click Browse Calendars Online to look for calendar templates. Scroll down to the Subscribe To A Free Internet Calendar area and click the link of a calendar you want to try. A prompt will ask your permission to proceed; click Yes, and the calendar is added to your Office Outlook 2007 Calendar view.

Displaying and Comparing Calendars

Office Outlook 2007 makes it easier to view others' calendars so you can easily identify opportunities for meetings and activities. The calendars available for you to view are displayed in the Calendars navigation pane. You can display or hide the available calendars by clicking the check box to the left of the calendar name. By default, when you display more than one calendar, the calendars are shown in Side-by-Side Mode (see Figure 10-13).

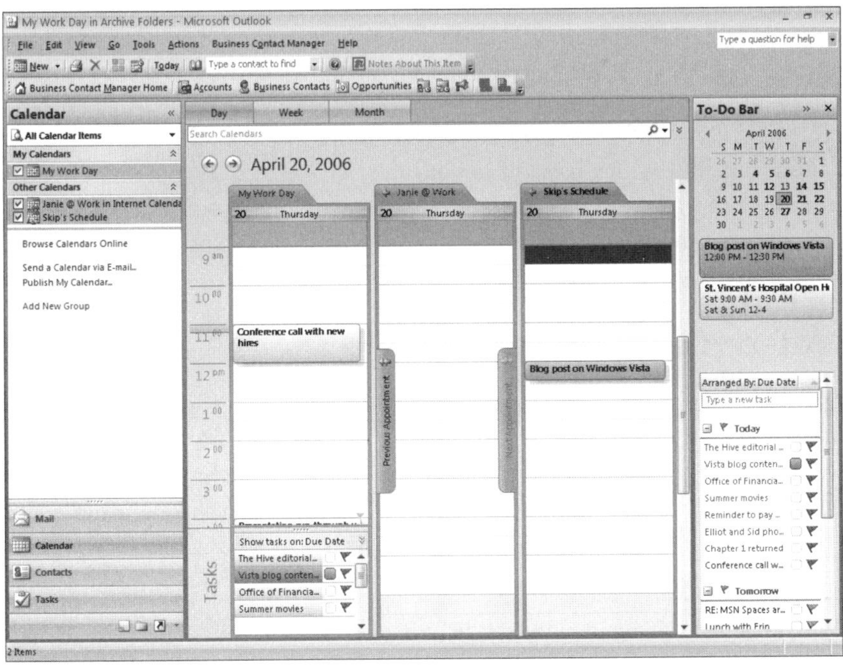

Figure 10-13 You can display multiple calendars in Side-by-Side Mode.

You can now layer calendars one on top of another using Overlay Mode to find open time slots easily by selecting the calendars and then clicking the green arrow on the calendar on the right. You can tell which appointments belong to which calendar by the coloring; the appointments from the underlying calendar appear in the same color as the underlying calendar's title bar (see Figure 10-14).

Figure 10-14 Overlay Mode lets you layer calendars to find available times.

Take Control of Your Inbox

As you can see, Office Outlook 2007 is about a lot more than e-mail, but e-mail takes up a large chunk of our time during the day. Office Outlook 2007 includes a number of new features that can save you a huge amount of time and effort–from setup techniques to content delivery to search options and junk e-mail filters, Office Outlook 2007 works faster and smarter to help you free up time you can spend getting more done.

Automatic Attachment Previews

Now instead of double-clicking an attachment and waiting for it to open in another application, you can preview attachments to your e-mail messages with a single click. This is a great timesaver and enables you to decide quickly which attachments you need to spend more time with and which ones you can file, respond to, or delete right away. To preview an attachment, click the attachment, and the file displays in the body of the e-mail message.

> **Note** Depending on whether the sender is on your Safe Senders list, you might see a message before the preview appears, warning you of a potential security risk. Click Preview File to continue the process.

Find What You Need Faster

The same indexing technology used in Windows Desktop Search and Windows Vista is used in Office Outlook 2007, giving you the fastest access possible to your information in all views (Mail, Calendar, Contacts, and Tasks). You will notice a dramatic decrease in the time it takes to display search results–now you can find what you need almost as fast as you can type.

A new search box is displayed at the top of the Inbox column and at the top of the Tasks List. Click in the search box and the display will change color, indicating that it is selected. You can simply type the word or phrase you want to find (see Figure 10-15). Even before you finish typing), results display messages (or tasks) that contain the word or phrase you're searching for.

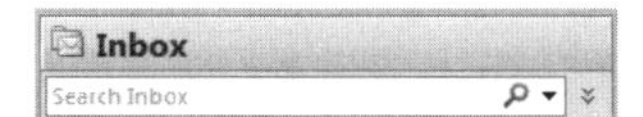

Figure 10-15 The faster search process locates messages or tasks that contain the text you type into the Search box almost instantly.

You can add search criteria to find specific items faster. Click the Add Criteria button to choose the criteria you want to add to your search (see Figure 10-16). You can also easily repeat searches you've done previously by clicking the Show Instant Search Pane button to the right of the search box; then point to Recent Searches and select the search you want to use (see Figure 10-17, on the next page). Additionally, you can change the defaults set up for the search process by choosing Search Options in the Instant Search Pane menu.

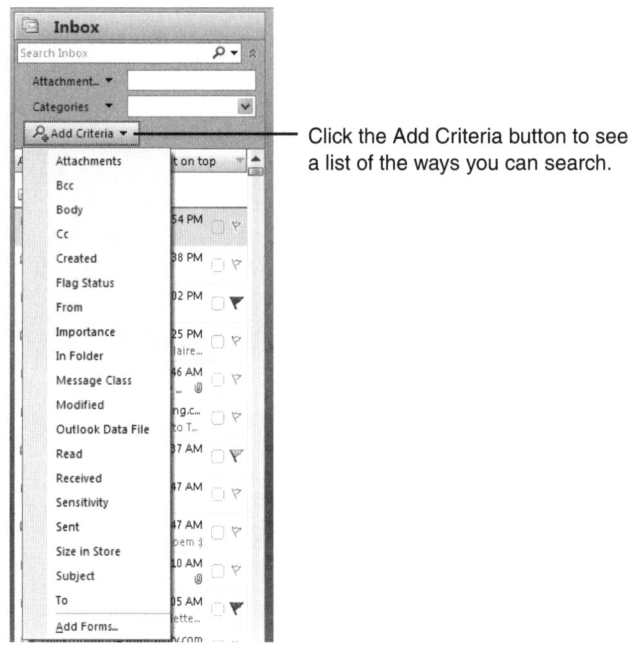

Figure 10-16 You can search faster and farther by adding search criteria.

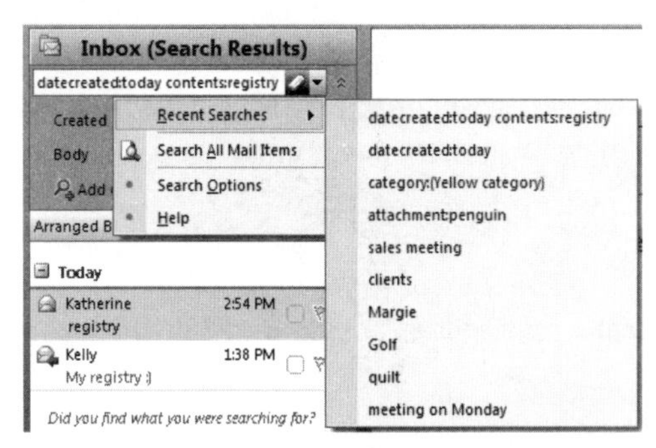

Figure 10-17 The Instant Search Pane has tools for repeating searches and setting search options.

Turning E-Mail into Action Items Instantly

Part of the challenge of working with e-mail effectively is dividing the messages we need to act on right away from the messages we can respond to later. In Office Outlook 2007, you can use the enhanced flagging feature to identify an important message as one you need to act on immediately. When you add the flag, the item is automatically added to the To-Do Bar.

Flagging Action Items for Others

You can also use the enhanced flagging feature to flag messages you send and receive. If you have just finished the draft of a new employee handbook, for example, you might send it in an e-mail to others working on the project, requesting their feedback by the end of the week. You want them to respond by a specific date, so you flag the message for follow-up. Because the message is flagged, when it arrives in their Inboxes, the message is added to their To-Do Bars as a task with a specific response date (see Figure 10-18).

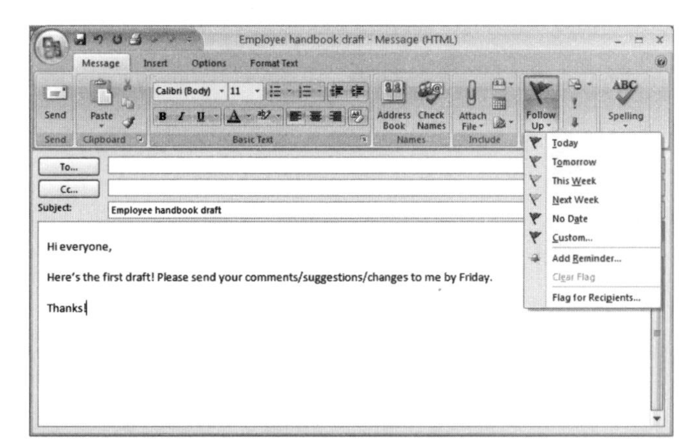

Figure 10-18 Improved flagging features enable you to send an e-mail message that creates an action item for others.

Easy E-Mail Setup

Setting up an e-mail account is now much easier in Office Outlook 2007. A new automated account setup feature simply asks for your e-mail account name and password, and then does the rest (see Figure 10-19). The wizard finds the server settings, automatically sets up the account, and then displays an updated E-Mail Accounts dialog box with the new account and the location for the account's PST file. There's nothing more to do except check your e-mail! The new mail folder is displayed in your Personal Folders list in the Mail navigation pane.

Tip Office Outlook 2007 can now retrieve your Web-based e-mail and download it to your Inbox, enabling you to compile mail from different accounts.

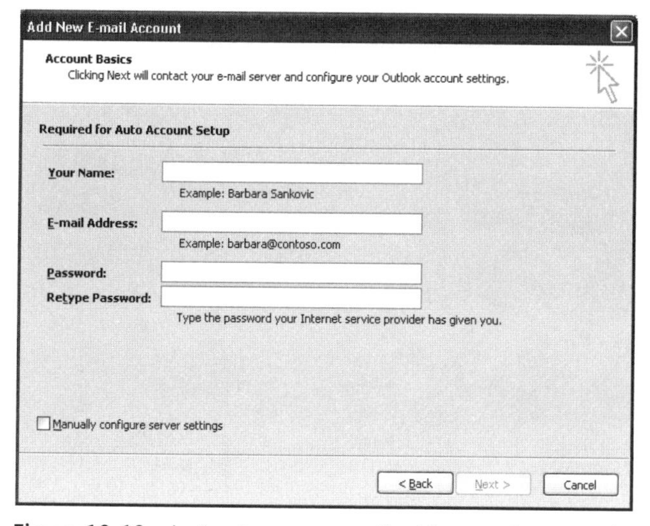

Figure 10-19 Just enter your e-mail address and password, and Office Outlook 2007 sets up the new e-mail account for you.

Creating and Sharing Electronic Business Cards

A fun and functional new feature in Office Outlook 2007 enables you to create, save, and share your contact information with others as an Electronic Business Card. In the New Contact window, click Business Card in the Write tab to customize the default card that is created for a new contact. You can add photos and other special design elements.

You can easily send electronic business cards to others via e-mail or attach your business card to your outgoing messages. Simply choose Options from the Tools menu and click the Mail Format tab in the Options dialog box. Click Signatures to display the Signatures and Stationery dialog box; then click Business Card in the Edit Signature area to display the Insert Business Card dialog box so that you can select the card you want to attach to your messages.

Receive RSS Feeds in Office Outlook 2007

Since Office Outlook 2003 was introduced, RSS has become a widely popular method of receiving content from the Web. With so many interesting–and necessary–Web pages to browse, we can spend hours online searching the sites we have come to rely on for dependable or interesting content. If those sites have RSS feeds available (meaning the information in published and distributed by the content publisher via RSS technology), you can receive those feeds directly in your Office Outlook 2007 Inbox, significantly reducing the time you once spent browsing–and giving you access to that great content whenever you want it.

To use the RSS feature in Office Outlook 2007, double-click the RSS Feeds folder in your Personal Folders in the Mail navigation pane. A window appears, describing the basis of RSS and telling you how to get started (see Figure 10-20).

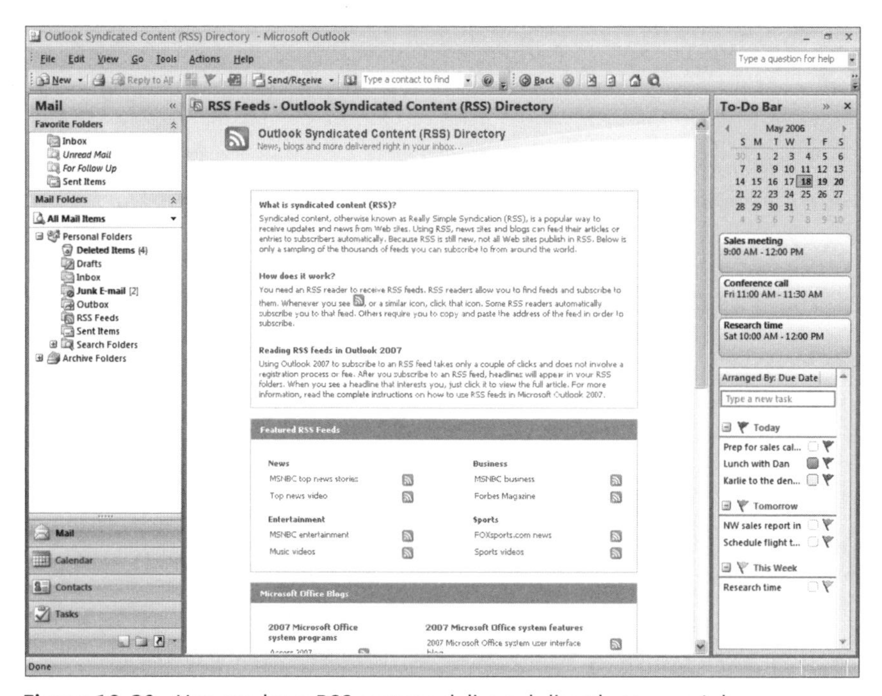

Figure 10-20 You can have RSS content delivered directly to your Inbox.

> **Note** When you use Microsoft Internet Explorer 7.0, your RSS feeds are synchronized both on the Web and in Office Outlook 2007 so that you have various ways to read and use the content you're most interested in.

Improved Junk E-Mail Filters

Office Outlook 2007 includes an enhanced Junk E-Mail Filter that catches incoming messages that could be junk mail–or its more dangerous counterpart, a phishing message–and then intercepts and eliminates it for you. The Junk E-Mail Filter scans incoming messages to determine their content and structure, and even tracks messages that look suspicious and disables any links that might lead you to a potentially dangerous site. When a message arrives that Office Outlook 2007 suspects might be a phishing message, a notification alerts you, and images and links in the message are disabled until you approve them.

On the Watch for Phishing

Phishing is a potentially dangerous form of junk e-mail that involves an unscrupulous sender who distributes an e-mail message that masquerades as a message from an organization you know and trust–perhaps your bank, a popular site that you visit often, or your mortgage company. The people sending these phishing messages often use the same logo, font, and design as the legitimate company's messages. They ask you to click a link that looks legitimate in the e-mail message, but actually links you to their site, in which they ask you to "verify" personal information. Sometimes these messages include warnings designed to alarm the recipient, such as "We believe someone has tried to access your account and we need you to log in and verify your personal information." Do not click the links in these e-mail messages. When you click to respond and then enter your personal information, these "phishers" gain access to your bank and credit card accounts, Web sites where your personal information is stored, and more.

Office Outlook 2007 includes phishing protection settings that are automatically enabled when you begin using the program. The options that control phishing protection are found in the Options tab of the Junk E-Mail Options dialog box (see Figure 10-21). Be sure to leave these two options selected to help protect you from phishing scams. To learn more, visit *www.microsoft.com/athome/security/email/phishing.mspx*.

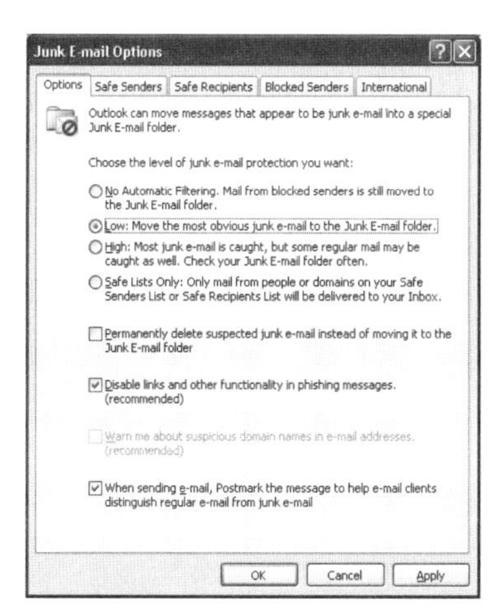

Figure 10-21 Two new phishing controls are in place in the Junk E-Mail Options dialog box.

> **Tip** Microsoft continually adds new updates and utilities to help you increase security on your computer systems. Be sure to check *www.microsoft.com/update* and Windows Marketplace (*windowsmarketplace.com*) regularly for new and enhanced utilities to help protect your system.

Automatic Postmarking

A new feature in Office Outlook 2007 automatically adds postmarks to messages you send. The postmark includes the list of recipients and the time you sent the message, which is what makes the postmark valid as an identification of that unique message–spammers send thousands of e-mails out at one time from the same computer, which makes a unique postmark impossible. The e-mail program of the person receiving the postmarked e-mail recognizes the message as authentically from you and not likely to be spam.

Improvements for Exchange Server 2007 Users

Office Outlook 2007 includes some additional new features that are available for people using Exchange Server 2007. Here's a quick list of some of the improved or added features:

Create different Out Of Office messages. Now you can better control the messages you give to people who are trying to contact you when you're out of the office or busy. You can schedule your Out Of Office Assistant for specific times–with a start and end time–so you don't have to remember to turn the feature on and off. Additionally, you can create different away messages so you communicate to different audiences in different ways. For example, if you're going off-site for several days, you might leave an internal message that encourages team members to call your cell phone or contact your assistant; for external contacts (clients and vendors, for example), you might provide a message saying that you are out of the office and will contact them when you return.

Include voice and fax messaging in your Inbox. Now you can arrange to have voice mail and received faxes delivered directly to your Inbox so Office Outlook 2007 literally becomes the communications hub at the center of your day.

2007 Microsoft Office Outlook Behind-the-Scenes Interview

Jessica Arnold, Office Outlook 2007 Program Manager

1. **Do you have a favorite new feature in Office Outlook 2007?** It's hard to choose one feature in Office Outlook 2007 that I could claim as my favorite because there are so many new features that I use on a daily basis. However, I probably use the new Instant Search capability more frequently than any other—probably about 20 times a day! Because of the flexibility of the interface, I no longer waste time looking for an e-mail that might be buried among thousands of other e-mails. Using Instant Search, I can use just a few keywords to locate the piece of information I need, no matter in which folder it might be stored.
2. **Do the changes come about as a result of user feedback? How so?** We take user feedback into account for every release of Office Outlook. When we looked at planning Office Outlook 2007 and redesigning the user interface, we went on customer visits and collected thousands of hours of data to understand what we could do to improve the user experience and positively affect users' daily lives. From this data, we identified trends and key areas for investment that the development team used to propose and design features that we believe will have a significant impact on the way our customers work.
3. **Does Office Outlook 2007 have what you think will be a "home run" feature that everyone will be talking about?** I think the improvements to time and task management will be incredibly useful for our users. The To-Do Bar, task integration with other Office programs, and the calendar really provide a great solution for users to be more effective and thus have more time to focus on the daily things that matter most.
4. **Do you have a fun or interesting story about what it was like for you to be involved in this major release?** One of the most interesting and exciting parts about being involved in this release is seeing all of the little things that go into shipping a product such as Office Outlook 2007. From the number of pixels that go into the follow-up flag icon on the user interface to the addition of new languages that Office Outlook 2007 will be offered in, it takes an amazing amount of coordination and collaboration among our teams to put together a product that we're really proud of. Seeing these pieces develop over the past two years and come together has been an incredible experience.

Chapter 11

Enhance Team Effectiveness with Office Groove 2007

What you'll find in this chapter:

- Using the Launchbar
- Easily create a Workspace
- Understand the Workspace window
- Powerful collaborative tools
- Using Office Groove 2007 with Office SharePoint Document Libraries
- A sample Office Groove 2007 work session

No matter what type of work you do, chances are that your job involves both projects and people. You might need, for example, to write a training manual, create a worksheet, prepare a presentation, research a proposal, or organize a sales force. All those tasks have a beginning, middle, and an end. And each one is likely to be something you work on collaboratively with others–whether you need a reviewer for your manual, a manager to sign off on your worksheet, peers to evaluate the presentation, a board of directors to okay the proposal, or a sales force to train.

Microsoft® Office Groove® 2007 is the new collaboration tool that helps you bring small teams together in a workspace to get your projects done easily and efficiently. Office Groove 2007 creates workspaces on your desktop PC, requiring no special server configurations. The files you and your team members work on collaboratively are stored on team members' computers, so participants have access to files whether they are online or offline. And each time a team member logs on, the files on that computer are updated so they show all changes made by everyone else on the team.

This is the tool you can use to get your project done, whether you're working in your office, in the coffee shop, in the boardroom, or on the deck. You can install Office Groove 2007 on all your computers and Windows Mobile devices so that you always have access to the latest information on your workspace, no matter which device you might be using. With Office Groove 2007, you can easily create ad hoc, self-hosted workspaces on a project-by-project basis, but the program also works seamlessly with Microsoft® Windows® SharePoint® Services and Microsoft Office SharePoint® Server 2007, enabling you to easily publish documents completed in Office Groove 2007 workspaces for structured workflows or long-term storage.

This chapter introduces you to some of the features in Office Groove 2007 that will help you complete your collaborative projects in a flexible and efficient way.

Tip Where do you get Office Groove 2007? Office Groove 2007 is available as part of Microsoft® Office Enterprise 2007 and as a stand-alone program to customers with EA agreements or who purchase software through Microsoft Volume Licensing. Small business customers, workgroups within larger organizations, and individuals can purchase Microsoft® Office Live Groove®, a yearly subscription offering that includes the Office Groove 2007 client application plus access to Microsoft-hosted data relay services.

Using the Launchbar

Begin by starting Office Groove 2007 as you would any other 2007 Microsoft Office system suite application; the Launchbar appears on your desktop to help you create and manage your activities in Office Groove 2007 (see Figure 11-1).

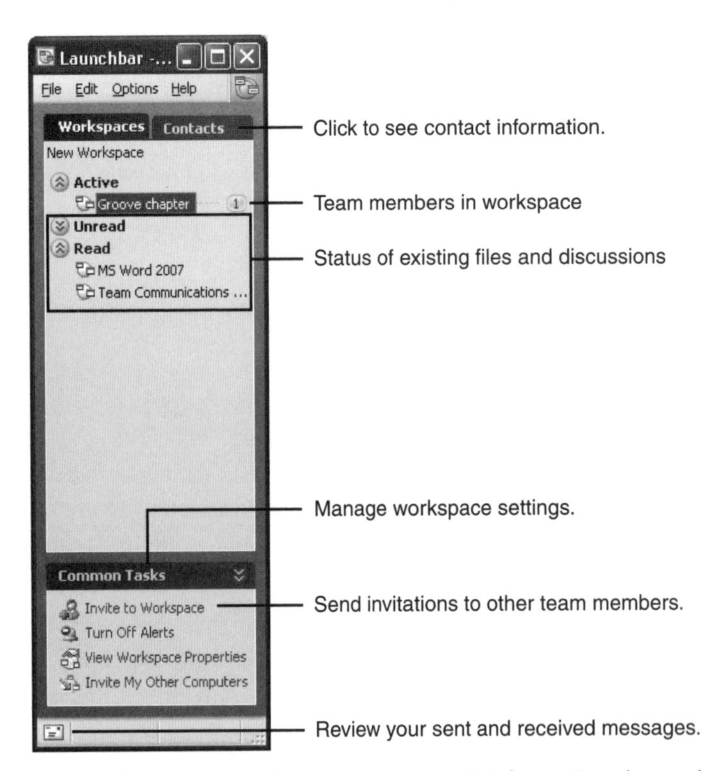

Figure 11-1 The Launchbar gives you quick information about what needs to be done in Office Groove 2007.

Easily Creating a Workspace

Creating a workspace in Office Groove 2007 is a simple process—with just a few clicks of the mouse you can set up a workspace team members can share. In the Launchbar, open the File menu, point to New, and choose Workspace. (You can also choose Workspace From if you want to create a workspace based on a template or an archived space.) The Create New Workspace dialog box (see Figure 11-2) gives you the options you need to create the new workspace—just enter a name, choose the workspace type you want to create, and click OK.

Figure 11-2 In the Create New Workspace dialog box, enter a name for the workspace and choose the type of space you want to create.

Understanding the Workspace Window

The Office Groove 2007 workspace window is organized to help you navigate easily among all your team communication and project tasks (see Figure 11-3). The title bar of the open workspace window displays the name of the current workspace; the familiar menu bar offers commands for managing files, working with tools, changing the view, and setting preferences. Use the Workspaces button on the menu bar to move among your various workspaces. The context-sensitive Common Tasks pane in the lower-right corner of the workspace also offers useful functions based on where you are in the workspace or what you've clicked.

If you create a Standard workspace, which is the most common way to begin a workspace, it automatically contains a Files tool and a Discussion tool. When you open the workspace, the Files tool is selected by default, and a set of buttons for working with files stretches across the top of the work area. Each tool has its own unique menu button just below the familiar Windows-style menu options. At any time during your project, you or your team members (depending on the permissions you've set) can add a variety of additional tools to your workspace (which you'll learn about in the next section).

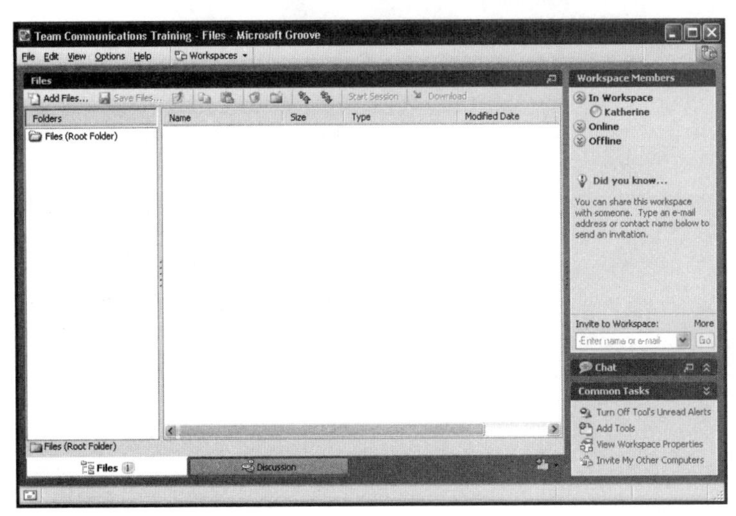

Figure 11-3 The Office Groove 2007 workspace includes tools to share files, host a discussion, and chat live.

The Workspace Members task pane on the right side of the window displays team members who are currently online and the Invite To Workspace box. The workspace called the Chat pane is just below the Workspace Members pane, and can be opened and closed using the up and down arrows.

Inviting Others and Assigning Roles

Inviting others to join your workspace is a simple task in Office Groove 2007. Simply click the Invite To Workspace box, type your contact's name or e-mail address, and click Go. (If you've entered the contact's information previously, the address will appear automatically before you finish typing it.) The Send Invitation dialog box appears so that you can add additional invitees, select roles, add a message, and click Invite (see Figure 11-4). Recipients who have Office Groove 2007 will receive the invitation that way. Those who do not will receive an e-mail message with the links they need to get started.

Office Groove 2007 enables you to assign three different roles to workspace members. As the creator of the workspace, you are by default a Manager and have all workspace-level permissions, including inviting or uninviting members and adding and deleting tools. Each member invited to a workspace is given a Participant role by default, which typically allows them to invite new members and add tools. The Guest setting restricts members to read-only privileges, so they cannot add to or delete information in the workspace or invite others.

Figure 11-4 When you invite others, you can specify their roles and add a customized message.

Tip You can change both workspace-level roles and permissions assigned to team members by clicking Set Roles in the Common Tasks area or by choosing Set Roles from the Options menu. You can also adjust the permissions of each tool by right-clicking the tool tab and choosing Properties/Permissions.

Office Groove 2007 and Data Safety

Is Office Groove 2007 safe? Many users today are concerned–and rightly so–about the safety of their information, particularly when they are working in an online collaborative group. Office Groove 2007 automatically encrypts all information shared within workspaces, both on team members' desktops and as the data passes over the company network or the Internet.

Powerful Collaborative Tools

Office Groove 2007 includes a diverse and powerful set of tools you can add to your workspace to help complete the various tasks your particular project requires. For example, you might add the Pictures tool to share images you plan to use in the annual report you are preparing for your nonprofit organization. Or you might add the Calendar tool if you are working on hosting a large event.

When you open a Standard workspace in Office Groove 2007, only the Files and Discussion tools are displayed in the workspace by default. You can add tools to your workspace by clicking the Add A Tool To This Workspace button just to the left of the Common Tasks toolbar and choosing the tool you want from the displayed menu (see Figure 11-5).

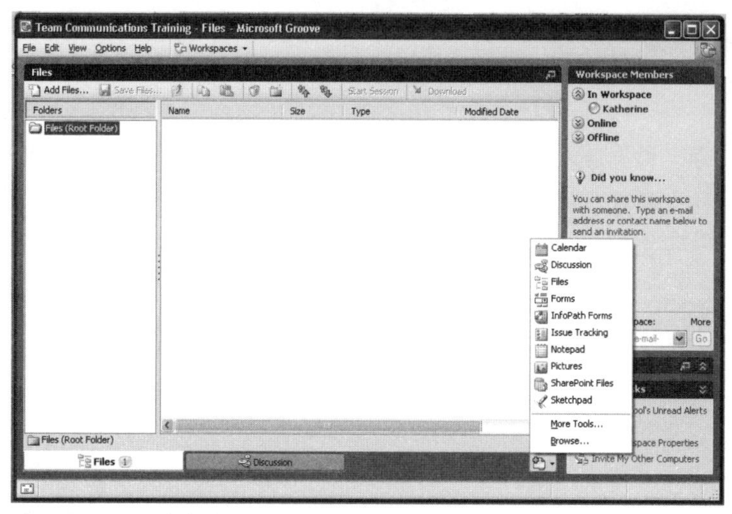

Figure 11-5 Click the Add A Tool To This Workspace button to display a list of tools you can add to the Office Groove 2007 workspace.

Sharing Files

The workspace area display changes depending on which tool you select. When you first open a workspace, the Files tool is displayed by default. This view enables you to create a file library your team members can use to post, share, review, and update all kinds of files related to your projects.

Note You can use files of all types with Office Groove 2007; any file that supports your project can be added to the Files tool in the workspace window.

You add files to the workspace by simply clicking Add Files; then choose the files you want to add (see Figure 11-6). The files are added to the workspace so others can view, modify, and discuss them.

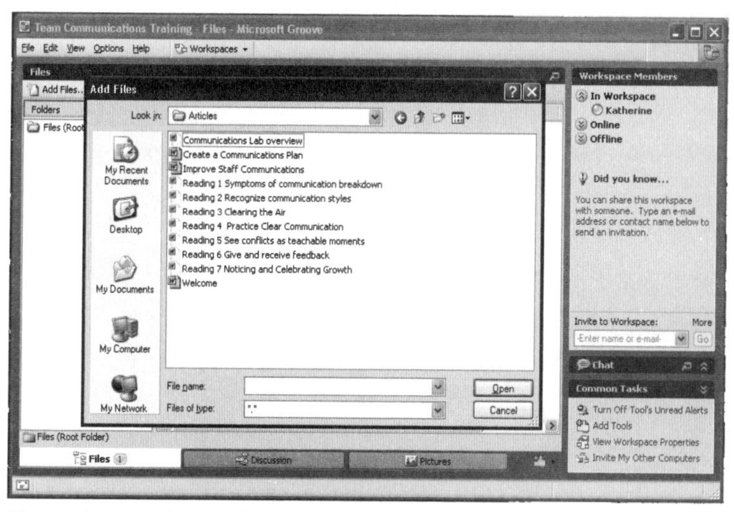

Figure 11-6 Click Add Files to select files you want to add to the workspace.

Hosting Discussions

The Discussion tool enables you to create and respond to a threaded discussion about various topics related to your project. You can organize the discussion by topic or by date so that you can easily see what needs your attention most. Each time a participant responds to the discussion thread, the conversation is indented so you can easily see the progression of the discussion and respond to the threads that are relevant to your tasks (see Figure 11-7).

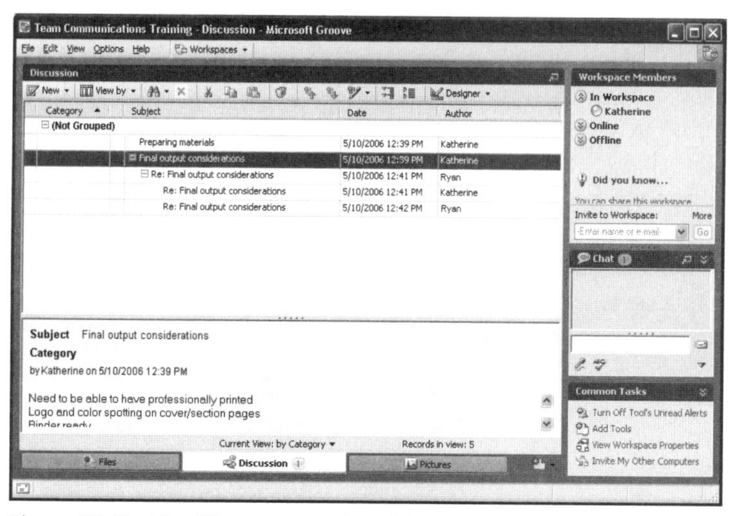

Figure 11-7 The Discussion tool enables you to host an ongoing threaded conversation about various aspects of your project.

Coordinating Calendars

The Calendar collects important information for team members by providing them with critical dates for the completion of a project. You can use the Calendar tool in Office Groove 2007 to put together a project schedule that helps keep everyone on track. Adding appointments and customizing the view is simple; just display the tool and right-click a specific day to display the Calendar options and select the one you need (see Figure 11-8).

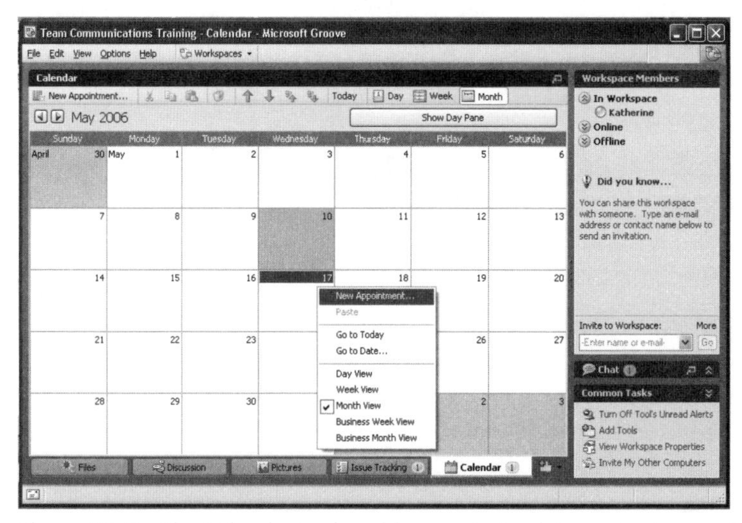

Figure 11-8 The Calendar tool enables you to track important team dates and project milestones.

Managing Meetings

You can use the Office Groove 2007 Meetings tool to plan, conduct, and record recurring team project meetings. The Meetings Wizard makes setup easy by walking you through the process. Because all workspace members can add information to a new meeting, you can develop agendas collaboratively rather than having one person collect input from the team. During the meeting, the person taking the minutes can insert the agenda into a note-taking space and record meeting minutes in real time. Participants can watch as the minutes are taken. After the meeting, action items can be recorded and assigned to team members. Agenda items, minutes, and action items from prior meetings can also be copied into future meetings.

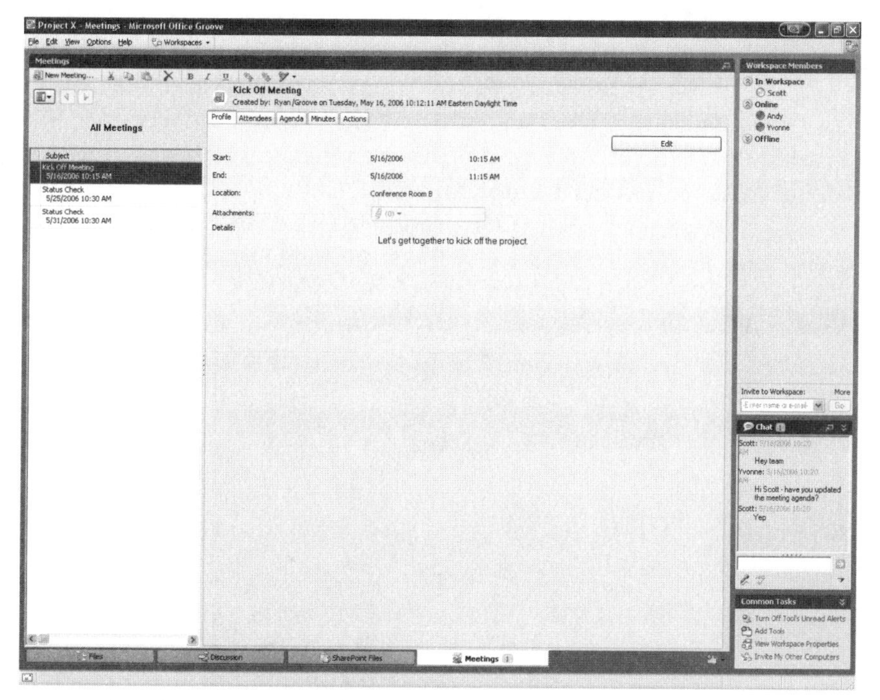

Figure 11-9 The Meetings tool in Office Groove 2007 helps you hold productive meetings in real time.

> **Note** Both the Meeting and Calendar tools help you and your team focus on the tasks, events, and milestones of the project or activity for which the Office Groove 2007 workspace is created. You and your team members will continue to manage and organize your personal calendars, tasks, and contacts using Microsoft Office Outlook® 2007.

Working with Forms

If forms are an important part of the way you collect and work with project-related information, the Forms and InfoPath Form tools in Office Groove 2007 will be helpful to you. You can create your own custom forms in the workspace window itself by using the Groove Forms tool, in which you can name the form, choose the fields you want to include, select the form style, and more.

The InfoPath Forms tool enables you to import forms you have created using Microsoft® Office InfoPath® 2007, which gives you the benefit of being able to work with forms that may already be in use in your business or department.

Tracking Issues

The Issue Tracking tool, a predesigned Groove Forms tool included with the program, provides a means of gathering information about tasks, challenges, or processes that require follow-up action. Whether you are working to resolve a technical problem, a production glitch, or a personnel challenge, you can document the issue, add supporting attachments, and track the progress of the resolution easily in Office Groove 2007. When you open the File menu and choose New to add a new tracking issue, the form shown in Figure 11-10 appears.

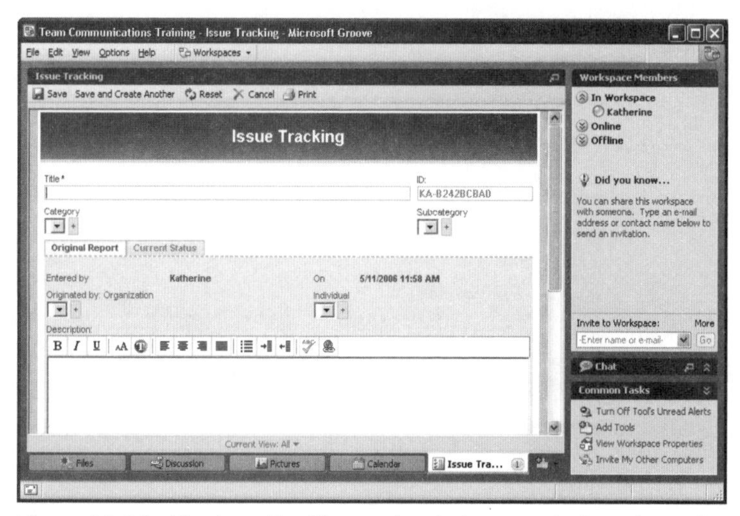

Figure 11-10 The Issue Tracking tool includes a predesigned template you can use to track items and responses in the workspace window.

Tip You can modify the issue tracking form to suit your needs by clicking the Add buttons, which display a small blue plus sign, and entering your own categories.

Creating a Picture Library

For some projects you need to be able to collect and organize graphics–perhaps charts for the business plan, photos for the annual report, or schematics for the new product you're preparing to launch. When you add the Picture tool to Office Groove 2007, you create a picture library that your entire team can access and reference as the project develops. Click Add Pictures to get started, and use the navigation tools above the pictures to move through the images you've added (see Figure 11-11).

Figure 11-11 The Picture tool enables you to add images, diagrams, and more.

Tip You can easily remove tools by right-clicking the tool's tab and choosing Delete.

Using Office Groove 2007 with Office SharePoint Document Libraries

Office Groove 2007 is a great tool for working on collaborative projects. You might use Office Groove 2007, for example, to develop and produce a new catalog; to prepare for an event; or to design a training course for your IT department. But your specific project is most likely one among many that are currently underway in your organization–and that's where Office Groove 2007's new seamless integration with Office SharePoint document libraries comes into play.

Windows SharePoint Services and Office SharePoint Server 2007 provide many businesses with the means to store, share, manage, and work with data securely on a large scale. When you use Office Groove 2007 with Office SharePoint Server 2007 or a Windows SharePoint Services V3 team site, you can check out documents into an Office Groove 2007 workspace, work on them collaboratively, and then, when you're ready, return them easily to the Office SharePoint document library. You can also choose to keep the files in your Office Groove workspace synchronized with the Office SharePoint document library throughout the project.

To set up Windows SharePoint Services, click the Add A Tool To This Workspace button in the workspace window and choose SharePoint Files. The Setup window appears so that you can begin the process (see Figure 11-12). You'll need to know the URL of the SharePoint site with which you want to synchronize your files, and you'll need the required access rights to the site.

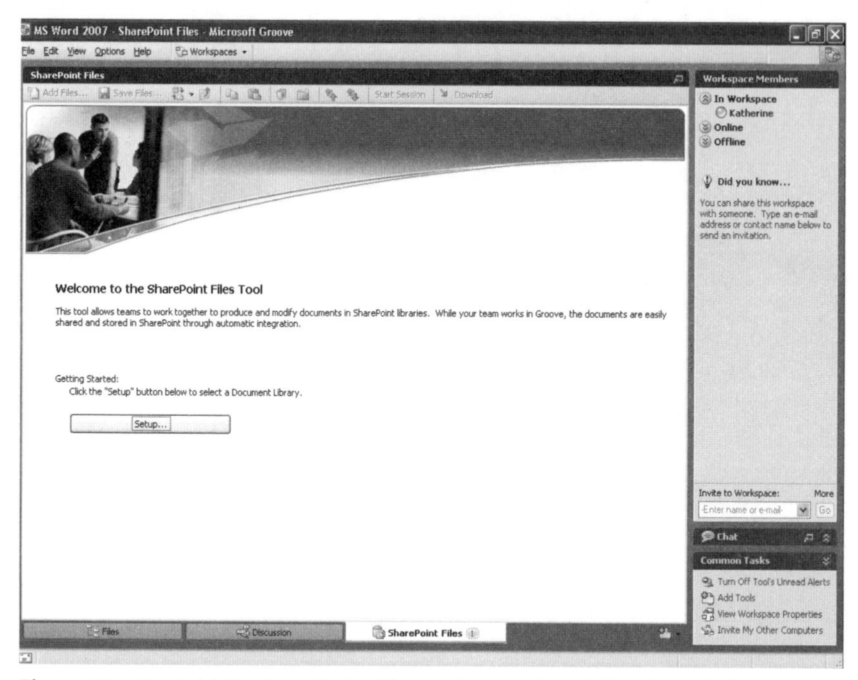

Figure 11-12 Add the SharePoint Files tool to work with files from Office SharePoint document libraries.

A Sample Office Groove 2007 Work Session

One of the great things about Office Groove 2007 is that it provides your team with a place to work whether you are all online at the same time or not. When you're offline, other team members can post and update files, send you messages, and continue to work on projects. When you log onto Office Groove 2007, all the changes will be downloaded to your PC automatically so you can review them—whenever and wherever that might be. This section explores some of the ways you can use Office Groove 2007 in a typical work session.

When you first sign on to Office Groove 2007, a number of text alerts might appear above the Office Groove 2007 icon in your Windows system tray, letting you know quickly which of your workspaces have the information and whether new messages have been delivered (see Figure 11-13). Clicking on workspace alerts will take you directly into the workspace and to the new information. Additionally, you can see quickly in the Launchbar which workspaces have unread content and how many team members are actively working in your workspaces (meaning that they have the workspace window open on their PCs).

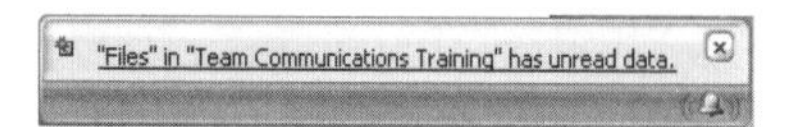

Figure 11-13 When you launch Office Groove 2007, a pop-up message lets you know that you have unread data in the workspace.

> **Tip** You can set up Office Groove 2007 to launch automatically when Windows starts by opening the Options menu, choosing Preferences, clicking the Options tab, and checking the Launch Groove When Windows Starts Up check box in the Startup Settings area. Click OK to save your settings.

Sending Messages in Office Groove 2007

You can send quick messages to Office Groove 2007 users by double-clicking the contact name in the Launchbar Contacts tab of any workspace (see Figure 11-14). Type your note in the Send Message window and click Files if you want to send along an attachment. Additionally, you can copy others on the message by clicking Add More. Click Send to send the message and an alert pops up on the recipient's desktop to let them know they have received a message from you.

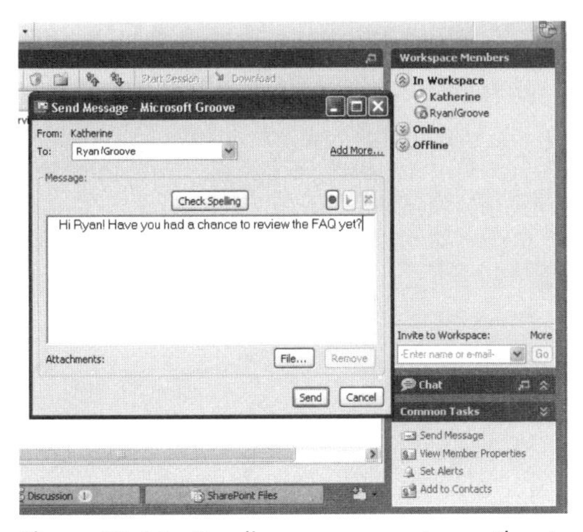

Figure 11-14 Sending a message to another team member is as easy as double-clicking the contact name.

Office Groove 2007 uses alerts to keep you informed about the status of the message you sent, which is especially helpful when you are working with time-critical information and want to know that another team member received the data you are sending. An alert lets you know when the message is sent, received, and even when the recipient opens it (see Figure 11-15).

Figure 11-15 Alerts let you know when messages you sent to team members have been opened.

> **Tip** You can review, organize, search, print, and discard past messages you've sent and received by clicking the Message History button (shown as an envelope) in the bottom-left corner of the Launchbar or any workspace.

Working with Alerts

When you log on to Office Groove 2007, you know immediately whether any changes have been made to the information in your workspace. Depending on your alert settings, you'll receive pop-up text alerts in your Windows task bar, as well as various unread content icons in your Launchbar workspaces tab, which signify how recently your workspaces have been updated. Although Office Groove 2007 will send you pop-up alerts only on the workspaces you use most often, it's best to customize your alert settings so that you are notified whenever content changes or events are added to the workspaces that are most important to you.

Alerts are fully customizable so that you can change the alert level and turn them on and off according to your preferences. You can determine how "sensitive" you want the alert system to be by indicating which events you want to be informed about—perhaps you want to know only when files are uploaded, or when a team member posts a question, or when SharePoint files have been modified. Alerts are enabled by default when you create a new workspace; if you want to disable them, click Turn Off Alerts in the Common Tasks area of the Launchbar.

To customize alerts for each workspace, right-click on the workspace from the Launchbar and choose Set Alerts (see Figure 11-16). You can then change the workspace alert level from Auto to High, Medium, or Low and also choose to be alerted when any new members enter the workspace—a helpful option when you're waiting on a time-critical update.

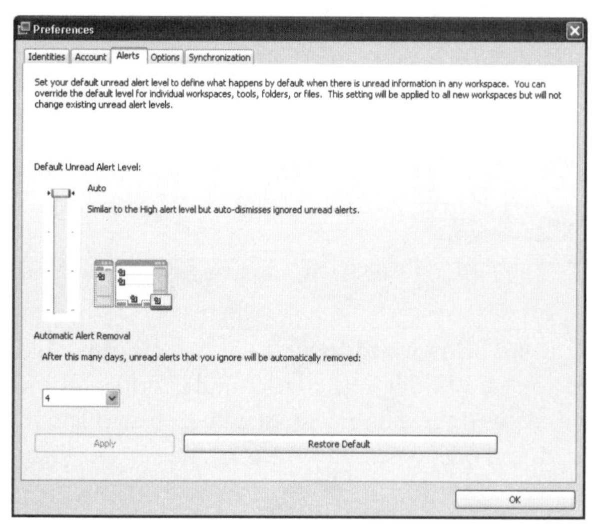

Figure 11-16 You can customize alerts to let you know when important updates have been made.

Reviewing Files

As you work in an Office Groove 2007 workspace, you can easily review modified files and post new ones. Open the workspace and click the Files tool to see the files that show a small unread icon to the left of the file name; this identifies them as unread (see Figure 11-17).

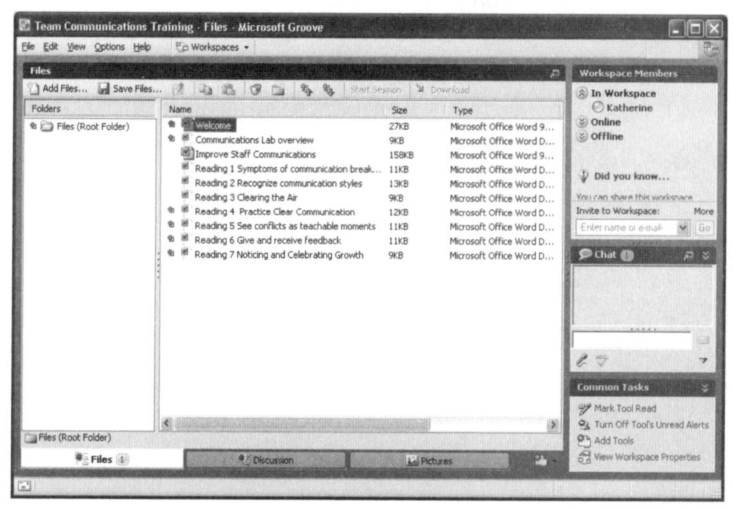

Figure 11-17 In the Files tool, unread files are marked with a small icon.

To view a file, you simply double-click it. The file opens in the application in which it was created. You can modify the file as needed. When finished, click Save and close the application. The next step is most important. Office Groove 2007 will prompt you to either save your changes over the existing file or to create a new version of the file. When doing a structured document review, it's best to save it as a new version and give it a descriptive title. After you save your changes, the file will be marked as Unread on your team members' copies of the workspace.

Chatting in Office Groove 2007

The chat feature in Office Groove 2007 is a simple, fast, and powerful feature that enables you to ask quick questions and get the answers you need from your team members while you're working in the project workspace. You can type in the Chat area in the navigation pane on the right side of the workspace window or you can click the Open Chat In A New Window tool to expand the Chat area and get additional tools for working with chat.

To begin chatting, click the up arrows on the right side of the Chat pane title bar. Click in the text box and type your message; then click the Send Chat Entry button or press Enter (see Figure 11-18). The text appears in the area above the text entry box. All members of the workspace who are currently online and logged into Office Groove 2007 will receive a pop-up alert that you are chatting in the workspace, and they can join you with a click of the mouse. They'll then see your text and be able to respond accordingly.

> **Note** Chat exchanges appear in all team members' workspaces, so even if members are currently offline, away, or busy with other things, the chat will be visible in the chat area for members to review when they return.

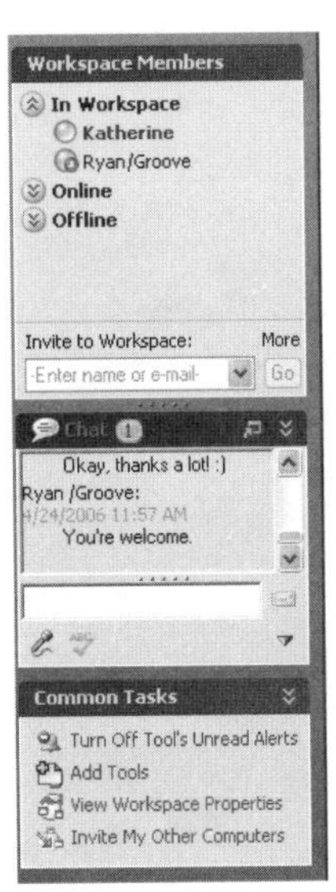

Figure 11-18 Use Chat to communicate quickly with team members who are currently online.

Viewing, Searching, and Printing Chat Transcripts

Your chat conversations are automatically saved in chat transcripts so that you can review them at any time. Click the Options button or press Shift+F10 to display the menu; point to Chat and choose among the Find In Transcript, Print Transcript, or Delete Transcript options.

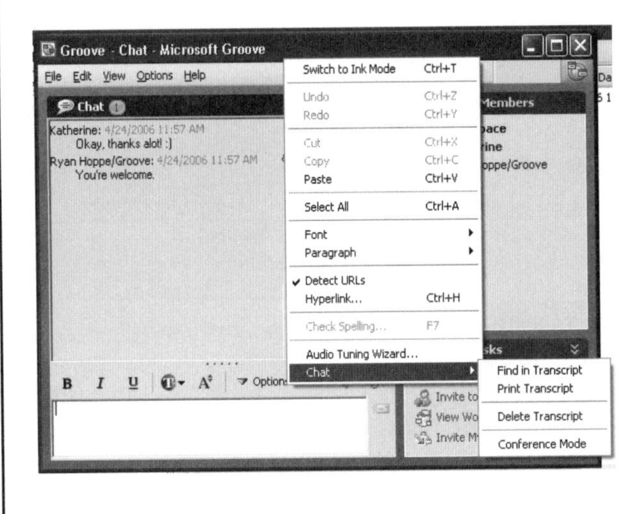

2007 Microsoft Office System Behind-the-Scenes Interview

Ryan Hoppe, Office Groove 2007 Product Manager

What are your favorite features in Office Groove 2007? Without question, my favorite new feature in Office Groove 2007 is the SharePoint Files tool. The standard Files tool is ideal for working collaboratively with your team members on one or more files. But the challenge is, how do you then share what you've developed in Office Groove 2007 with a larger group of people? With the new SharePoint Files tool, you can "publish" your final documents, either to a Windows SharePoint Services teamsite or to Office SharePoint Server 2007, with just a couple mouse clicks. This way, the work you do among your small project team in Groove workspaces becomes part of the corporate record without a lot of overhead.

Who do you envision average Office Groove 2007 users to be and what are they trying to accomplish? Pretty much anyone who works with information and relies on other people to get their jobs done can gain value from Office Groove 2007. But of course, the people who will gain the most value from the product are those that work on a number of team projects with people inside and outside organizations, and may sometimes be working while disconnected from a network. For example, a marketing manager who travels frequently and works with a number of external vendors like public relations firms or advertising agencies. Or a sales rep who often works from customer sites and works with various partners to respond to new opportunities. In these cases, the key challenge is that the team is not always connected to the same network and systems. Office Groove 2007 becomes the "glue" that connects these cross-organizational, mobile teams together – effortlessly.

What type of feedback led you to realize a product like Office Groove 2007 was needed? How long has the program been in development? Office Groove 2007 was actually conceived way back in 1997 by Ray Ozzie, now a CTO with Microsoft. At the time, Ray and the Groove development team realized that the workplace was changing from a purely centralized environment to more of a decentralized environment. A number of trends were fueling this change such as outsourcing, partnering, telework, an increase in travel, and a general desire to tighten connections across the value chain. Nearly 10 years later, the decentralized work environment Ray and his team foresaw has become reality. Groove was conceived from the bottom up to support this new work environment. The goal was to make a product that allowed teams to work together easily and effectively regardless of what company they work for, where they might be connecting from, or what kind of data they need to share.

What has it been like for you to be part of such a major release? It's been quite challenging, thrilling, and rewarding to participate in the launch of Office 2007. One of the original goals of Groove Networks back in 1997 was to achieve ubiquity. Success meant having all information workers using and gaining value from Groove on a daily basis. With Office Groove 2007 included in 2007 Microsoft Office Enterprise, which is the most comprehensive suite, the product and its new and improved capabilities will be exposed to such a wide audience. I'm really looking forward to the launch and the opportunity to speak directly to our new customers and learn how the product has helped them overcome their collaborative business challenges.

Do you have any fun or interesting stories (or surprising features/ tips or tricks/) you'd like to add? Many customers in the past have expressed the need for file versioning in Groove. This is a challenge, because one of the major benefits of Office Groove 2007 is the ability to access and edit files while you're disconnected from a network. Locking files, as a result, becomes very difficult when one or more members of a workspace are offline. In Office Groove 2007, there's a subtle yet powerful enhancement that I believe will improve the document versioning experience significantly. When you open a document from a Groove workspace and make changes, you now have the option of saving your changes atop the existing version OR saving the file as a new version. I've been running the beta version of Office Groove 2007 for several months, and I've already noticed in practice that this small feature has streamlined the process of reviewing documents among a team. And, of course, when you're ready for a rich, structured document workflow, you can take advantage of the new SharePoint files tool.

Appendix

A Quick Look at Additional Changes

There's still more to cover in the 2007 Microsoft® Office system! This appendix gives you a quick look at some of the additional applications you'll hear more about in the coming months. Be sure to visit the Microsoft Office system preview site (*www.microsoft.com/office/preview/default.mspx*) to learn more about the programs, suites, and servers available with the new release.

Microsoft Office Visio 2007

Microsoft® Office Visio® 2007 is the new version of the popular diagramming tool included with the Microsoft Office systems. Changes in Office Visio 2007 include these:

- The Getting Started user interface helps you find the right diagram for the job.
- New shapes and templates help you easily visualize and communicate information, systems, and processes and give your diagrams additional power, flexibility, and professional appeal.
- AutoConnect helps you create diagrams faster by combining the three main steps–choose, connect, and space shapes–into a quick single step.
- A new diagram type called PivotDiagrams enables you to generate a diagram based on the structure of your data.
- Data Graphics Gallery task pane gives you a new level of control over where and how data fields are displayed in the diagram
- Integration with Microsoft® Office Project 2007 and Microsoft® Office SharePoint® Server 2007 enable you to effectively communicate information in reports based on project data from those other sources.

Microsoft Office System Behind-the-Scenes Interview

Eric Rockey, Program Manager for Office Visio 2007

What are the major new features of Office Visio 2007? Is there one feature you think everyone will love? In Office Visio 2007, our goal was to make it far easier for people to communication business information using Office Visio diagrams. To do this, we focused our efforts in three major areas. First, we looked at how we could allow people to achieve "better results, faster" by making it easier to author great-looking diagrams quickly in Office Visio 2007. The second area, which is a major investment for Office Visio 2007, is the work we have done to easily display business data directly on top of Office Visio diagrams. This will really revolutionize what people will be able to do with Office Visio. Finally, with Office Visio 2007, you can use diagrams to communicate with everyone, even those who do not have Office Visio 2007 installed. We have added a number of options to make it easier to distribute Office Visio diagrams. These are all great features, but I think everyone's going to be amazed at how much faster AutoConnect allows you to create your diagrams in Office Visio 2007.

Will Office Visio 2007 be included as part of the Microsoft Office system? Office Visio 2007 is part of the Microsoft Office system, but it is not included in any of the suites (Microsoft® Office Standard 2007, Microsoft® Office Professional 2007, etc.). Office Visio 2007 is a bit more specialized than the products in those suites. Instead, Office Visio 2007 is sold as a stand-alone application in two versions: Office Standard 2007 and Office Professional 2007. There is also a version that ships as part of Microsoft Visual Studio called Visio for Enterprise Architects.

Do you have a sense of who the typical Office Visio 2007 user is? What does he or she use the program to do? Office Visio 2007 really has a number of typical user types, largely based on the different diagram types that we ship (we currently ship more than 50 different diagram types). IT professionals use Office Visio 2007 to create network diagrams, visualize databases and software systems, create Web site maps, and create floor plans for network equipment. Business analysts use Office Visio 2007 in a key role to create business process diagrams (flowcharts) to document and optimize their systems because business process reengineering is an increasingly important aspect of a well-run company.

Do you have a fun or interesting story you can tell about what it's been like for you to be part of the Visio development team? For me, it's fun to work on a product that has such a loyal following. I'm always amazed at how passionate people are about Office Visio, both on the team and as customers. A lot of people think Office Visio is all about business, but we have these customers sending us examples of games such as Asteroids (Visteroids) or Tetris (ShapeTris) that have been created as programmable diagrams in Office Visio!

Microsoft Office SharePoint Server 2007

Microsoft® Office SharePoint® Server 2007 is an enterprise-scale system that enables organizations to manage content, streamline processes, and facilitate collaboration in powerful new ways. Used with Microsoft® Windows® SharePoint Services V3, Office SharePoint Server 2007 provides a comprehensive suite of server applications designed to work seamlessly with desktop applications to enable users to connect, collaborate, create, and control business critical information in a secure and effective way.

As you've read throughout this book, one of the major investment areas of the 2007 release is increased integration with Windows SharePoint Services. Collaboration is the wave of the future, and the enhanced support for Windows SharePoint Services V3 in the core applications enables you to take full advantage of the wall-less office, building the best possible teams across all boundaries and giving them the tools they need to work efficiently, effectively, and securely toward a common goal.

Microsoft Office InfoPath 2007

Microsoft® Office InfoPath® 2007 is a forms tool that enables you to gather, share, and continue to use data you collect in documents, worksheets, and even e-mail messages sent via Office Outlook 2007. Microsoft Office InfoPath 2007 integrates easily with the other applications in the 2007 Microsoft Office system to provide you with forms capability no matter how you might be reaching out to your audience.

In addition, Office InfoPath 2007 works seamlessly with both Office Groove 2007 and Microsoft Office SharePoint Server 2007. This gives you an intuitive and accurate way to gather data from team members, customers, vendors, and others, and synchronize and integrate that data directly into your applications. Office InfoPath 2007 includes tools to help you with the design process as well; you can choose a form from the pre-designed gallery and modify it to suit your needs; you can create a form from scratch; or you can modify an existing form your business currently uses, updating it to make the most of the features in Office InfoPath 2007.

Microsoft Expression Web Designer

A free trial of Microsoft® Expression® Web Designer may also be part of your 2007 Microsoft Office system package. Microsoft Expression Web Designer is an innovative new Web design tool with a simplified interface that enables you to design, create, update, and maintain Web sites easily.

To find out more about Microsoft Expression Web Designer and learn about its companion products, Graphic Designer and Interactive Designer, go to *www.microsoft.com/products/expression*.

Microsoft Office System for Microsoft Windows Vista

The Microsoft Office system and Windows Vista, the next-generation operating system from Microsoft, have been going through their beta cycles at the same time. As we near the release date for both products, excitement is building and users are eager to see how both releases will work together to provide an optimum experience in both application and system software.

Although older versions of Microsoft Office will run on Windows Vista, the 2007 Microsoft Office system is designed to take full advantage of the powerful capabilities of the new operating system. Here are just a few of the improvements you can expect to see when you use the 2007 release with Windows Vista:

- Dramatically faster process times when searching or updating files
- Easier and broader search capabilities
- Improvements in file organization, management, and selection
- Simplified file operations using the common dialog box design in Windows Vista
- Really Simple Syndication (RSS) support in Internet Explorer 7 and Microsoft® Office Outlook® 2007 enables you to receive RSS feeds on the Web or delivered to your Inbox
- Dramatic improvements in media capabilities–including thumbnail representations, keyword cataloging, and easy transfer features for working with photos, video, music, and more in the documents and presentations you create

Note To learn more about the capabilities of Windows Vista, go to *www.microsoft.com/windowsvista/features/forhome/gallery.mspx*.

Microsoft Office Live

Microsoft® Office Live is a new online service currently in beta that enables small businesses to create and maintain a professional Web presence. Office Live offers three service programs, enabling businesses to choose just what they need for their type of product or service:

- Microsoft® Office Live Basics gets you started with a domain name, five e-mail accounts, and traffic reports on your Web site traffic.
- Microsoft® Office Live Collaboration builds on the basic service by giving you the tools to create a collaborative site and manage projects, customers, vendors, staff, and more.
- Microsoft® Office Live Essentials helps grow your business by including both the basic and collaborative services with specialized traffic reports and 50 e-mail addresses.

During the beta period, Office Live is free; after the trial period, Office Live Collaboration and Office Live Essentials will be charged at a monthly subscription rate. To find out more about Microsoft Office Live services, go to *officelive.microsoft.com/default.aspx*.

Index

N

O

Katherine Murray

Katherine Murray has been writing about technology since the mid-1980s, which means she's seen a lot of menu bars, nested dialog boxes, and new user interfaces. She's excited about the great changes and wide-open potential in the 2007 Microsoft Office system and feels that it truly represents a major shift in the way we will work in the future—a future that promises a global workplace, a mobile workforce, with room for workstyles and tools that enhance and develop the potential of individuals and groups. In addition to Katherine's many books on technology, she is an avid blogger (and the co-author of Share Your Story: Blogging with MSN Spaces, published in 2006 by Microsoft Press) and a columnist for a number of Microsoft sites. You can visit Katherine's technology blog, BlogOffice, at www.revisionsplus.com/blogofficexp.html or visit her MSN Space at spaces.msn.com/livingspace.

What do you think of this book? We want to hear from you!

Do you have a few minutes to participate in a brief online survey? Microsoft is interested in hearing your feedback about this publication so that we can continually improve our books and learning resources for you.

To participate in our survey, please visit:
www.microsoft.com/learning/booksurvey

And enter this book's ISBN, 0-7356-2265-5. As a thank-you to survey participants in the United States and Canada, each month we'll randomly select five respondents to win one of five $100 gift certificates from a leading online merchant.* At the conclusion of the survey, you can enter the drawing by providing your e-mail address, which will be used for prize notification *only*.

Thanks in advance for your input. Your opinion counts!

Sincerely,

Microsoft Learning

Learn More. Go Further.

To see special offers on Microsoft Learning products for developers, IT professionals, and home and office users, visit: *www.microsoft.com/learning/booksurvey*

* No purchase necessary. Void where prohibited. Open only to residents of the 50 United States (includes District of Columbia) and Canada (void in Quebec). Sweepstakes ends 6/30/2007. For official rules, see: *www.microsoft.com/learning/booksurvey*